Friends and Kindred

Friends and Kindred

Memoirs of Louisa Kathleen Haldane

Edited by Naomi Mitchison

K&B

Kennedy & Boyd
an imprint of
Zeticula
57 St Vincent Crescent
Glasgow
G3 8NQ
Scotland.

http://www.kennedyandboyd.co.uk
admin@kennedyandboyd.co.uk

First published in 1961
Copyright © Louisa Kathleen Haldane 1961
This edition first published 2009

ISBN-13 978-1-904999-99-7 Paperback
ISBN-10   1-904999-99-9 Paperback

An extended family tree can be found at
http://www.kennedyandboyd.co.uk/images/NML/tree.pdf

This book is for my daughter

NAOMI MITCHISON

—indeed it is hers already, for she has recast much of it and deleted notes on friends which I have enjoyed writing, and which I think most of those still alive would have enjoyed reading if it had come their way to do so. Anyhow, if my reminiscences are of interest to people who have never seen or heard of me, they will enquire how the writer became the author, and her friendships probably demonstrate this better than many words of explanation. To Naomi's name I add that of her daughter, my dearly beloved granddaughter,

LOIS GODFREY

who has also from time to time urged me to write on the non-contemporary happenings during my ninety-seven years' sojourn in this troublesome world. With measureless love to you both.

LOUISA KATHLEEN HALDANE

Acknowledgements are due to the Editors of *The Scotsman*, the *Glasgow Herald*, the *Manchester Guardian* and *Twentieth Century*, in whose pages parts of this book have appeared.

Contents

❋

9

Illustrations

�֎

CHAPTER I

Families

❊

I was born in Harley Street, London, on February 15th, 1863. My father used to read up the symptoms of some disease, brood over them, and then believe he had got them. When he saw a new doctor he told him that he was suffering from *so and so*, and ten to one the doctor began to treat him for it, before he found out whether the patient's diagnosis was correct.

It can't have been long after his marriage that he thought he had cancer. Anyhow, just before I was born it was the prevailing idea—pleasant for my mother! This of course is hearsay, but I can remember several cases of the same sort and there was always 'a pernicious spinal complaint', of which he was ready to complain. I have heard some doctors call it 'male hysteria'.

His mother and sisters were staying off and on in London and were full of sympathy for 'poor dear Coutts'. My mother had none of her own people near her and was desperately lonely and frightened (I feel pretty bitter about this episode). She had a very bad, long confinement—she was no longer young, several years older than my father. She was bitterly disappointed not to be able to feed me. I had a wet nurse, the usual fashion in those days, even when there was no real need for it. My mother and the wet nurse 'sat opposite one another and looked into each other's faces while the baby sucked'. I tell the tale as 'twas told to me.

I was christened by my father's old uncle, Spencer Drummond, and named Louisa after my grandmother. 'No other

13

name would have been possible', but Uncle Pen, who was devoted to my mother, insisted that I should have her name too. She did not like her own name of Harriet, and wanted Kathleen. I suspect that she was feeling 'very Irish'—one of her sisters-in-law was in the habit of exclaiming 'Murder and Irish' as one might say 'Death and Damnation'. My mother told Uncle Pen that Kathleen was Irish for Harriet, and he believed her! Years afterwards I heard him tell someone: 'We christened the dear child Kathleen—Irish for Harriet you know.'

My Trotter forebears were an armigerous family in Berwickshire, until one of them married Jean Moubray, heiress of Bush and Castlelaw in the Pentlands, after which they seem to have moved their headquarters to Midlothian. But one of them evidently stayed on at Kettleshiels, Berwickshire. I have a frank of Lord Cockburn's addressed to 'Lady Kettleshiels at her house in Edinburgh'. I presume her home was still Kettleshiels and she was only on a visit to her town house. Among the Midlothian Trotters for two or three generations there were fairly large families of boys, of whom several served in the Army or Navy, and as many went out to Bengal in the Honourable East India Company. The daughters married into families much like their own. They were cousins of Dundas of Arniston, of Lindsays and Bethunes, of Stuarts of Allanbank and Coltness, of Elliots, Drummonds and Murrays. They all seem to have travelled whenever they could afford it. If the eldest son was not going directly into the Services, he did a tour of Europe, armed with introductions to 'persons of quality' at each stopping place.

Some of the wives wrote 'meditations' on the obscurer texts in the Old Testament, but the family was definitely Episcopalian, and left theological discussion to those whose business it was. In their third generation in Midlothian, my uncle, John Mowbray Trotter, who married Mary (Mimi) Abercromby, only child of Lord Dunfermline, one time Speaker of the House of Commons, and afterwards Ambassador at The Hague, felt very strongly that the theological rift between the gentry and the people was the worst thing possible for the country. I believe that it was only in that generation that Scotch families began as a rule to send their sons to English Public Schools, and that this probably accentuated the antagonism between the two brands of theology. When he was at home my uncle always went to the kirk—the Established Church of Scotland in the village, and was ready to discuss the sermon with anyone in Colinton. When the family was in India, I, on more than one occasion, occupied the family pew alone, and was made shy by the warmth of the greetings which I received when the kirk skailed.

They were certainly not a literary family. The only two books which, as far as I know, were produced among them are *Trotter on the Currency* and *Farm Book-keeping*. Still less were they artistic, though cousin James Stuart of Allanbank, to whom my father was devoted, and who was a genuine, if minor, painter, drew wonderful galloping horses, and illustrations of 'Marmion' for the children's scrapbooks. But even more than theology, politics mattered to all the men in the family, and men and women alike were staunch, and possibly slightly bigoted, Tories. They drank sentimentally to the 'King over the Waters', but they were ready to take the oath to the later Hanoverians without too many mental reservations, and whatever they may have done in the '15, very few of them were out in the '45.

Rather later there was closer contact with the Crown when the Prince Consort took great interest in the Niger expedition. The first exploration of that great river was under the command of my great-uncle, Admiral Sir Henry Trotter. The Queen sent a life-sized bust of the Prince Consort which was to be placed in the Admiral's cabin. It would have half-filled it, but fortunately it arrived too late to be embarked. It was in this house forty or fifty years ago, and I should think it is here still. My father's writing-table, at which I am now sitting, was made by the Dreghorn house-carpenter from the fittings of that cabin.

Families

My father was Coutts Trotter of Dreghorn, Midlothian, son of Archibald Trotter, Scots Greys, and grandson of Alexander Trotter, younger, of Bush. My father was a typical man of leisure. There were always interests for him to take up, and suggestions being made to him about them. He was interested in many subjects, but never enough to work for them seriously. He had a steady stream of books to review from the 'Athenaeum', and he steered the Scottish Geographical Society through its early years. But before coming down to my father's own times I want to write about his grandfather who was Paymaster to the Navy and who bought Dreghorn, while my other Scottish great-great-grandfather, the first Lord Melville, was Treasurer to the Navy. At Lord Melville's impeachment for malversation of public monies, and subsequent trial, the Paymaster was also involved. It is apparent that my father and my uncle, Colonel John Mowbray Trotter, were both concerned about their grandfather's reputation. Only one side of the correspondence survives, a packet of letters from my uncle written between 1890 and 1899, when my uncle was ill, immersed in County business and in schemes for the betterment of conditions for ex-Servicemen. In one letter he wrote, 'I agree with all you say about the Melville papers but my work increases yearly out of all proportion to my health and power of getting through it . . . our business is not to whitewash our grandfather but to put his papers in order and learn what they prove . . . from what I know of the papers I can assure the family that our great-grandfather's memory will gain much by this investigation. He left a careful statement of all his transactions evidently with the intention that we should read it and understand the case. . . . It would have been better for his reputation had he been tried himself . . . what strikes one is his reticence in answering questions about his intromissions with public funds. But it has to be remembered that he would have been prosecuted himself had the Crown lawyers been able to convince the Government that he could be charged with illegal practices . . . and without doubt he held in view the State trial and financial ruin of Warren Hastings ten or eleven years

My fair-haired mother with her darker sister, my Aunt Annie

Dreghorn

earlier and he was rightly advised by Counsel not to give any part of his own case away. . . . His kindness to young men and lame dogs in all walks of life in India and in Scotland and his recognition of claims of kinship are points which strike me most about him. His papers seem to me to show he hoped posterity would do him justice when the events he was connected with became records of history and not Party questions. Whether such things concern him now—who can tell?'

Before I read these letters, I had thought it more comical than tragic that two of my great-grandfathers should be in a *cause célèbre* together. I was often at Melville, intimate friends with my cousin Blanche Dundas, niece of General Lord Melville and sister of Harry Lord Melville, whom I shall often mention in the following pages. If I had known the contents of the letters I would certainly have urged my father to take up the role that his brother assigned to him, but I should not have succeeded in persuading him to do so. He was usually very ready to acknowledge the claims of kinship, but if these became oppressive, he shifted the burden. How well I remember the yearly ritual of the visit of a poor lady, with which an important meeting at the Athenaeum Club, or at the Asiatic Society in London, always coincided!

As a small girl all I heard about the Dundas-Trotter complication was from my grandmother, who was much more interested in her own grandfather than in her husband's father. Two of her stories are quite fresh in my memory. In the last hour of the Melville trial, the House was equally divided on the impeachment; 'The Speaker gave his casting vote for "guilty" with the tears choking him.'

And, in lighter vein, the story was that, entering the House together one morning, Pitt said to Dundas, 'I can't see the Speaker, Hal.' To which Dundas replied, 'Damn it, Will, I see two.'

My great-grandfather's youngest brother, 'Uncle Robert', was the representative of the East India Company in Cape Town, and there he married his deceased wife's sister, which was perfectly legal in the Cape, but caused some awkwardness

B

when they came to stay at Dreghorn. When this poor lady died he made a third marriage to someone of the same name, though she was not another sister. All my mother would say on the subject was that 'Uncle Robert showed a want of imagination'.

The Paymaster married Lilias Stuart of Allanbank. This is impressed on my mind because her portrait, life-size, in a blue 'classical' costume—a willowy lady with a firm mouth —used to hang on the staircase at my grandmother's and on the frame was the legend 'Mrs. Trotter of Dreghorn, née Lilias Stuart of Allanbank'. I speculated about the number of things to which Mrs. Trotter might have said 'nay', and made up a story in which she was anything but kind to poor young Lilias Stuart. I was quite a big girl, and read French, before the meaning dawned on me!

The eldest son of the Paymaster, Archibald, was my grandfather. He got his commission in the Scots Greys in the year of Waterloo, and of course saw no active service. He seems to have been sent wandering all over Europe with introductions to all our Embassies, and to all the German princelings and other men of note in both Germany and Italy. He married Louisa Strange, daughter of James Strange of the East India Company, grand-daughter of the first Lord Melville. Objections were made to the engagement and it was broken off, but she threatened to 'die of a broken heart' and the objections were withdrawn. My impression from reading some of his diaries is that he must have been most courteous, unselfish and charming, but possibly not very enterprising or determined. He died quite young and his three brothers were extraordinarily kind to his widow.

One of my father's stories of his grandfather, was that an Admiral whom he had known when he was in the Navy Office, wrote that he was travelling to Scotland, and that he would do himself the honour of waiting on his old friend Mr. Trotter. Of course, hospitality being what it was in those days, he was asked to stay at Dreghorn, and Mrs. Trotter was no doubt delighted to put up her husband's old friend the Admiral.

Families

The Admiral's father had followed the fortunes of the Paymaster and was now his butler. It would never do for the father to wait on his son at dinner, so the Laird and his butler took counsel together and decided that the footmen should be trusted to wait at dinner, but, when the cloth was drawn, the Admiral's father and the port should come in together, and so it was done. Neither father nor son was in the least embarrassed, and the record does not tell how many bottles they emptied before they went for a stroll on the Pentlands and the Laird went to bed—or did the Laird go to bed and leave the Admiral and his father to crack a final bottle?

My father and his next brother were first taught by the village schoolmaster at Colinton. They were then sent to a school called 'The Grange' in northern England. It was a fashionable school among Scotch people, possibly because it removed boys from the constant sound of the Scottish accent. All the parents seem to have known one another. The school fell into bad repute when three boys were drowned—one boy trying to save his younger brother—while the master in charge of the bathing parade looked on helplessly. Several boys were removed at once, and I think the school shortly came to an end.

My father went on to Rugby, then under Tate, Dr. Arnold's successor. It must have been on account of the Arnold tradition that he was sent there. I wish I had kept more of his schoolboy letters to his mother, which in some ways were extremely adult, very religious, and giving full accounts of the people who asked him out, but saying nothing of his schoolfellows and little of his work. In every letter there are complaints about his digestion. From Rugby he went to Haileybury, the East India Company's College, and passed out head of his year with the Gold Medal, given by the Company, for the best essay. He was always destined for the Indian Service. His brothers were—two in the Indian Army, one in the Royal Navy and one in the 93rd Highlanders. As far as he was concerned, his cousins at the Bush had done well in India, so why should not he? He was expected to make enough to be able to

19

live at Dreghorn. Money seems to have been a worry to the family, but I have never understood why they were quite so hard up. The Paymaster must have been either fearfully extravagant or improvident—or did he just overbuild, like so many of his generation?

In due course my father went out to Calcutta and got ill, as so many of the cadets did. He came back to England while others stuck it, or died. I do not think he was more than two or perhaps three years in India altogether, but he made the voyages there and back, four voyages round the Cape of about five months each.

It must have been some years after he came back from India that he met my mother. In the interval he went up to Balliol, but I do not think that he kept even three terms. He said that the undergraduates were mere schoolboys, and that he felt out of place and wished that he had gone to St. Mary Hall where the atmosphere was more suited to a grown man. An old acquaintance of his, Dr. Chase, a don of St. Mary Hall, was Master there when I came up to Oxford and he asked us to dinner. I remember this dinner party very clearly because there they offered *white* port to the ladies at dessert, whereas elsewhere white port was only offered to the men diners. Port of both colours was entirely wasted on me, but I objected to discrimination!

My father and mother met at some watering place in Germany where the Keatinge family were staying *en famille*, as the custom was. I suppose that my grandfather, Judge Keatinge, was taking the water or the baths for his gout. They never spoke about this episode, and I only heard it from an old friend of my mother's, Mrs. Palmer, who was extremely satirical about my father's having anything serious the matter with his health: 'an attractive young man, and Harriet was very sympathetic with him'. I gather everyone saw it was 'a case' and they got engaged very quickly. My father, accompanied by his mother, went to Ireland for the wedding. They were married in Dublin and went away to some place in the vicinity, Kingstown, I think, where her two sisters visited them the next day.

My mother's father was the Right Honourable P. C. Keatinge of Narrymuir, County Kildare, Judge of the Court of Probate in Ireland.[1] His wife was a Miss Joseph. I am as certain as I can be of anything of which I have no proof that Granny was not the kind of person who would be described as 'a rich Jewess'. She was certainly a very strong member of the Protestant Church in Ireland. Her parents were buried in the cemetery at Thun, in Switzerland, and on their tombstone is the verse beginning:

'*In the Resurrection, there is neither Jew nor Gentile,
Bond nor free. . . .*'

I went there once with my mother and we found the grave. Like my father, my mother was one of a large family; he was the eldest of eight children, she the youngest of seven. None of my mother's family, except the youngest brother, showed any trace of Jewish blood.

My mother's eldest sister, my Aunt Laura, married Sir John Keane of Cappoquin, County Waterford. When people said someone was 'stately', I always thought of her, and I was rather afraid of her, not so of jolly Uncle Jack.

By the time I was seven or eight, this Aunt and Uncle had acquired a romantic attraction, for I had heard how in the time of the last 'potato famine', when there was fever in the village, they had sent the children to Dublin, but had stayed on at Cappoquin themselves, and had bought grain, wheat or oats, and made porridge of it and eaten with the tenants; but even with this example, some of the people refused the strange food, and starved themselves, as natives did in Southern India when offered grain when the supply of rice failed.

I think that Granny must have brought up her family very strictly, for I never succeeded in hearing any stories of their

[1] See the Leadbeater Papers, Vol. 1, on 'Southern Gentlemen and Loyal Protestants'.

childhood days, which some of them must surely have told, had they been at all colourful ones! What my mother seemed to remember so painfully clearly, that it overshadowed most earlier recollections of him, was an occasion when my Uncle, Richard Harte, the General, came on leave 'with a nursery of children and several native servants'. 'It must have been too lovely—I wish I'd been there,' I said enviously. But my mother answered rather grimly that Granny did not like to have the house upset, and I heard no more at that time.

I do not now (1958), understand why, during the last forty years, I have never done more than glance at the top sheet of the big bundles of my Uncle Harte's letters, which my mother left to me. She collected his letters to their father when she went to Dublin at the time of his last illness, and tied them up with those to herself. She never destroyed a single sheet of his handwriting, though she was most un-Victorian in the way she disposed of other correspondence, some of which would have been of quite historic interest had it survived; but I should be the last to blame her, for I have torn up ruthlessly myself.

His letters begin from 1840, and he was in India by early 1842. His letters are always carefully dated with the day of the month, and it is only after he wrote from India that the recipients noted the date of the year on the back of each letter. He had a nomination for Woolwich, but was rejected on account of an injury to his right eye ('the result of too close an interest in gunpowder during my schooldays'). He always shot from the left shoulder.

He received a direct commission in the Bombay Horse Artillery and went to Addiscombe, where cadets for the East India Company's army trained. What he writes about his life while receiving tuition (we should say cramming), for the college entrance, is of special interest to me because about twenty years later I heard very much the same conditions discussed by my Scotch grandmother and her daughters, about my uncle on their side, John Mowbray Trotter—no less beloved than the General. John was preparing for the

Indian Army—no longer the E.I.C's Army but the Queen's.

This reminds me of the first conversation of which I have any distinct recollection; I remember it very clearly indeed. I think that my aunts considered their conversation with their contemporaries so far above my head that I should not be interested in it; so far they had been quite right, but this was a different story altogether, involving someone I loved, so I woke up and listened. I can see the long drawing-room with the aunts and my grandmother grouped round the fire, and one aunt said 'Run along now dear and get on with your cross-stitch' and the other said 'Don't sit on the stairs, it's too cold.' To my question 'Where am I to sit?' grandmother answered, 'Run along to the end of the room, dear child, and do one more whole row of cross-stitch in pink, and be careful not to tangle the wool.'

So I went, with my hated cross-stitch, and discovered that grown-up conversation could be interesting enough to make me very angry.

The aunts said that Johnny had written to his mother, of the lady under whose roof he was lodging, that she was very kind to him. Hers was quite a small cottage and he and two others had their own rooms, beside a room to work in, which he was afraid was really the lady's own dressing-room. 'Indeed she has only kept "a butt and ben" for herself, and she has sweet eyes and hair.' One of the aunts sniffed—she had a habit of sniffing—and said that we had heard of several ladies who took in young army cadets; their eyes and their hair were not mentioned, but they were said to be devout Church workers and to have a most remarkable influence on their young men and to hold serious talks with them on Sunday evenings. What a pity that Johnny was not staying with one of these ladies. My grandmother said she would get him an introduction to the one of whom she had heard most, and she hoped that he would be invited to the Sunday evening talks. She would write at once to a mutual friend for the introduction. It was an opportunity not to be missed!

I felt furious with my aunts; why did they grudge Johnny

the pleasure of looking at his hostess's eyes and hair? I liked beautiful people myself; my uncle was certainly beautiful, and I didn't admire my aunts!

And in those older letters my elder uncle Harte writes to my mother: 'Mrs. Bridge, whose small cottage we are living in, is a kind old lady and does her best to make all four of us comfortable. There is another inhabitant of the cottage, Miss Bridge or 'Mary, my dear'. She is about eighteen and makes very good tea. Mrs. Bridge does not come down in the morning, so at breakfast we have Mademoiselle to ourselves.

'The college is about three-quarters of a mile away, so it doesn't take us long to run there, and we come back for dinner at three o'clock, after which the others go to the mathematical tutor, and I do some mathematics and read Fortifications. I have written to Papa to ask whether I am to stay in London after the examination, but I can make no plans until I hear from him—' He did, however, plan to see Adelaide Norton in *Norma.*

I am going to put in a few letters describing Harte's first voyage through the Mediterranean, and the overland journey to Suez in May, 1842.

He writes: 'My dear Mamma. I am the only artillery officer on board; there are some infantry cadets, and some merchants going out to China. It has been so calm that no one has been sick, which makes it much pleasanter. We expect to pass the *Orient* today, returning from Egypt, but we shall not be able to get any papers or letters as she is in quarantine, and we must not land at Gibraltar until we have had pratique.'

'We are only allowed six hours at Gibraltar, but one of us knew some artillery officers, who showed us all the best parts of the Rock, and finally let us out on a private beach where the boat we had arranged for did not come to meet us. So as no one is ever allowed into the fortress at night, we shouted to some fishermen who came to pick us up. We expect to reach Malta in five days'.

Families

After leaving Gibraltar, he writes: 'There is a report among the passengers that the Canal of the Nile is dry and if so, we shall have rather an adventurous journey. We shall have to ride all the way, but I am afraid there is no such luck. Since we left Gibraltar it's been very pleasant, as we have followed the shore all the way, the Captain to oblige us went a bit out of his way and took us quite near Algiers'.

Four days later he writes from Malta: 'About the passage to Egypt, we are not sure yet but most say the Canal is dry, in which case we shall find it very hard to make the passage.'

The next letter tells of the journey from Alexandria to Suez, partly in a very overcrowded boat, but chiefly on camel-back. They dare not leave their luggage behind and finally pick it up, and all got to Suez to find their ship had been boarded by a crowd of passengers for Calcutta, whose own ship had failed to pick them up. But he writes: 'A fellow-passenger has given me the use of his cabin to dress in, so I am quite "à mon aise", though the Calcutta passengers have taken all the other cabins. There are altogether sixty passengers, of whom thirty-two are deck passengers, like me. They charge us fifty pounds, in the cabins, it is seventy'.

He signs himself 'your attached son' . . . .

He married extremely young, a sister of Eldred Pottinger of Herat. Like her brother, and so many of the finest men of the generation, she was a very devout Evangelical. That being so, I do not understand why she was so terribly concerned when her husband refused to have their children baptized by 'a Clergyman for whom I have no respect'. I should have thought that ordination would have made little difference to such a man as Eldred Pottinger, and that his sister would have objected, as her husband did, to receiving in their house a man who 'sets a bad example to the natives'. Eldred Pottinger would surely have preferred lay-baptism by a practising Christian, but apparently his sister did not, and there was trouble between the parents of many little Keatinge babies.

25

Families

I gathered that when she came home, Aunt Harte thought her relations-in-law were 'very lax'.

Later I shall be writing more about my uncle, who was, along with my other uncle, John Mowbray Trotter, the person who meant most to me.

CHAPTER II

Scottish Background

❋

The family house, Dreghorn, was bought by my great-grandfather the Paymaster out of money said to have been 'improperly employed'—but shall we ever know now? It was on the north side of the Pentlands and marched with Woodhouselea at the summit of Allermuir. Woodhouselea looking south got all the sun there was; it did not strike Dreghorn during the three winter months. I was never in the house but I was always told it was 'most inconvenient'. The kitchen of course was as far from the dining-room as possible and on each floor several very large rooms led out of one another but did not communicate with the passages. Yet it must have been nice in summer. The ground sloped down to Lothian Burn and there were fine oak trees and all the open air of the Pentlands.

The Paymaster enlarged the original house, adding a tower. It changed hands several times, finally ending as the headquarters of Scottish Command. When my daughter Naomi heard that Scottish Command were evacuating it and about to blow it up she asked if it would be possible to get a piece of carving from the building but was refused. The only record of some very charming interior decoration in plaster and wood are photographs taken by Mr. Colin MacWilliams of the Historic Buildings Record of Scotland. The wood carvings seem to have been very similar to that in Colinton House (now Merchiston School) always attributed to Grinling Gibbons. It seems probable that the same carver worked in the two neighbour houses at the same time.

When it became obvious that my parents would not be able to live at Dreghorn the place was put up for sale. My mother told me that on the day of the sale my grandmother and my aunt sat waiting for the telegram announcing that it was sold so that they might 'lift up their voices and weep together'.

One of the disadvantages of my childhood was that I never had a settled home. I must have spent nearly half of it in hotels or lodgings and most of the rest in hired houses frequently changed. The earliest of these that I remember is Springfield (Polton, Midlothian) where a portrait of me with a little dog on my knee was painted. I loved 'Worry,' dearly, or perhaps really I only loved his master, my young Uncle John Mowbray Trotter, whom I loved all his life more passionately than I think I ever loved anyone else. Worry lived with us when his master went to India. My portrait was done by a German artist who seems to have gone from one country house to another painting children.

All this meant constant travelling. We travelled first-class, of course, and a manservant and my *bonne* or my mother's French maid went second. There was no smoking except in smoking carriages and these were not much more numerous than those marked 'Ladies Only'. It was assumed that the Railway Company was bound to put on a 'Ladies Only' if requested to do so. I once demanded and got one; a Third Class passenger who remarked 'Ye're no feared o' a man, are ye?' was very severely told off by the Platform Superintendent of the 'Cally' (Princes Street Station) Edinburgh. There was no heating on the train but at every station porters came along with trolleys loaded with tins of hot sand, and as the train slowed down rows of people hung out of the carriage windows signalling to the porters. One advantage of travelling with a manservant was that our foot warmers were replenished at frequent intervals. There was no restaurant cars but on long trips there was always one stop of twenty minutes or so when the travellers made a rush for the Refreshment Rooms.

My mother disapproved of 'station food', and we carried a luncheon basket which always contained a carefully roasted and carved chicken. The skill with which this was tied together again with red tape was one of the thrills of dinner on the train! In those days red tape was not official, but all respectable households used it to tie up their parcels. There was one station—was it Carlisle?—where during a five-minute stop we always bought hot teacakes, and Abernethy biscuits that were quite unlike the modern product bearing their name.

When we arrived in London we might find that the friends with whom we were going to stay had sent a brougham to meet us. If not, my parents and I went on in a hansom, and the servants followed in a four-wheeler—on the floor of which there was usually damp straw—and behind the four-wheeler the cab-runner raced. There were always cab-runners waiting outside London stations ready to follow any cab with luggage in it, in the hope of being hired to carry up the luggage when it reached its destination. Sometimes there was a row between the cabby and the cab-runner, and sometimes a second man attached himself to the cab, and the two fought till one of them dropped off.

When the cab drew up the wretched cab-runner was in very poor condition, and I always felt that he was not paid enough, even if our hosts had not already engaged a man to carry up the trunks. If this were so, the cab-runner only got a compassionate shilling or sixpence, and he looked so hot and muddy! In fact, the cab-runners spoiled for me the drive through the lighted streets. Edinburgh to London was a twelve hours' journey, so except perhaps at midsummer one never reached London before lighting-up time, and the drive down gas-lit Piccadilly was as exciting as being taken to the illuminations—the only Edinburgh occasion when little girls were taken out at night.

. . . . .

Scottish Background

I fancy my father always had it in mind to settle in Scotland, preferably in Midlothian. Quite late in the day, when I must have been eleven or twelve, Dryden,[1] part of the Bush property, was for sale and negotiations were well advanced for its purchase when the surveyor reported that the house was not only undermined by the workings of a newly opened coal seam, but that it was full of dry rot. Its roof and floors collapsed shortly afterwards. If it had been at all habitable it would have been a most suitable home for us. The house, good solid grey stone, was not too large, the woods surrounding it were lovely, and I suppose there was some sort of home farm as well as a walled garden. It was close to Rosslyn, and to Glen Corse, the Royal Scots depot, to Woodhouselea, Bush, Colinton, Hawthornden and Melville, and we should anyhow have dwelt among our own people.

Long before this. however, my father had bought and sold one house, and we had lived in two hired ones. When we left Springfield he had asked his mother to 'look out for a suitable place' while we were abroad. She wrote that she had bought a house for him. She and the aunts had gone to look at Rosetta, a small property in Peebleshire. On a fine sunny summer day I have no doubt that it looked most attractive, and they bought it—just like that! My father must have put up the money for the purchase, but he had no further say in the matter, and my mother resented it exceedingly. The valley of the Edelston was well known to be the most rheumatic district in Scotland, and after each of the two summers we spent there she was carried out of the house after a bad attack of rheumatism (it was always called rheumatic fever).

This, as far as I know, was the one drawback to the place—but surely it was a sufficient one; otherwise the neighbourhood was pleasant. On one side we had Sir Graham Montgomery, a keen Conservative giving a lead to the county. He gave my mother one of his dachshunds, descended from the famous

---

[1] 'Who knows not Dryden's groves of oak and Melville's rocky glen, Dalkeith which all the virtues love, and caverned Hawthornden.'
                                                                    Scott.

breed of a German princeling. On the other side of the valley
was Cringletie, and cousin Wolfe Murray, a dear and delightful person, one of the Queen's Bodyguard of Scottish Archers.

His children were not so nice. His eldest daughter frightened
me with stories of a madman who was supposed to live in the
house. I must have been a particularly credulous child, for I
believed this improbable tale, and was in acute terror when
we played hide-and-seek in the passages. Her young half-
brother used to get under the table at nursery tea and pinch
my legs. I did not complain because I wanted to deal with the
nuisance myself, and hoped to kick him hard enough to make
him stop; but when he got his hand up my drawers I had to
complain, and was scolded for not doing so earlier.

There was a scare of a mad dog while we were at Rosetta.
The poor beast ran across the lawn where I was playing, pur-
sued by what I remember as a shouting crowd of men and boys
—there were probably not more than a dozen of them. My
father carried me in by the drawing-room windows and for
days no-one talked of anything but hydrophobia. I understood
that anyone who was bitten would be 'smothered between two
feather beds to prevent his going mad'. I had nightmares
about this for years afterwards. What I remember best, though,
is the big nursery where there was room for a large dolls' house
which my mother had built for me by the village carpenter,
and for all the wooden toys which people brought me from
India. How different this was from a hotel bedroom! One
basket of Indian bricks, red, green and yellow, highly polished,
survived to be played with by my grandsons, Denny and
Murdoch.

Wherever we came from, the end of at least one of our
yearly peregrinations was always my Trotter grandmother's
house in Edinburgh. For years she lived in Melville Street
(the street called after her grandfather). When I was quite a
small child in Edinburgh I used to come down to the drawing-
room before dinner and when dinner was announced I said
goodnight and was kissed by the couples as they left the drawing-room arm in arm, the last couple turning down the gas

Scottish Background

to a mere flicker. The tiger skins on the floor lay carpet-like when the light was full on, but in the semi-darkness, when a coal dropped in the grate, the glass eyes in the tigers' heads shone, and the slightly raised heads between the spread paws seemed to move. I crouched as near the fire as I could get, but I did not dare to turn with my back to the biggest tiger until one night I could bear the strain no longer. Perhaps my nurse was later than usual in fetching me to bed. Anyhow I jumped up, seized the largest tiger's head and banged it on the floor. Of course I was caught—one always is caught.

My grandmother finally moved to 10 Randolph Crescent, a house my father had bought for her, and into which he and my mother moved after her death. This part of Randolph Crescent was built on the edge of the cliff overhanging the Water of Leith. I thought it a most romantic house after my father had taken me down into the basement, four storeys below the front of the house at street level, where there was a cavern-like place, with stalactites hanging from the roof, and in the middle of the stone floor a mysterious-looking trap-door!

My father grabbed me when I was going to jump on it, and explained that it covered a well, he didn't know how deep, and that the trap-door was to prevent people from falling in; but he was not sure whether the planks were good—they might be rotten. 'I must have this looked to,' he added. I very much hoped that I might have a chance of 'looking to' and it came when an old man was found who said that he had orders to come 'whiles' and test the boards and bolts of the trap-door.

My father arranged for a more regular inspection, once a year I think, and the old man became a family institution to me, and to my son after me. He always let down a jug with a string tied to the handle, and, after politely offering it to us first, he drank the contents. He said it 'kept him right for a year'. 'Esparto grass and drains,' my father murmured. The Water of Leith was dirty and smelly in those days, and we certainly never saw a trout in it, even well above the town. However, not even the interest of the trap-door and the

32

My father

My godfather, the Rev. Spencer Drummond, 'Uncle Pen'

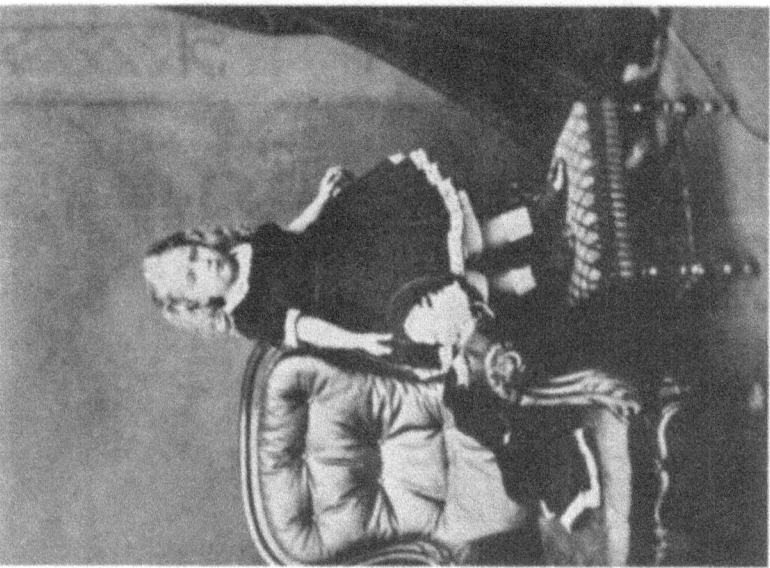

I.K.T., about two years old

stalactites made me forget that he had promised to show me St. Bernard's Well, which wasn't a well at all, but a kind of drinking fountain. My father was so pleased with the place that he had a comfortable seat—'for the old folk' he said—placed close to our back garden door. I wonder whether it still exists. I have a vague idea that he gave a little endowment with it.

With these early days in Edinburgh, I very closely connect three old gentlemen, who would figure in any social history of the time—Admiral Ramsay, the Dean, his brother, and Dr. John Brown. The Dean was of course an Episcopalian, but he would have fitted as well into the David Wilkie picture of the Moderator installed in St. Giles'. He and the Admiral used to give me new fourpenny bits, which they seem always to have carried in their pockets for their child friends, but I do not understand why, when either of them was in trouble, I should have been sent to visit him. When the old Admiral was ill, and again after his death, I went to the Dean's. My *bonne* took me to his door and then retired and waited till I reappeared. I have no idea what we talked about, and I hope the visit did not last long enough to worry the Dean very much.

Dr. John Brown, author of *Rab and his Friends*, known to everyone as 'Rab', really, I think, liked my visits. There was something of the eternal boy about him till the last, and he always had stories to tell about his dogs, or about my uncles and aunts when they were children, and he had been family doctor. I think Dr. Brown was an Elder of the Free Church, or do I merely imagine this because he was so fond of the word 'freedom'? When my *bonne* complained that I would stand on the bridges in Princes Street Gardens, while trains passed underneath (a habit which my son and daughter both indulged in, in their time, and which is carried on by my great-grandchildren), he would say 'Ah! Let the child have freedom. Children should be allowed to run free, to be free!' My *bonne* objected that it was an amusement shared, as she said, by *tous les petits galopins* of the place and most indecorous, besides dirtying one's frock and gloves.

Scottish Background

My grandmother always had a children's party shortly after we arrived in Edinburgh, and I was told how kind it was of Ga-ga to give the party 'for me'. But of course grandmother was meeting some of her social obligations in giving these parties! We always had a long wait for our tea until the latest guest had arrived, and during one of the waits my mother produced a box of crystallized apricots and told me to hand it round to all my 'little friends'. Presently I saw that when I reached the end of the long row of chairs there would not be an apricot left for me. One of the Fraser-Tytler's saw it too and broke hers in half, and shared with me. I always remembered this unto her for good.

I remember only one Christmas tree from the early period of my childhood in Edinburgh. (Ninety years ago Christmas was observed in Scotland by Episcopalian families only.) Every detail connected with that Christmas tree is so clear in my memory that there must have been something 'extra special' about it.

Sheriff and Mrs. Archie Davidson were living at Redhall, Slateford. Their youngest daughter was my contemporary, and the 'Christmas tree party' was given for her and her little brother. My mother and I drove out from Edinburgh, but as it came on to snow, we had to leave the party early so as not to keep the horses waiting, and I missed the great final thrill of helping to blow out the last remaining five or six flickering candles on the tree.

I don't think our hosts can have been very expert candle lighters, for we had at last finished tea and some bold spirits were hammering on the drawing-room door clamouring 'Let us in!' long before the tree was ready and we were admitted. Then, of course, it was lovely, and one or two branches caught fire and smelled delicious, and elderly ladies murmured about how dangerous it was, and said 'Keep the dear children away from the candles', which made it all the more exciting.

All the presents had, as I remember, to hang on the tree. It didn't count if they were piled on the floor under the lower branches as we used to pile them in later years; the result was that some of them fell off, a doll's head was broken, and a box of coloured pencils burst and scattered its contents. We fell over one another trying to pick them up, and the rightful owner was sure he had not got them all back.

Just before we left, the Father Christmas on the topmost bough began to sag and had to be taken down. Our hostess murmured that she would keep him for next year, but a tall man said: 'Nonsense! Where is the wastepaper basket? The children want the effigy. Let them draw lots for it!' And while I was being buttoned up into my long gaiters in the dressing-room, he came in to announce that I'd drawn the lucky number. My mother said: 'Oh no, Colonel, she has had her little share.' But I wanted that Father Christmas, and the Colonel must have seen a covetous gleam in my eye, for he tucked it under my arm. I had that Father Christmas for many years—then a housemaid dusted him—and in the carriage going home my mother blamed me for having accepted him too readily. 'You ought to have asked whether none of the others wanted it. It was not nice of you,' she said.

Greatly daring, I retorted: '*You* said I'd had my *little* share. I don't think *that* was nice.' And between excitement and consternation at my own audacity, I wept a little.

My mother answered quite gently: 'You know that I did not mean *little* in that sense' and I was left to puzzle about a word which was so often applied to myself and my possessions. The nurse in the dressing-room had said 'Stand still, there's a good little girl, and I'll put on your little coat, and your dear little warm hood.' I had wanted to tell her that my clothes were *not* little—they fitted quite well. But one did not argue with other people's nurses!

After that first Christmas tree I often saw one at my grandmother's, but they were intended for the entertainment of my younger cousins, and I was soon considered old enough to be allowed to 'trim' them. That was great fun, though I always longed for more tinsel and more candles than the aunts allowed. There were no candle clips until well into the new century; we used to wire each candle separately on to a branch.

Scottish Background

It was not easy and it hurt one's fingers, but if one managed to get the candle to stand straight one felt very grown-up and capable.

As to the decorations in my grandmother's house: what she really revelled in were mirrors framed in plush, with water-lilies and kingfishers painted on them. Part of the lighting in the drawing-room consisted of tiny naked gas jets, forming haloes over the heads of two of Thorwaldsen's angels. These angels must have been fashionable at the time, for I remember them in other houses. I understand that the original ones in Denmark are life-size, and are fonts, the kneeling angels holding large shells for christening water. My grandmother's were fastened to the wall at each side of the drawing-room fireplace, and their haloes would have been big enough for the angels to jump through.

The curls from the heads of her two younger sons were mounted on a stand under glass. The crested Lowestoft china, of which at that time she had still quite a quantity, was not put under glass. I gather that several of the Trotter families in the county used the dark blue Worcester china, with the red line, of which I have one cup and saucer. It must have made a lovely breakfast table, and I suppose they ordered it down from the makers in large family crates. Bush certainly used it, and Arniston, as well as Dreghorn.

There were five framed prints of 'The Virgin Martyr' hanging in different rooms. She is depicted floating on a pond, her halo just clear of the water. In the background, two figures in dark cloaks and sombreros are evidently getting the fright of their lives.

I was her eldest grandchild and my grandmother worked a cross-stitch chair seat for me, and painted illuminated texts for my nursery walls. I remember one long frame which held on each end a verse of a hymn, surrounded by wreaths of convolvulus, and in the middle a photograph of the 'Infant Samuel'. My earliest and most vivid impression of her is a slight figure, sitting very upright on a hard sofa, wearing a modified widow's cap with mauve ribbons, and a really lovely

36

Kashmir shawl. As far as I remember, most well-dressed elderly ladies wore one of these 'chuddahs', and it is said that Queen Victoria made a present of a 'chuddah' to each of her god-daughters on her marriage. The Queen had a constant supply of them, for when, after the first Sikh War, Kashmir was handed over to Ghulab Singh in acknowledgment of his support, 'he not only paid seventy-five lakhs of rupees, but made a yearly tribute of six pairs of shawls, twelve goats and a horse.' I should like to find out what the fate of the horses was, and whether or when the tribute of shawls ceased.

My grandmother used to sit making shirts for missions, and I pitied the little black boys who would have to wear them in 'hot Africa', for they were made of stuff called galatea, which was very hard and stiff; and as the seams were not oversewed, they must have been terribly scratchy!

A large, square work-basket stood on the stool in front of her and in each corner of it there was a little bag; two of these held pins and buttons and the others pieces of liquorice or marshmallow. We called marshmallow 'pâte de guimauve' and pieces were cut from a long stick of the lovely 'marshy' stuff, which we longed to be allowed to suck.

I, and any other child who visited her, was told to take a piece from one of the corner bags, but we never knew which one contained horrible liquorice and which the pâte; and whichever we took out we had to put directly into our mouths, without even waiting to say 'thank you'! I have been nearly sick trying to swallow the horrible black stuff too quickly, and the aunts thought it a good joke and laughed.

The grandmother sang hymns, or else a most intriguing song, to which I listened over and over again. 'Not a button, not a button, not a button do I care, for Sir David Hunter Blair.' I was never able to find out who Sir David was; I don't know to this day.

On these kinds of occasions, the aunts used often to ask whether I did not love 'Gaga' better than anyone else in the world, and they were definitely put out when I said that I loved 'Mammy' best.

On other occasions they asked whether I loved Papa or Mama best; but that question I always refused to answer. I can remember various occasions when I heard grown-ups ask the same kind of embarrassing questions of other long-suffering children; so it must have been a fashionable form of indiscretion.

In my aunt Mrs. Forbes' house there was a curious piece of furniture which my grandmother must have given to her. It was a white marble mantelshelf, supported by two caryatids, which were portraits of my grandmother and her sister Mary, Mrs. William Pitt Dundas. Their mother was the daughter of the first Lord Melville, and married first Mr. Drummond of Albury. Her sons by this marriage were, Henry Drummond, one of the original apostles of the Irvingite creed and founder of Drummond's Bank, and the Reverend Spencer Drummond, who christened me. She married *en seconde noce* James Strange of the Hon. East India Company. Her two daughters by this marriage were my grandmother Louisa and her sister Mary. At some period they spent a considerable time in Italy, at Florence, where they had some cousins called Ciccarporci. The two Scotch girls mixed in the 'best society' and a sculptor begged to do their portraits—hence the caryatids.

Aunt Mary fell in love with an Italian, 'a most suitable marriage, only unfortunately he was a Roman Catholic'. They agreed to elope, but Louisa gave her sister away to the parents —she was the 'dutiful one'—and they all went home to Scotland.

Mrs. Strange held strong religious views—there is a volume of her *Reflections* among the old books; and somewhere I have seen a letter from one of her sons, recommending the book to a friend. Aunt Mary married her cousin, William Pitt Dundas, who had always wanted to marry her. She was the dearest and kindest little old lady, and in spite of having nine children of her own, she made time to care for me too. Once when we had all been staying in the country and I was going home by train with my parents, she kept me back for a day and I drove home—a two days' drive with her and uncle Pitt. The joy and excitement of this was half spoiled by the long, cautionary addresses which preceded it. My mother told me how shocked Aunt Mary would be if I did not comb out *all* the tangles in my hair, and my father said that I really must not bore the old gentleman with much chatter. The latter injunction went by the board when I was sitting silent opposite uncle Pitt in the carriage, and he exclaimed 'What ails the lassie? Have ye lost your tongue?'

For our second day's drive we had to make an early start. On the way to bed, Aunt Mary called down to me 'My dear, don't be late in the morning. Whenever I have to begin the day unusually early I say my prayers overnight.'

CHAPTER III

Abroad

❋

In time I came to know the main railway lines between Scotland and the South very intimately, because we were constantly using them, but we never *travelled*, and I cannot remember the time I did not long to do so, and sitting quietly in my corner—'back to the engine, dear, don't forget that; and don't try to look out of the window, you will get so dirty' —I made wonderful plans for crossing the Atlantic and still more perhaps for going East—it was a map of India which hung above my bed.

According to my early recollection, the object of going abroad was to 'take the waters', usually at some 'Badeort' in Germany. To which of these places we went seems to have depended on which of the Webers we consulted.

There were in my childhood two Webers, German doctors who came to London for a few weeks every year for consultations. One heard people asking one another: 'To which of the Webers do you go?' Of course the patients of the one thought the other Weber nothing but a quack.

It must have been in 1868 that 'our Weber' sent us to Ems. The place became notorious later when Bismarck dispatched the 'Ems telegram' which launched the Franco-German war, but in 1869 he and the old King of Prussia were taking the cure like ourselves, and there I met with my one small Continental adventure. We were sitting in the Kursaal garden one afternoon when the band struck up 'Heil dir im Sieges Krantz', which is the tune of 'God Save the Queen'. As he always did when he heard it played, my father stood up and took off his hat. I think a few Germans did likewise, or possibly the other hats raised belonged to Englishmen; but most people sat stolidly still on their chairs, though some said, 'Oh, look at the Herr Englander! How polite he is! He stands uncovered while the 'Heil' is played, as they do in England when they hear their national songs. Lieber Gott, it looks well, too!' To a friend who was sitting near us my father remarked in a loud aside, 'Very decent of these people to play "God Save the Queen". They must have noticed how many English there are about this year.'

Presently the old King of Prussia, with Bismarck beside him, came down the garden, followed by a group of officers. He looked a friendly, elderly soldier, much the sort of person I was used to at home, but as a king he was extremely interesting. Is there not a king in nearly all fairy tales?

'If you think him so interesting, go and drop a curtsy to him,' my father said. I do not know whether he really intended me to do so, but I ran forward and made my bob just in front of the old gentleman. He picked me up and gave me a kiss. I very much resented being lifted and kissed by most elderly gentlemen, but I did not mind the King of Prussia at all, and ran back contentedly to my father, who stood with his hat off, and more or less at attention, till the group had passed on, laughing and saluting good-naturedly. I do not think my mother was pleased when she heard about this.

We were on a short driving tour in Eastern France when one evening we heard laughter and shouts from behind rows of vines—uninteresting vines, for all the grapes had been picked. My father said, 'I believe this is the vintage, and they are pressing the grapes. Let us go and see.' We were hailed in quite incomprehensible patois, but the tone was obviously friendly. 'You know all about this,' my father said, and he quoted:

> '*And in the vats of Luna*
> *This year the must shall foam*
> *Round the white feet . . .*'

Abroad

Yes, of course I knew the 'Lays' and here were the 'laughing girls', although they seemed older than I had visualized them. They beckoned and held out welcoming hands. 'You'd better join them,' my father said, and I had just begun eagerly to take off my shoes and stockings, when three or four old men came leaping, prancing, gesticulating and screaming through the must. They had long, very hairy legs, and strange-looking feet with claw-like, long-nailed toes.

I can think of only one word to express what I felt. I was 'scunnert' and got behind my father, saying 'But—their Sires *haven't* marched to Rome! I'll wait till they have all started.' My father told me not to be silly, but I retorted, '*You* can drink that must when they've made it into wine. I *won't*.' This time I think that my mother rather sympathized with me, and afterwards Henry told me confidentially: 'You were quite right, Missy. Them Frenchies! Stick to beer!'

About 1869 we went to stay at the big English hotel in Cannes. I do not remember which particular modification of the Franco-Italian frontier had taken place shortly before this time, but the frontier itself looked like any other of the narrow gullies on the coast, and had the usual rough stone bridge across it—only here there was a French sentry at one end of the bridge and an Italian at the other. I thought them very unimpressive soldiers, not to be compared with privates of the Black Watch or the Royal Scots, but they smiled amiably when a little girl walked boldly—though I will not say without trepidation—across the bridge into 'another country'. Her father waited for her in France, but it was true that she had gone to Italy by herself.

That summer sea-bathing had been prescribed for me. My red flannel nightgowns were made into bathing dresses (grownups wore bathing dresses made of thick blue serge with patterns of white or red braid). I was allowed a few minutes of delightful splash and paddle, and then I was seized by a horrible old 'baigneur' who carried me into the sea and dipped me, head under, three times. He shouted all the while at the top of his voice: 'N'ayez pas peur, la petite M'zelle, n'ayez pas peur.'

42

Abroad

To this I screamed back 'Les Anglaises n'ont *jamais* peur!' and kicked as hard as I could until he deposited me back in the bathing hut with my *bonne*. I cannot believe that this kind of bathing can have been particularly salubrious!

This type of bathing machine was mounted on wheels, and there were shafts between which the horse, which dragged it into or out of the sea, was harnessed. Outside each door were steps, and one tried to persuade the proprietor of the machine to drive it into the sea so that the water reached the topmost step and one got out into fairly deep water. One could only wade out as far as the rope attached to the side of the door would reach, and only swimmers ever let go the rope—and how few swimmers there were among the lady bathers! One couldn't hire a machine for more than half an hour, and if the proprietor thought you were going to overstay your time, he harnessed his horse to the landward side and started to pull the machine up the beach, so that one had to scramble ignominiously and painfully into the moving machine—ladies, of course, bathed at one end of the beach and men at the other.

At the 'English' hotel in Cannes there was at this time a Russian lady, known to the English children as Princess Olga Dolgoruki. She walked about in the *salle-a-manger* in the evening, when some kind of crawly insect after bashing itself against the hanging lamps, would fall on the floor with a horrid scrunch. Then Olga Dolgoruki would stamp on it with her immensely high heels, ejaculating 'Peste! Il a vécu'. The impression she made on little English girls was that this was not the behaviour of a lady, whatever she might call herself.

We stayed at San Remo till Easter. My mother and Lady John Russell decorated the English church—a hotel sitting-room, I think—and I learned to get rid of the smell of the lovely wild white garlic by dipping the stems in boiling water—also that Lord John was called the 'Pie Minister'. It was not till years later that I realized that Lord John's appointment had nothing to do with things as nice as pies. The other English children at San Remo stayed on the sea front or in the gardens of the large 'English' hotel. Our hotel was small, with a marble balcony overlooking the harbour, and very Italian sanitary arrangements. My father and I collected wild flowers on the hillsides, and I learnt enough elementary botany for old Miss Henslowe, the botanist, to think me 'an intelligent child', and to present me with Miss Pratt's *English Flora*, in four volumes, with coloured illustrations!

When we walked through the queer, steep, narrow little village streets, the women at the doorsteps, and marketing at the little stalls, called to one another. They came up and touched my frock and my long flaxen, blue-ribboned curls and said 'C'e un angelo!' They probably took me for a *vouée à la vierge*, who till the time of her first communion only wears white and blue, the Virgin's colours, and for years after this I could still pass for a *vouée* if I wanted to join in a religious procession, or to see some church ceremony at close quarters. I had only to wear a white summer dress and a blue bow, and to hang round my neck a silver medallion bought when I chose my birthday present at Hamilton and Inches in Edinburgh. Or perhaps it was my tow-coloured hair that did the trick!

The religious orders had been banished from Italy about this time, but two old monks had been allowed to remain at San Remo because of the good work they had done during an epidemic of smallpox. They were friendly old gentlemen, with white beards and sandals. They and my father talked Latin together, and on Easter Eve they gave the Eaton boys and me rings of plaited palm leaves, and each of us a 'Saint Esprit', very like a grasshopper, also made of palm leaves, with Venetian glass eyes.

From San Remo we went to Grenoble, where I got typhoid, and was, I believe, dangerously ill; and from there to Geneva to consult a well-known child specialist. It seems to me that I lay in bed in Geneva for weeks and weeks, but it may not have been so long. I remember that my father went to 'every shop in the town' to try to get plain biscuits. I wasn't allowed bread. He came in triumphantly one evening to say that he had found a shop which stocked Huntley and Palmers and had ordered a tin—but when it came the biscuits were 'Mixed, with Icing', so of course, I wasn't allowed to eat even one!

I do not remember where we went from Geneva, but the plan was to go home *via* the Rhine, and there was much discussion about boats, and the easiest way to travel. Then one day Henry, our manservant, came in to report 'The Frenchies all say that they'll be on the Rhine in a week' and that it wouldn't be at all wise to try to get home that way. So we set out across France. I heard afterwards that ours was the last 'ordinary' train to connect in Paris with trains to Calais. The only thing which I remember about the drive across Paris is the Colonne Vendome which my father pointed out, bidding me remember that it was made of 'Guns from every nation in Europe except ours'. When shortly afterwards I read about 'He that won a hundred fights nor ever lost an English gun',[1] I felt that this was something real, something that I had been in touch with!

The Gare du Nord was packed with excited people—soldiers screaming '*à* Berlin', and gendarmes trying to keep the crowds moving. Henry came to the door of our *fiacre* and said 'This won't do for Missie, I must carry her' and lifted me down. I was always at loggerheads with my French *bonne*, and to irritate her I sometimes said 'Vive Bismarck'. Henry whispered in my ear 'For God's sake, Missie, don't say "Vive-you-know-who"', or the Frenchies will scrag me', and I felt proud and powerful, because if I could so easily make trouble for Henry, I could 'contrariwise' protect him by not saying the dangerous words. Wild horses would not have dragged the name of Bismarck over my lips!

A gendarme got us into the crowded train at last, my poor mother taking me on her knee because there was not a vacant seat. I was desperately hungry, but there was scarcely anything which the doctors permitted me to eat, till eventually my father succeeded in getting a mug of hot milk without coffee in it; but the mug was handleless and burnt my fingers and I dropped it! There was no more to be had, and the train started, and my poor mother kept, I suspect, a very irritable, hungry

[1] Tennyson's *Burial of the Duke of Wellington*.

little girl on her lap through the long journey. The next thing I remember is being wrapped in a plaid and told to look at the white cliffs of Dover.

I was very much puzzled as the war went on to know which side I was 'on'. Cousin Margaret Trotter, who was always called 'La Grande Marguerite' (she was an immense woman), lived at Saint Germain, and had done a great deal for the place—given a cottage hospital I think—but at the time of the siege of Paris the '*bas peuple*' came and demanded money of her and terrified her maids, so Sir Coutts Lindsay asked for German protection for her, and as soon as Paris surrendered, the Crown Prince came to see her, and quartered a couple of German officers on her ('gentlemen' she reported, 'who knew how to behave in a lady's house'). The local people were furious, and said she was fraternizing with the enemy, but she sent for the Mayor and told him that she had only accepted German protection because he was unable to supply it, and he acknowledged (as the story goes) that she had been a most generous friend of the place, had deserved better of the people, and was '*Une dame des plus courageuses*'.

I believe Sir Coutts Lindsay was responsible for the pigeon post to beleaguered Paris, where copies of *The Times* in miniature photograph were delivered by the birds.

I am sure that we went to Scotland after escaping from France, for I made 'charpi' (threads pulled out of old linen, and used as sphagnum moss was used in the Boer War) with my grandmother and aunts. The Germans wanted their 'charpi' made into neat little bundles, but this was supposed to be too difficult for me, so I only made for the French, who were not so particular.

At the end of the war we saw something of Archibald Forbes, who had been War Correspondent with the German Army, the first neutral country correspondent to have accompanied an army in the field. I remember him as a strong, friendly, outspoken man, possibly not quite so popular with my mother, because he was so outspoken. She much preferred

Sir William Russell of *The Times*, who took me to the zoo to visit an infant family of brown bears, which he scratched familiarly on their heads. This must have been a tremendous treat, but still I always looked on Archibald Forbes as *my* War Correspondent, though I don't think he ever paid any attention to me, and certainly never took me to the zoo!

After the Franco-German war, when going abroad was once more the fashion, 'our' Dr. Weber directed our steps towards Homburg, a Badeort where at least four springs of water with different chemical compositions rise within a few hundred yards of one another. Every patient was directed to a special spring, and ordered to drink just so many tumblers-full before breakfast. Most of them took exercise between their first and second tumblers, and my parents always found acquaintances to talk to during their walks. But it was dull work for me, and I amused myself by sampling all the springs, and pretending that I much preferred the 'Stahl-brunnen', which was colder than the others and not nearly so much frequented, and the Mädchen in charge of the glasses was friendly and talkative. We had rooms at Homburg instead of staying at an hotel, so there was not even the fun of the *table d'hote*, with the chance of curious food, and the possibility of making friends with some other young things. Even the country walks were spoiled the year when the North of Europe had a plague of lemmings. Homburg was supposed to be quite beyond their range, but one constantly saw dead 'field-mice' on the paths, and trod on them if one ventured on to the grass, and there was no Pied Piper to deal with them.

On just one lucky summer my mother met an old friend, the Polish Countess Plaaten, and her girls were encouraged to practise their English on me. Only unfortunately I could seldom understand them, as they had learned English from an Irish nursemaid, and had acquired a shocking brogue! In Catholic families the nursemaids and nursery governesses were nearly always Irish. People did not risk their children coming under an alien theological influence: my French *bonne,* for example, was a 'black Protestant' who believed in hell!

Countess Plaaten gave my mother a set of onyx brooches mounted in black and silver enamel, the ornaments of 'la *nation en deuil*'. I liked Poles, and always asked whether there were any staying at the hotels to which we went, and tried to make friends with all members of that gallant distressful nation.

We must have stayed at Homburg on three or four different occasions; long after the year of the lemmings was the summer in which I tried to find out what people did in the Kursaal. I never discovered what the dreadful hush-hush game was which was played there, but I picked up all sorts of interesting hints about Lord Rosebery's wooing of the handsome and beautifully dressed Miss Rothschild, whose family refused to allow the engagement because they wanted to keep entire control of her fortune. At last, so gossip said, she threatened to withdraw all her wealth from the family business in one enormous cheque, at which they relented, and one saw the couple walking and driving about together. I fancy that I thought it a case of young love being frustrated by selfish elders, for I had great sympathy with the resolute young lady!

L.K.T. with 'Worry'

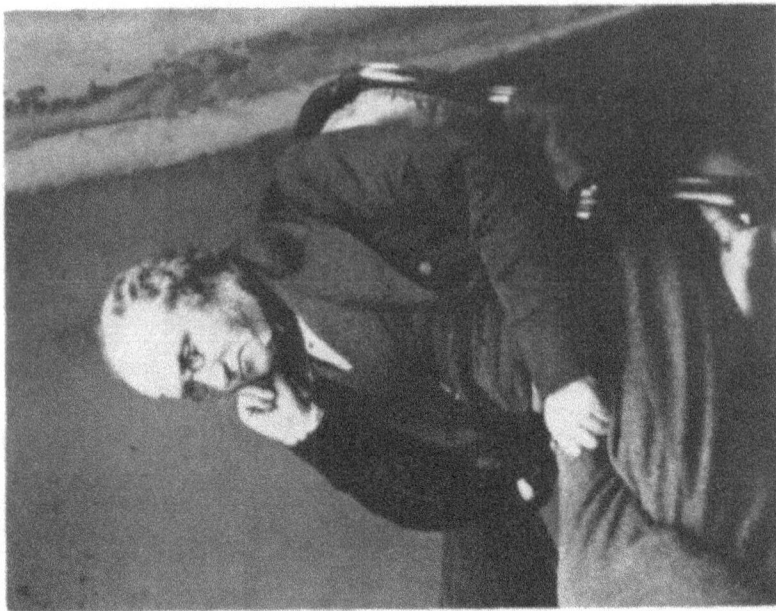

Dr John Brown, 'Rab'

Admiral Ramsay

CHAPTER IV

Irish Background

As I remember it, my mother and I went every year to Ireland to stay with my grandfather Judge Keatinge but possibly we did not go so often. My grandfather's house was in Merrion Square, 'the Mayfair of Dublin', and all sorts of nice things happened at that house. My cousin Alys, my contemporary among the other children, crept into the dining-room with me; we watched while two footmen polished the mahogany table till the reflected silver winked back at us and the old butler said 'For the love of the Saints, Missie Darlin', keep your blessed fingers off my table. Sure, I'm expecting *twinty* to dinner this very day.' There was an old housemaid who rather than go to a doctor used to appeal to my bachelor uncle 'Have ye ne'er a cast pill you could oblige me wid, Mr. William?'

Upstairs in the drawing-room the Chinese wallpaper had strange trees growing from floor to ceiling, with life-size parrots and macaws, as well as less recognizable creatures, climbing their branches; an ideal room in which to tell oneself stories of 'going to the tropics'.

One day the Judge asked which we would like—'Half-a-crown or sixpence?' Wise with schoolroom teaching, Alys said half-a-crown, while I considered that six pennies were surely more worth having than *half* something! When the two coins were laid on the table, I was naturally disappointed by the size of mine, but I had been enjoined always to say

'Thank you' for a present—I was to remember that I was thanking the donor for his kindness, whatever the present might be—so I thanked, and when we were alone again my cousin was slightly scornful of my ignorance; but the next morning I was called into the breakfast-room and my grandfather gave me an hour-glass. This time my thanks were heartfelt. I wish I had that hour-glass now, but it disappeared in one of our many changes of abode. My mother told me years afterwards that the Judge had said that the gift was 'in recognition of the child's self-control on the occasion of the coins'.

The Dublin family must have dined at least as early as five o'clock for I came down to dessert (at the end of a long dinner) and sat beside my grandfather and was given grapes, and something to drink out of a salt spoon—port, I suppose, as it was red and tasted hot. I wore a short-sleeved muslin frock and my Uncle Maurice used to put his hand in at the loose neck and say it was my post office and he was posting his letters. I hated him and his nasty pawing fingers!

I have one other pleasant recollection of that visit to Dublin. My cousin greatly admired my bronze kid boots with gilt buttons, I thought them 'dressed up and babyish' and was delighted when the buttons came off and could not be matched.

One summer we went to Wildbad in the Black Forest. My mother was taking the baths for her rheumatism, and so was the Princess of Wales. There was much criticism and head-shaking among the German medical men because the Prince would bathe in the Enz—before breakfast too!—and it was worse still when he arranged to go down the river on one of the rafts which took wood from the Forest to join the immense rafts on the Rhine. When one of these rafts was due to start, the Enz was dammed up for a day till the raft was launched. Then down it came—a little bow wave and a rush of water bearing the crushing, straining tree trunks poled by shouting foresters. No wonder the Prince of Wales wanted to take the trip! Dr. Acland—later Sir Henry Acland, Regius Professor of Medicine at Oxford—shrugged his shoulders and told his

Irish Background

German opposite number that he would not interfere with any English gentleman who wanted to get his feet wet, still less with the Prince when he desired to bathe.

It was an immense pleasure to my mother when the Judge, after a bad attack of gout, decided to join us at Wildbad. My grandfather had his manservant Michael with him, and an outsize wheelchair, in which his bad foot was propped on a pile of cushions, leaving room for me to sit on the floor beside his good foot; and Michael pushed the chair with both of us in it. The Judge was bored by the well-laid-out 'Anlagen', where people stopped the chair and made conversation, and liked to go a mile or so up the valley to the water meadows, where tiny streams purled quietly between the boundaries of the fields, and I could pick a bigger bunch of wild flowers than even grandpapa could hold and—better still—there were little green lizards to hunt.

Michael had retired to a discreet distance and was, I think, occupied with his rosary when he suddenly made a rush at me, screaming: 'Missy, Missy, don't you touch it! 'Tis poisonous it is! A snake, a snake!' He was armed with one of grandpapa's sticks, but I stood my ground and said: 'It's a dear little lizard, Michael, and you shan't hurt it!'

Grandpapa had been dozing, but he woke up to grunt: 'Don't be a fool, Michael.'

'But sor, sor, it's one o' them snakes which Saint Patrick drove out of Ireland—praise be!'

I said: 'I'm sure Saint Patrick never did such a silly thing. He'd be very angry with you for trying to hurt it.'

Grandpapa kept the balance true: 'If it had been a snake it might have been a poisonous one, although I think this improbable, and Michael's intentions were good, so we'll say no more about it.'

'But I've lost my lizard,' I complained.

Grandpapa looked at me very gravely and said what I remember as this: 'You cannot say that you have lost something which you have never owned, nor,' he hesitated for a moment—'nor captured.'

The word 'captured' stuck in my mind, so that before we got back to the 'Anlagen' and the talkative people, I asked, 'But Grandpapa, when would the lizard have been mine?'

But Grandpapa had had enough of the subject and he said 'You are as inconsequent as Michael.' So I thought that perhaps it was wrong to try to catch lizards.

At Wildbad, Dr. Acland sometimes took me with him when he went to her nursery to visit the little Princess Louise, but what I longed for was to have her two brothers to play with. The big balcony at the front of the hotel was part of the Princes' suite. My grandfather's balcony was beside it but much lower down, so that Prince Eddy and Prince George could pelt me with withered flowers from their window boxes, but I could not throw them back and had to content myself with making faces at them! They were not allowed to play with the other English children in the place (neither was I!), but on the last day of their stay the rule was relaxed and we met in the woods. They said 'We've always wanted to play with you' and we fell into a good game at once. There were goats in the wood—we started to hunt them, and presently Prince Edward said he would be a great hunter 'when I am King of England.' Prince George said 'Well, I am going to sea.' 'Oh do,' I said, 'that's much nicer. I'll go too,' but he shook his head, and said he was afraid that was impossible, but if I'd wait for him. . . .

I think it was the goat-herd who interrupted our hunt, and then my *bonne* and their governess came up with us, and the fun was over. They gave me an envelope of coloured and skeleton leaves, which they said they had collected for me, and we went sadly back to our dinners.

Prince Eddy died quite young, and Prince George was afterwards George V; he was nearly two years younger than I.

I think it must have been on the last of my visits to Dublin that my grandmother died. I was sent with my nurse to stay at a friend's house. My mother told me to be good and go to sleep as soon as I was put to bed; she would not be there to say goodnight, but I should find her in bed beside me when I woke in the morning.

When I woke she was not there, and I heard footsteps and lay still and heard the housemaid whispering to my nurse that Mrs. Keatinge had died in the night, and that Mrs. Trotter would soon be coming to lie down; she had been up all night, poor lady, and she had sent word that she wished to tell me herself of my grandmother's death—nurse wasn't to mention it.

Now I had no affection for 'Grannie', but I understood that when people died you were 'sorry' for them. They were always spoken of as 'poor' so and so. I felt that 'Mammy' would expect me to be sorry, and I knew that I was *not* sorry. What was to be done about this?

I enjoyed tricking my nurse by pretending that I had not overheard her gossip, and by not expressing surprise when I found her in bed with me, but when my mother came in, very shaken and tired and crying a little, I *was* sorry. I did not let her suspect that I had already heard the news which she 'broke' to me. I cried a little out of sympathy, and said that I had loved Grannie. Out of this grew the first 'conviction of sin' that I remember to have had.

We went abroad in the autumn and stayed for some time at San Remo, where I had the unusual pleasure of playfellows of my own age. The Eaton family were Roman Catholics, and I have since wondered whether I may have heard something about confession from Steenie Eaton, the elder boy, which started the idea—I am quite positive that I had not brooded for some months over the events in Dublin—but I suddenly felt I must confess at once, I couldn't bear concealment one moment longer! The boys were having tea with me. I dropped a piece of the puzzle we were doing, ran to my mother and said that I must tell her something. I can almost hear her saying 'Not now, dear' and of stammering 'please, please, *now*' with my arms round her neck; but she pushed me away and said 'Not now, dear.' When I had 'little friends' to tea, was not the time to tell a secret; I must go and play nicely. I burst into tears. The younger Eaton boy laughed at me, but Steenie, the gentleman, said they would go home. My mother, however, would not allow that. She said I must learn—I can almost hear her saying 'Learn to attend to your guests.' That at any rate was what she was trying to teach me. So I went back and tried to play, crying all the time, and the moment that the boys were fetched, I flung myself on to my mother's shoulder and poured out my tale of iniquity; a long story. I had listened to the servants talking, a thing strictly forbidden, I had pretended not to know that Grannie was dead when Mammy 'broke' it to me, and I had said that I was very sorry about Grannie, and I wasn't really!

To my intense surprise my mother said that she had guessed that I did not love Grannie much—and she did not seem to mind this so much as I had expected—but I had been deceitful, and I had acted a lie, even if I did not actually tell one, and it was all very dreadful, and it made her sad that her little girl could behave so. I was dreadfully tired after all the crying, and was sick.

My visits to Cappoquin were many years later. After my grandfather was dead and the old connection with Dublin had ceased to exist, my mother and I went several times to stay there with her nephew. On one of our visits we lunched at the Trappist monastery on the hillside above the Black Water. As far as I remember, the story of the foundation of this monastery was something like this:

When the religious orders were being suppressed in France, two Trappist monks begged of the Protestant Squire at Cappoquin for leave to start a House on his land. They undertook to cultivate a perfectly barren mountainside, to look after the poor in the vicinity, to allow certain privileges to the Keane family—and that both men and women of the family should be allowed to visit the monastery at any time, if they expressed the wish to do so. The relations of the family with the monastery had always been very good. The Fathers had sent holy water to be sprinkled over the nursery when the children were ill, and had on various occasions tried to reform any insubordinate young men recommended to their care by their landlord.

My mother had visited the monastery once, many years before, but of course I was very anxious to do so, and my cousin Fanny Keane wrote to the Abbot asking for an invitation, which we received on a beautiful sunny day. We drove to the foot of the monastery hill, through a strip of what seemed to me to be quite frightfully bad farming, reaching as far as the monastery boundaries. Once inside their gate, the change was astonishing. The ground was desperately poor; where, here and there, a patch of specially steep hillside was left uncultivated, it produced nothing but coarse grass and juniper bushes, growing among grey stones, but a few inches further away the ground was being spade-dug, and every plant looked as if it had received individual attention. They used no mechanical farming, it was all 'spade work and sweat of their brows'.

Lay brothers looked up from time to time at us and saluted civilly, but returned no greeting and scarcely paused a moment as we passed; and a few ordinary workmen answered civilly, but for Irishmen, very shortly and quietly. We were received by a Lay Brother, who asked us to break bread before going up to the Abbot's room. It was a monastery rule that no one left the monastery without breaking bread—in our case the bread was the most delicious home-made loaf, fresh butter and milk which was half cream. When he saw that we had finished, the waiting Brother showed us up to the Abbot's room, a small one, furnished only with plain unvarnished wooden chairs and tables 'of excellent design', my mother remarked. There was a prie-Dieu and a large crucifix, and, most surprisingly, piles and piles of newspapers. The Abbot himself was a striking-looking man, tall and handsome. He bowed as he welcomed us, but kept his hands out of sight in the loose sleeves of his habit.

My mother remarked on the piles of newspapers on the table beside him—there were half a dozen still unopened.

Irish Background

'You understand that I have to keep in touch with our Houses all over the world', he said. 'I ought really to know the languages of the East as well as those of Europe.'

My cousin asked whether he could not get one of the Brothers to make extracts for him from some of the papers. He seemed to have a week's work on the table by his chair. 'There is seldom anyone else in the House who has access to the newspapers. It is my work,' he said quietly.

'But if you were ill or when you went to France,' began my cousin, and stopped awkwardly. She had forgotten that no one was supposed to know that the Abbot ever left home.

He smiled at her, almost laughed. 'No one has any right to speak of my travels outside the monastery walls,' he said, 'but there is nothing mysterious about them. About the papers— why should we add another unnecessary topic of conversation to those which are always too available to the Brethren?'

He told us that when he was elected Abbot he had to re-learn the map of Europe; for instance, he had never heard of the Franco-German war, though it had been lost and won ten years before. I wish I could remember more of the talk, but I did not realize what an interesting occasion it was.

It was on another visit years later that I almost disgraced myself by being too frightened to go into the Pict's house which my cousin Fanny Keane had discovered in the woods at Glen Shelane. That remarkable woman out by herself had literally stumbled against the Pict's roof and then and there had entered the house! They had invited all the available anthropologists to visit it, and it was said to be in very good preservation; but unluckily there were no traces of the inhabitants—in fact it was so thoroughly swept and garnished that people were inclined to think it had been known and visited by some of the local peasantry before my cousin found it.

The most striking thing in my early visits to Cappoquin was the relation between the people of the village and their squire. On Sunday afternoons when we were sitting at tea, half the village seemed to stroll past us to the gardens. They just walked in—there were no lodge gates—and wandered about at will through the glasshouses. They were not so friendly when I was there fifteen years later.

The most lovely place in the neighbourhood is Dromannor, the Villiers Stuarts', where there were three daughters half a generation younger than I, of whom Adela Keane used to say one clever, one handsome and one nice! I contacted the family again in London and was very glad to go with Mrs. Villiers Stuart to the drawing-room, when I was presented on my marriage. It was the last drawing-room at which the old Queen appeared. Lady Abercromby presented me, but in name only, and I should have been terribly bored and felt terribly out of things and aggrieved had I had to drive to Buckingham Palace by myself. Instead I had a jolly drive, with friends of the Villiers Stuarts talking to us through the windows, and went back for the 'show' tea at their house, and found that the 'nice one' was just on the edge of growing up—as nice as ever, and extremely good-looking. She became Lady Scott and I did not see her again until I had made friends with her two sons as Oxford undergraduates. Their father was Sir George Scott.

CHAPTER V

Childhood in England

❄

I don't remember my first nurse. It seems a pity, as from her photographs she must have been a most 'comfortable' woman, with smooth, neatly-brushed hair and an enormous bonnet. But I understand that before she left when I was three I could 'almost read'. Then one of those wretched doctors who were always being consulted about me, said that my brain was over-active, and I must not be allowed even to look at a book until I was seven. There seems to have been something mysterious about the age of seven. We were supposed to have changed the whole composition of our bodies during those years! When I was nearly eight I had my first governess, Miss Andrews, and I hated learning to read. I knew that all my contemporaries could do so already, and I loathed having to do 'baby lessons'. I don't think that Miss Andrews was really a very good teacher but perhaps the rules and regulations of the schoolroom hampered her. I was not to be over-excited and I had to lie flat on the floor three or four times daily for twenty minutes at a time. This was because one of those wretched doctors said that I had curvature of the spine.[1]

By now it was the autumn of 1871. Continental travel was of course disorganized by the Franco-Prussian war; there were discussions as to where we were to go for the winter months and then it was suddenly decided to 'try Bournemouth'. I believe that the rise of Bournemouth dated from this time, as

[1] This was one of the diseases which my father thought at different times that he had himself.

so many people who usually wintered abroad were diverted there by doctors' orders.

At first we stayed in rooms, where it was difficult to find a place for me to do my lessons. It was decided that my governess, Miss Andrews, should have a fire in her bedroom during the day, and that we would do lessons there; but it was horrid having to lie on the floor close to her boots and shoes. She always gave me a towel under my head, but the carpet smelt of lodging-house.

Then later we moved to The Firs, an old-fashioned country house with six or seven acres of ground—garden, shrubbery and a big field. Even then the town had almost surrounded it, but once the gates were closed we seemed almost in the country. There were masses of rhododendrons, a row of very fine sweet chestnut trees, a rose bed, with all the old-fashioned cabbage and moss roses, and a kitchen garden with as many strawberries as any child could desire. There were beehives, and birds nesting in every bush. The gardener was a surprising person who really liked birds, 'but them horrid little daisies I can't abide.' So I grubbed daisies in the lawn in return for his not minding when I cut the strawberry nets to let out entangled thrushes. The Firs was more like home than any of our other hired houses.

I was very backward and slow at lessons. I remember the sheer impossibility of remembering French verbs, and it seems to me, looking back, that I really did try, not only because I 'ought', but in self-defence. Sums were as bad, though I rather enjoyed the early propositions of Euclid, and I apparently distinguished myself by identifying some objects that lay thick on the ground in parts of the garden. They were between the size of a grain of barley and a coffee bean, and some were coloured bright pink. When he couldn't make anything of them, my father sent some up to the Secretary of the Linnaean Society, who pronounced them vegetable, but could not get any nearer to an identification, and asked for more specimens. I had been sent out to collect these when I rushed in one day to exclaim that I had seen sparrows eating the berries of some ivy on an old garden wall, and had found the seeds in their droppings. The Linnaean Society never succeeded in explaining why some of them turned pink! It asked for more specimens and expressed the hope that the young scientist would be encouraged! I suppose this encouraged any semi-scientific leanings I may have had, and I know I absorbed Kingsley's *Madam How and Lady Why* with intense interest, as well as various other very junior science books.

Then I had a new governess. I don't know why Miss Andrews left. Perhaps she was 'not quite a lady', or possibly I had got too fond of her, and was experiencing the first taste of a trouble which I long failed to understand—my poor mother's craving to have my unlimited devotion. It wasn't enough that she should be first with me, she wanted to be all in all. It made life at times very difficult. She was anxious that I should be friendly, more especially that I should like the people she liked, but they and I must beware of becoming too fond of one another!

Miss Smith, Miss Andrew's successor, was a younger woman who really enjoyed going out in a fisherman's boat with my father and me, and did not mind scrambling about the cliffs and getting wet and sandy. Once when we had sailed to Studland Bay, I climbed up the chalk cliff in search of a flower my father wanted. The chalk crumbled, and I landed on the shingle with a shower of flints and bits of chalk. I heard my father screaming 'Oh my God, my God, she'll be killed!' And I said, 'No, I won't!' and rolled over on to my back. When Miss Smith helped me to my feet my father was shaking and nearly crying, which I thought very silly. If anyone had a right to cry it was I, and I didn't, though one knee was badly cut and the blood running over my torn stockings. When we got home my mother was angry with Miss Smith for letting me 'get into danger', while I was grateful to her for not treating me as a baby!

They cannot have disinfected the knee properly, for after a few days it got septic and the doctor was sent for, and I had to lie up. I got a sore throat, and I was told that it was 'my own fault' because I had 'obstinately refused' to wrap up in a shawl while I was lying out in the garden—but the next day I developed scarlet fever (and when I understood that this, and not my obstinacy, was the cause of the sore throat, wasn't I pleased!) In those days scarlet fever was one of the serious diseases, considered more dangerous than measles is now, and my mother told me that Miss Smith had 'gallantly' offered to share the nursing with her, but that she had refused until Miss Smith got her father's permission. He was a doctor and he wired that she was to 'nail her colours to the mast'! She kindly played draughts and read to me—nothing exciting allowed, of course; but I never cared for her as I had cared for Miss Andrews. She was a very earnest Evangelical and when a revival was started she could hardly contain her excitement. Many of our friends were involved in it. Admiral Grey, the Thrings, the Cairns—Lord Cairns was afterwards Lord Chancellor—and a dashing young sailor, Captain Sherbrook, who married a Cairns daughter. They were always having meetings and Miss Smith went to them—occasionally even in lesson time, with leave granted. Of course I wanted to hear everything about the meetings, but 'My dear, your mother has asked me not to talk to you about my experiences, and you know our first duty is to obey.' One day a very nervous young woman told my mother that Captain Sherbrook wanted to come and see her. Might she receive him in the schoolroom? My mother was very much upset—such things were really 'not done' and she could not see her way to allow it. At this point my father cut in 'I can't have a sailor *I don't know* hob-nobbing with a girl living in my house! I believe he is quite a good sort of young fellow. I'll talk to him.' So Captain Sher-brook was allowed to come, and, looking over the bannisters I saw hearty greetings take place between the two men. They both laughed, and, still laughing, came up to the schoolroom. My father opened the door and said, "Here is Captain Sher-brook, Miss Smith,' and to me, 'Run along and don't bother them. His sense of humour often saved a situation, but my mother was sometimes hurt by it. Lady Alice Sherbrook's baby died, and all the revivalists were much concerned, and offered rather effusive condolences. When we were out together Miss Smith went up to Captain Sherbrook and said—very gushingly it seemed to me—how grieved all his friends were. I felt this was tactless and intrusive, and edged away, but all the same I was quite glad when he took my hand and held it while he talked to Miss Smith!

Miss Smith was in disgrace for a short time because, having taken it on her plate, she didn't eat her trifle at lunch. She explained that she had taken a very strict temperance pledge for the sake of her brother, who 'needed all the help she could give him'. My mother approved, but said if Miss Smith had had enough forethought to explain the case to her beforehand, an awkward situation would have been avoided. 'As it was, she could not but feel offended that any girl should refuse the food at her table.'

But how I wished we had been teetotallers when a dreadful doctor ordered me a tumblerful of porter every day. I have never hated anything as much as I hated the taste and smell of that drink, but the shame of the thing was much the worst part of it. Everyone's attention was called to it—it was a kind of bad joke to be taken very seriously, for when we went out to luncheon, my bottle of porter was solemnly taken too, and was poured out for me by our host's butler. I begged hard not to go to that lunch party, but was told not to be silly and make a fuss.

Mr. Pullen, our host, was a rather crusty and alarming old Yorkshireman who was wintering in Bournemouth with his very considerable stable. He lent me a pony and took me out riding, but I suppose I must have been a particularly cowardly or clumsy child, for I seldom really enjoyed riding. Or was it that with the riding master the hired ponies had particularly hard mouths and the hired saddles were never really comfortable, nor were the long chamois leather trousers I wore for riding and the long heavy skirts of my riding habits. Then my hat always blew off unless I used at least one hand to hold it on; no doubt I should have been told that the broad-brimmed hat was given me to shield my complexion!

But I do remember one ride with Mr. Pullen that I did really enjoy. I was well and truly run away with along the sands, but managed to stick on till we raced into one of the small streams which meandered across the shore. Here Mr. Pullen came up with us, and caught at my rein, asking indignantly why hadn't I slowed down when he told me to do so. I explained that I had tried, but that I thought the pony was stronger than me, 'and really it was a lovely ride, I've never had such a nice one before', on which he patted me on the back and said he'd make a horsewoman of me if I'd come to Yorkshire! Alas he went home, and I resumed my rides on the hired pony, with the riding master who was supposed to take me and two other small girls on ponies for 'private lessons', but usually picked up five or six grown-up people as soon as we were out of sight of our parents' windows, and devoted all his teaching powers to them.

All the same, any exercise must have been far better for me than the porter or unlimited milk drinking, milk puddings and suet roll, for I was by this time a fat, heavy child. My father was keen about some kind of water cure, and once for a short time I was made to wear a compress round my neck, but happily that craze did not last very long. The interest in homeopathy persisted, however, and he was always ready to dose his family and friends with the contents of a little green bottle. I was sent upstairs one day to take two pillules from a bottle on his dressing-table—'Mind, only take two'. When I came down and he said 'You only took two, I hope?' I answered that the bottle had been half full and I had finished it. And what will happen now? I thought hopefully, but I do not think he can have been a really convinced homeopath, for he was not as upset as I hoped, and only asked me off and on during the day how I felt. It fell equally flat when I scratched my arm with a Malay kris I had been told was poisoned. They bathed the scratch, scolding all the time, but nothing happened.

Childhood in England

The only time I scored off the grown-ups, and I still remember it with satisfaction, was when I said that I had felt an earthquake, and was told not to be silly, and when I persisted, not to make myself out to know better than grown-up people. The next morning's *Times* reported an earthquake on the South Coast! No one apologized to me of course.

One of the many odd things to look back on is that I was allowed to visit at a small hospital for incurable consumptive patients. It was rather terrifying, and at times one saw some fairly ghastly things, but I have no doubt that the patients, most of them, liked the healthy child who sat on the foot of their beds, said little pieces of poetry to them, and brought flowers and fruit. Then suddenly I heard that I must not go there any more, as I might 'catch their coughs'. I thought this most unreasonable. Was not visiting the sick one of the things which we were told in the Bible to do? I suppose it was at the same time that visits to a children's hospital were stopped. It was called the Hospital for Hip Diseases (obviously tubercular joints), but I never connected the two hospitals in my mind until years afterwards, and the prohibition in the case of the children's hospital seemed particularly irritating, as Miss Smith and I had just started teaching some of the children to read. The place was an offshoot from one of the big London hospitals, and a few patients had been sent down before the wards were really ready. They were understaffed, and the nurses made us very welcome. Miss Smith was allowed to go on with our scheme, though I was not.

We went to Brighton periodically for my father to visit a homoepath doctor in whom he had great faith. I hated great hulking Dr. Hilberts, who said I had one shoulder higher than the other; but Brighton was enlivened by 'Uncle Penn', my father's step-uncle, the Reverend Spencer Drummond. He lived in the old part of the town in a small house, over-crowded with old china and books, and run by three devoted old servants. There was always a roast bird of some kind when we went to luncheon with him. The maid who waited at table had her own ideas about children's diet, and when the old gentle-

64

Lady Keane, my mother's elder sister

Judge Keatinge, my mother's father

Cousin Lou (Mrs Mure)

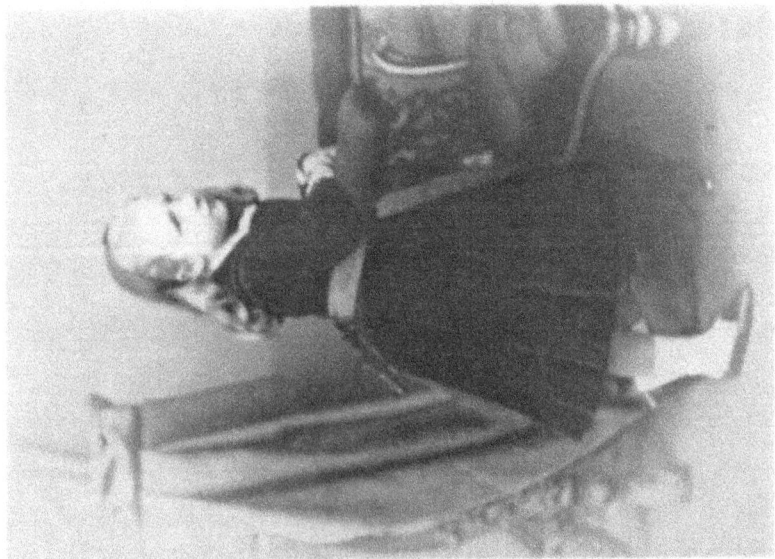

L.K.T. six years old

man was carving I heard her say 'You're helping the little Miss, Sir, one slice is enough'. Then she would deposit a huge helping of some green vegetables beside the slice of chicken or pheasant, spoiling the delicious bread sauce with peppers in it. Presently he would ask 'could you not fancy another slice from the breast, my dear?' and apparently on one occasion I was heard to answer 'I'd like a bit more from anywhere, please Uncle Penn, and will you tell Emily not any more greens.' On which Emily, thinking of the honour of the house, said indignantly, 'It isn't greens, Miss. It's the best spinach', and Uncle Penn intervened 'You see my dear, everything green is not what is domestically known as greens.'

He took me to see my first conjurer, and we were ushered, with great respect, into reserved seats in the front row, which did not prevent the conjurer from producing eggs, a whole basketful of them, from Uncle Penn's long white beard. 'Sir, Sir, remember you are dealing with the oldest clergyman in Brighton', said the uncle, not quite sure whether he was being treated with proper respect. 'Do you usually carry these, Sir?' asked the conjurer, producing several bunches of sausages. Uncle Penn was duly astonished and offered to turn out the pockets of his huge black coat, to show that they were quite empty. This they appeared to be until the conjurer, very politely said 'Excuse me, Sir,' and putting his hand in brought out a Chinese-looking box, and said something about the Reverend gentleman's well-known interest in the Temperance campaign. The audience clapped, but I rather spoiled the effect by asking anxiously whether it was real Chinese tea, because Uncle Penn only likes that!

On one ever memorable Easter Monday I watched 'hundreds and hundreds' of men marching past the little house. The volunteers were using their Bank Holiday for the small amount of training which was all they could persuade the War Office to give them. They had a Field Day on the Downs before we saw them, and my aunts said how tired and dirty the poor lads looked.

The old uncle came and stood beside me: 'Every fit man

should have some military training', he said. 'All honour to these volunteers, and may our Government some day come to understand that no boy should escape having to defend his country. Now here come the London Scottish! You may give a cheer for Cousin William if you can see him.'

I did see Cousin William, and I hoped that he heard me. He was certainly looking out for the little house, for as he passed close to our area railings, he looked up and saluted.

Possibly the goat carriages which I remember still park along the edge of King's Road, and some of the attractions which I remember are still carried on. One showman wore elaborately folded paper hats of many colours. From time to time he took off the one that he was wearing, gave it a twist, and behold! in his hands it became a bag or a ship or a lion! What he liked was to go through his whole series of manipulations before someone standing at a window. If Number Twenty-One offered him five shillings for this, he was pretty sure of extra shillings from Numbers Twenty and Twenty-Two, though they had not been responsible for ordering the performance, and the child whose father had ordered it felt immense satisfaction at conferring such a favour on her neighbours! There were also marionette shows and a Punch and Judy. The Punch and Judy show was the more amusing, but my mother thought it 'really not very nice', and preferred the marionettes; which enacted the more romantic stories and which were 'quite pretty'.

Brighton had a special craft too. It made little boxes and pin trays of lobster shells, and a real triumph—a stuffed lobster which stood up on his tail, carried a walking stick and a quizzing glass, and was an obvious 'masher'! I was allowed to present one of these to my uncle General Keatinge, when he came to say good-bye after a leave. He wrote later that he had parted with great regret with the 'masher', but that a great man in the District had liked it so much that he felt he must leave it with him. It was a very wholesome thing to have an inter-racial joke!

.   .   .   .

Childhood in England

The account of my childhood wouldn't be at all realistic if I did not mention cousin Louisa Janin. She was one of the Murrays of Cringletie, but, unlike most of her family, she was not good-looking. She was more exactly like a parrot than I have ever known another human being to be like an animal; but she must have been a very clever woman; and she had many devoted friends. I fancy she was quite hard up, and she certainly had no settled home. She stayed with us for long and frequent visits and there seemed always to be a welcome awaiting her somewhere when she chose to move on. She entertained my father, though they often had fierce quarrels; and my mother found her very helpful and a great standby when he had a nervous breakdown. She had made a mesalliance with a Frenchman, Monsieur Janin, and there was one daughter whom she said she had married off 'before she gave me any trouble'!

She knew everybody—at any rate everybody north of the Tweed—and she had stories of them all, which she told so dramatically that when I was first taken to the theatre I told my mother that it was just like listening to Cousin Louisa talking. Perhaps I was not so wide of the mark, as the play was *Othello*. Why my grandmother, with whom I was staying, allowed me to be taken to *Othello* I cannot imagine; I can remember her saying that it must be all right 'because it's Shakespeare', but my mother was horrified when she was told; just as she was at my listening to some of Cousin Louisa's tales! But what could she do about this, when we were in rooms at the time, or in a Continental hotel, and there was no convenient place in which to segregate me?

Cousin Louisa couldn't stand children, and her scathingly sarcastic remarks rankled, so that I remember very clearly the one occasion when I won her praise. Little girls used to have their ears pierced as a matter of routine, but I think mine were done rather younger than usual, because piercing the ears was said to be a cure for styes. We went to a jeweller's in Brighton to have it done and I made a fuss—probably a very unnecessary fuss—for I should anyway have resented having my face touched by a nasty jeweller, and Cousin Louisa looked down her parrot beak and told my mother not to pet the silly child. Then some days afterwards, while I was still wearing the very large gold rings which were inserted temporarily till the ear lobes healed, a much beloved old friend, Mr. Carrick Moore of Corswell, chucked me under the chin, caught his finger in the ring, and gave the ear a painful wrench. I said nothing, because I was very fond of the old gentleman and I knew he would be distressed if he saw the trickle of blood on my neck. Cousin Louisa said 'Child, you might be a boy!' enormously high praise because boys were always supposed to be very brave.

Then some ten years' later, when her French husband had died, Cousin Louisa married one of her devoted old friends, Colonel Peter Scarlett. They stayed with us at Bournemouth, and when she was in the middle of a story, Cousin Peter would sometimes give a little cough, and look up with a pained expression, and we lost the point of the tale while she jumped up and threw her arms round his neck, 'like a silly schoolgirl', my father said superciliously. They only had a short few years together, but they were very happy ones. Dear Cousin Peter!

CHAPTER VI

Education

I learned very slowly. When I started with Miss Andrews we 'did' a book called *Magnall's Questions.* I learned by rote the answers to questions such as : What is Bread? What is a star? One had to get the answers word-perfect. Then we did *Little Arthur's History of England,* followed by Miss Yonge's *Kings of England.* Of course I liked the stories out of *Tales of a Grandfather,* but the padding between them was very dull; and later my father started the schoolroom on Freeman's Series of Histories of European Countries, which must have been quite informative, but were really a frame upon which history lessons might have been hung. After this came *The Greatness of England,* followed by *The Greatness of Russia.* Of course the mere names started me wanting to find out whether, and why, England didn't (or couldn't) still attain 'First Greatness'. Had she lost it? If so, what was being done about it? Were people trying to keep up the greatness? (I saw no sign of this in the lives of the people about me.) Surely that was the most important thing anyone could possibly do? Were people *trying*? Perhaps they were, only they didn't talk about it? I could never get my governesses interested in this kind of question.

I recollect one occasion when I was convicted of grossly breaking the rule against listening to 'servants' gossip'. The Tichborne Case, the *cause célèbre* of the moment, was being discussed; I blurted out 'but don't you believe that the poor man really *is* the squire, and that rich people are just keeping him out of his home because he's a working man from Australia?' Consternation on the part of the elders and 'you see what comes of her listening to gossip'. They laughed and joked about what I thought a serious case of injustice until my mother said she would explain it all to me, if I waited patiently for bedtime, when if she was not busy we always had 'a nice talk'.

She began by saying that what had really happened was that 'people who ought to know better were trying to take the home from a poor little boy'. I agreed that if this were really so it was too bad, but that Henry and Euphrasie were agreed that the man from Australia was the real squire . . . they so rarely agreed about anything that I thought. . . . My mother smiled. 'I can explain this to you, darling,' she said. 'The woman who takes the side of the man from Australia is *French*. Now do you understand?' I did—at least as far as Euphrasie was concerned, and transferred my sympathies to the 'poor little boy'. But it did not explain what I called the rights and wrongs of the thing, and though I allowed my sentiments to be enlisted for the poor little boy, it was years afterwards when I thought about the case again, that the legal side of it troubled me, till I got my father to go through some of the evidence with me. I think he was rather pleased that I should take what he called a masculine outlook when I said that I understood that the Law was not meant 'just to be kind to people', but to be fair all round, to nasty people as well as to nice ones. Fairness was what really mattered. He asked what I thought the country would be like if it had only good laws and everyone obeyed them, and apparently I answered at once 'Jack should have Jill, nought should go ill, the man should have his mare again and all go well.' It was the most tremendous talk on law that I ever remember to have had, and I became very anxious to know more about it, but it didn't come much into one's history lessons with one's governess.

I think that Miss Andrews got under £40 a year and she had a book called *How to Dress on £15 a Year as a Lady, by a*

Lady. She told me about her sister who was a missionary in India, and about her brother in the Merchant Service, and I certainly began to get a wider lookout on the world around me.

We seem to have spent that summer at Plean in Stirling-shire, and one day my cousin Richard Keatinge came to stay with us. He was the eldest son of my mother's eldest brother, tall and rather good-looking, with a somewhat vacant face. I do not think that he had ever had much of a chance or had been to any well-known school, and 'nothing was expected of him'. He was going out to Australia, to some of the De Salis family, his mother's people, who had land in New South Wales. Somehow I was given to understand that going out to Australia wasn't at all the same thing as going out to India.

From an early date I was always sorry for Cousin Richard, so even as a child I tried to be 'nice' to him, and felt angry when people scored off him, and he only looked vague and never had an answer ready. During this visit of his, things went wrong. My parents' attitude was condescending rather than friendly, and one evening they went out to dinner and he and Miss Andrews sat in the drawing-room and played the piano and sang together. She let me stay up, and I enjoyed it immensely, and had no idea that I was acting chaperone; but when the parents came in I was sent off to bed at once, and everyone looked grim. I felt that we three were in disgrace and in the morning Miss Andrews was very subdued and I think she had been crying. Years afterwards I reminded my mother of that evening, and asked her what had been wrong? She said vaguely that Miss Andrews and Richard should not have sat up together. Why didn't he go for a walk!

Plean, Stirlingshire, was one of the places we took furnished for a year with the idea of buying it if it proved suitable. But the drains were found to be out of order, or non-existent, and it was supposed to be due to this that I had a return of the typhoid, or low fever, such as I had at Grenoble, so as soon as I could be moved I was packed off with Miss Andrews, to Edinburgh, and a children's party was put off till I could be vaccinated.

The family were rather keen about vaccination. My father was done when he was abroad, had what amounted to a slight attack of smallpox, and carried several pock-marks in which I took a great interest. There were many pock-marked people to be seen in Edinburgh. My French *bonne* and I used to count how many we met walking down one division of Princes Street! My vaccination was delayed from day to day because the child who was to supply the vaccine was slow to take. I heard a lot about that child, but its name was never mentioned. When at last I was done I took violently and was naturally interested in the next child in the series, the one who was to get the 'stuff' from my sore arm. But the doctor wouldn't tell, and Miss Andrews looked shocked and said 'Hush' as if I were asking an improper question.

Plean was close to the Field of Bannockburn, and I used to repeat 'Scots wha hae' to myself, looking through the garden door to the Field of Bannockburn. I learned poetry by heart very easily and liked having poetry read to me better than anything else. My mother read me most of the early Tennyson's—*The Lady of Shalott, The Charge of the Six Hundred* and *The Lotus Eaters*; and my father read nearly all of Scott's poetry, the *Lays of Ancient Rome*, and the *Lays of the Scottish Cavaliers*. He was vexed because I yawned over *The Cottar's Saturday Night* and asked for *Tam O'Shanter* instead, but he introduced me gently to Shakespeare, and I learnt 'The quality of mercy' because *he* liked it, and bits of *Henry V* because *I* did! Someone gave me Lamb's *Tales* on my ninth birthday and I was much offended, though I confess to having made use of it twenty-five years later when the OUDS performed one of the more obscure plays.

Some of my questions on my reading must have puzzled my father sometimes. I wanted to know whether 'a wet sea-boy in an hour so rude' could really go to sleep on 'a high and giddy mast'? My father said honestly that he did not know.

But a governess's reaction would most likely have been 'Oh, never mind, it's only poetry.' When I asked what was False Sextus' 'Deed of Shame', my father said 'Oh, he was very rude to a lady!' But the walling up of Constance in *Marmion* was harder to explain, and that episode became one of my nightmares, displacing the mad dog.

I fail to understand on what principle my reading matter was selected. Till I was over seven, the doctor's orders about no excitement were still supposed to be attended to. I can hear one parent saying to the other 'Don't let the child excite herself', but what could have been more exciting than the *Charge of the Six Hundred,* or *Edinburgh after Flodden,* and the *Lady of Shalott* was surely quite likely to haunt the dreams of an imaginative child.

Of actual children's books I only remember two—Mrs. Trimmer's *History of the Robins,* which I fancy was to be found in all nurseries of that period. It was distinctly boring, but there was a charming book which made me cry, called *Conrad the Squirrel.* My impression is that it was probably really well-written and had a sort of fascination for me. I liked the more sentimental parts of Hans Andersen's stories. I remember being surprised when I saw that another book was called 'Grimm's Fairy Tales'. I had always believed it to be 'Grim Fairy Tales'.

Until I was almost grown up I was not supposed to read any book without asking leave, and whole ranges of children's books, such as the Little Women series, were forbidden. I was once surprised reading *Lilian's Golden Hours* which had been lent me by another child. As far as I remember, it was a rather sentimental story for schoolgirls. I was allowed to finish it, which I thought very kind, as of course I had been disobedient, and expected it to be confiscated as soon as it was discovered. My mother, however, discussed it with me, and pointed out that some incidents were quite unnatural, and she wanted to know why I wanted to read about such silly things?

When I read my first grown-up novel—without permission,

of course—I think it was Ouida's *Tricotrin*—I was surprised to find that grown-ups liked to read about events quite as unnatural.

However, my 'reading matter' was controlled long before this, and I think that the doctors must have been partly responsible for the extreme care which was taken to keep all exciting stories from me, though *Marmion* was passed and parts of Burns. Is it possible that these were considered literature, and the story books tended to be vulgar? Anyhow, I cannot have been more than four or five when a magazine called, I think, *The Infant's Magazine*, which my grandmother sent to me, was discontinued because I was impatient to know the fate of the hero in the next number. I was told that the story was not about a real little boy, so it didn't matter at all what the magazine said about him, and that I must not be silly.

This rationing of reading matter is one of the things which I have never been able to understand or, I am afraid, to forgive.

One summer when we were going abroad for at least six weeks, I was given a Sunday book and a week-day one to last till we returned. I must, I think, have been eleven. The Sunday book was a set of allegories—my parents liked allegories. And the other was called *Stories for Summer Days and Winter Nights*. I remember one of the stories quite well, and that the last one in the book was a very dull account of the Battle of Waterloo. I had hurried through the rest of the book in my eagerness to get to that one, and was bitterly disappointed with it. The number of troops engaged on each side was given, but not a name of a single regiment, an incident, or a detail of the fighting. It might have been an answer in one of *Magnall's Questions* to the question 'What is Waterloo?' I do not know whether that question occurs in Magnall's—I never got as far as the 'W's'—but it was a comfort that my mother agreed that it was dull, and on the first possible occasion she read Byron's *Eve of Waterloo* to me.

Along with my other two books on that summer journey I

had a much-read volume of the *Bibliothèque Rose*, in which
any doubtful incidents were inked out, or pasted over so carefully that it was impossible to unstick the gummed paper
without tearing it. There was nothing to fall back on but my
father's travelling Shakespeare. I wish I could say that I
became an enthusiastic Shakespearian, but I did not. The
edition was in double columns, in very small print, and I fear
I only read 'for amusement'. I don't think that my mother
ever knowingly allowed me to read anything which she had
not vetted until I was seventeen or eighteen, and not willingly
even then.

Nobody today remembers *La Bibliothèque Rose*, the pink
paper-bound books by Madame De Ségur. The appearance
of a new volume was an eagerly awaited event, and I have a
very vivid recollection of my father bringing one in and
handing it, not to me as I expected, but to my mother and
saying 'Not nice for the child', and when I eventually got the
book some pages had been pasted over with brown paper. Of
course I longed to read those particular pages and there was
a picture missing too. Then one day I peeped into the copy of
the book which my little French girl friend, Mimi Desforges,
had been reading, and was disgusted by the story and by the
picture, only I did wish that my mother had shown it, and
discussed it with me. I should have agreed that the very
domestic concerns dealt with were not fit subjects for a funny
story and that the picture was 'not nice' on a drawing-room
table, and really I had imagined it was something much worse!
I did wish, however, that I had been taken into her confidence
and not left to guess. Another thing which puzzled me was
what my father meant when he said that something was 'not
fit for the child, much *too French*'. It was a French book,
wasn't it, so how could it be 'too French'?

I have just got what I find to be the last volume of the
Bibliothèque Rose to be published, *Les Vacances*. This is a
new edition, no longer '*rose*', and with new illustrations, as
inappropriate to the period as those which appeared in one of
the new editions of *Alice in Wonderland*. But luckily the new

illustrations did not catch on with lovers of Alice, and I cannot but think that if there is a republication of the *Bibliothèque*, the old pictures will reappear as the old ones in Alice have done. There is a new ending to *Les Vacances* too. Madame De Ségur apparently made up her mind that she had no more to say about our old friends, so she arranged marriages for all the girls to the most appropriate of the boys, and there were enough boys to provide husbands for all but one of the girls. Only Madeleine, one of the *Petites Filles Modèles*, was left unmatched, so, to complete the picture, a new boy had to be introduced for her.

Now I come to consider it, this is a most extraordinary arrangement! They were all cousins, and what can Madame De Ségur have been thinking of—surely she cannot have been a Protestant? No! I am sure she was 'dévote', and there is a mistake somewhere. The family would have needed dispensations for all the weddings but one. Paul and Sophie were happily unrelated—but all the rest!

I used to go to *déjeuner* with Mimi Desforges but I felt much too old to allow myself to be lifted, as she was, on to a high chair so, without waiting for her *bonne* to help me, I scrambled ungracefully on to the stool which had been set on a chair to raise me to the desired height. I knew that I did it badly and that Monsieur Desforges laughed *at*, not *with* me; but anyway, I hadn't been lifted up like a baby and I did not wear a bib as Mimi did—but I got into disgrace because I just could not eat the pudding! I told my mother afterwards that it was covered with a white fluff like the stuff you get when you squash a puff-ball, and it tasted of medicine—obviously it was a white wine sauce and probably extremely nice. My father used to try to make friends with Mimi, but she said she did not like 'ce grand Monsieur'. I, on the contrary, had two great friends, the Marquis De Nicolai and his brother. I do not think that they were climbers, but they walked in the lower slopes of the Alps, and brought bunches of *alpenrosen* to my mother, and the old Marquis discussed 'the muddy end of a glacier' (the moraine), with my father, while I pulled at his hand, and demanded to be taken on to the nice white clean ice.

On occasions such as this I think my *bonne* usually hovered in the offing, so that if my father wanted to get rid of me he had only to signal to her, but I counted on the old Marquis, who would not, I knew, let my *bonne* get hold of me if he could avoid it, for he objected to her strongly. I had left out one verse of Lord Houghton's '*Goodnight and Good Morning*', when told to recite it to him, the verse when the sun is referred to as having 'God's time to keep'. My mother told me to say it properly, I tried to explain to her that perhaps I ought not to say just that verse to the Marquis. I probably spoke half in English and half in French, and said that Euphrasie, my *bonne*, had said that it was rude to talk about God to Roman Catholics. Whether it was said to be rude to God or to the Roman Catholics, I could not explain. Then the old Marquis, half understanding what I was saying, exclaimed 'Sacré Nom! Ma petite Louise, elle s'imagine donc que je ne crois pas au Bon Dieu. Quelle horreur! Ah cette bonne! Ma foi je voudrais. . . .'

But what he would have liked to do to Euphrasie, I never heard, for my mother said 'Ah, taisez-vous donc, Monsieur Le Marquis. La petite n'a pas compris.'

'Je crois bien qu'elle n'a pas compris', he said, getting up and walking away. But I ran after him and said 'Revenez donc, Monsieur Le Marquis, I'll say all the poetry I know to you if you like.' He thereupon taught me a couple of verses in which *La Reine des Cieux* occurred. I wish I could remember them, but my mother told me not to repeat them to my *bonne*, and said that even some people in Scotland might be shocked by them, and so for want of being repeated they are forgotten.

In 1876, before we went back to Bournemouth from Scotland, I had my only experience of school. This was at Madame Froebel's in Murray Place, which was (as far as was possible at that date for a school for *girls* to be fashionable), the most fashionable in Edinburgh. I suppose that Monsieur Froebel was a son or grandson of a schoolmaster who popularized the Pestalozzi educational theories, and was the founder of the Froebel System, about which there was much talk in those days. He and his wife were very anxious to get me as a boarder, and took me aside and privately coached me with arguments which might induce my parents to send me there. I knew it was quite useless, but tried some of the arguments just to see!

When we got back to Bournemouth I found that Miss Smith was going to be married, and there was a new governess coming; a 'finishing' governess, who did not usually take girls under sixteen, and I was told I must really make the most of this opportunity. Miss Schweitzer was the plainest woman I have ever met. She was large-boned and angular, with a flat yellowish face and black boot-button eyes. She generally looked peevishly down her flat nose, but when required she could produce an entirely mechanical smile, as when she gave a curtsy lesson (which was part of 'deport-ment'). She claimed to launch into the world young ladies trained from every point of view, including the expression of their faces when they read their 'chapter' before beginning the lessons of the day. Deportment was very important indeed. She was a first-rate instructor, the first I had ever come across, and I was ready to learn all she could teach me, but not to be 'trained' or 'influenced', so after a while we had a violent quarrel, after which she announced 'En suite vous serez mon écolière et non mon élève', to which I responded 'Parfaite-ment, mademoiselle', and from that time we got on sur-prisingly well together.

My parents were really very long-suffering, for they took her with us when we went abroad in the summer, and she was at no pains to be a pleasant travelling companion. I have terrible recollections of long sessions in museums, when I got so tired that in desperation I sat on the floor, and I am sure she was a terrible trial to my poor mother. Of course I saw more of her than they did, for we dined at the mid-day *table d'hote* and they at the evening session, but I got some fun out of the conversations which we overheard among fellow diners concerning our nationality. They generally decided that 'Die Lehrerin' was herself German, but the *reitzendes mädchen* (attention centred on my hair, as it had in the old days in San Remo) was Scandinavian. Why not English, someone would suggest? Because no English girl could speak German like that. She did not seem to be 'Echt Deutsch', but she must be the next thing to it. My parents were quite pleased when this was reported to them, but I longed to stand up and say quite clearly 'Civis Britannicus sum'.

When I was sixteen my mother said that I had worked so well for two years that if I wished it, Miss Schweitzer should leave either in March or three months later. I chose the latter alternative, for I really enjoyed my lessons, and at home the teacher interfered less with the amenities of life than she did when travelling.

When we came back from abroad, I had a young English woman, with whom I was supposed 'to read', and in the evenings a schoolmaster came to try to teach me arithmetic and free-hand drawing. My father was determined that I should sketch, as he and my aunts did. I never had the least wish to sketch, but a short time ago I found a book with extraordinary, life-like, caricatures of Miss Schweitzer on the back of elaborately painstaking drawings of trees all labelled pine, fir, larch, oak, elm, etc.

It must have been just after Miss Schweitzer's departure when I was sixteen, that my father had a 'nervous breakdown' while we were at Homburg. My mother got into a desperate state of collapse, and I wrote to their doctor and told him that though, of course, my father must finish his cure, I wanted him to order my mother off to Switzerland at once, on any pretext, otherwise 'I wouldn't answer for the consequences'! He must have been an English doctor, for I couldn't have undertaken to explain the inexplicable in any foreign tongue. He came to pay his usual call and looked at me so fixedly that

Education

I thought he was going to give me away; but he was an understanding person, and said that my mother's heart or liver was not responding to Homburg water. He felt rather anxious about her and thought she ought to go to a high altitude at once—and to Murren in the Engadine we went.

My godfather, Coutts Trotter, happened to be there, and I went for some good walks with him, but when he left, life was very monotonous. My mother took a couple of short constitutionals every day, but thought, quite rightly, that I needed more exercise. She liked me to take her maid with me for walks, otherwise I might only go for a mile or two along the Interlaken path and back again. She breakfasted in her room, I in the *salle à manger*, and I couldn't very well help answering when some other breakfast eater spoke to me! Arthur Arnold, brother of Sir Edwin Arnold, author of *The Light of Asia*, and *The Song Celestial*, generally talked during breakfast. We took some short walks together, and he proposed a longer one, for which he would supply sandwiches; but my mother thought this 'wouldn't do at all'. I was to explain to Mr. Arnold that my mother objected, I said I thought that she must do this herself, but she said no, that would be disagreeable for her. I remember suggesting that it would be *very* disagreeable for me; but she said that Mr. Arnold would understand—that there had been no proper introduction. I was certainly not to go on that expedition, I ought never to have allowed it to be suggested.

Quite naturally the poor man was irate. 'Does your mother think I'm not respectable?' he asked. I remember speculating on what qualities went to make up respectability! Luckily for me, my uncle, Colonel Keatinge, V.C., C.S.I., joined us shortly afterwards; it was the second time he had met us in Switzerland, and it became an annual custom. Though he was her favourite brother, my mother was usually very generous about the time and affection he bestowed on me. One summer we went up the Rigi by the new funicular, saw the sunrise and walked down. Another year we went together to the Engadine, where an old friend of theirs, Mrs. Palmer, was

living. She was a widow who, like my uncle, had been through
the Mutiny, and they had much to talk about, and for me to
listen to. On hearing that she had been abducted, her husband
had shot himself—fortunately not fatally. My mother thought
this terribly wicked, and too dreadful to be alluded to. Mrs.
Palmer merely said that few men loved their wives sufficiently
to do such a thing, and there was some coldness between the
two old friends. I think it was about this time that I realized
how possessive my poor mother's affection for me was. It
made me very sorry for her. She could not bear my becoming
at all attached to Mrs. Palmer, and refused to let me accept a
cheque for £5 which she wrote for me. I was to buy 'something
pretty to wear', and when finally I was allowed to accept £1,
she was worried at having caused Mrs. Palmer to destroy a
cheque, and with me as the ultimate cause of the trouble. This
sounds simply funny, but she always had an immense respect
for her cheque-book and used to ask me to help her when she
had to use it.

During these years between my sixteenth and twentieth
birthdays, I did all the business on our travels, took railway
tickets and engaged rooms and bargained for carriage and
horses when we went up to Pontresina. I'm no bargainer, and
I've been driven to despair and got into trouble when my
mother went through her bills and wanted me to query them.
When he first came home, my uncle was inclined to back her
up. I think he felt that no one expected you to pay the price
at which things were offered to you. Later he took my part
and if we couldn't afford the best suite in the hotel, we did
with something else. I only once persuaded him to come on a
glacier with me, which he persisted in doing in ordinary nail
boots, and found them more troublesome than he expected,
but we had long tramps in the lower slopes, eating omelettes
at out-of-the-way inns and not coming home till dark. Those
weeks in the years when I was between fifteen and twenty
were far the happiest of my girlhood: they ended when he
married again. The chapter that follows tells more about him.

CHAPTER VII

General Keatinge

I have already quoted some letters of my uncle's when he was a boy of seventeen, starting for the country where his working life was spent. In the coming chapter, I would like to emphasize that I write of events as they were thought of then, and as I think of them still. In 1845, when the Mutiny broke out, he was stationed at Nimar, where—a strange occupation for a lieutenant of Horse Artillery—he began 'to bridge the streams and build the roads of India', a labour of love to which he always returned when active service allowed him to do so.

Sir Henry Durand gave him his first orders 'to do all in his power to prevent troops whose loyalty was doubtful' from joining the Mhaw Brigade, which was believed to be on the point of mutiny. This he did by 'fortifying a gap in the hills and holding it with a rabble of police and armed workmen till the native troops surrendered their arms.' His troop of mounted police accompanied him throughout the campaign in Central India, and enabled him on several occasions to ride long distances through enemy country.

For this and other services he received the thanks of the Governor General in Council, and was promoted Brevet Captain and appointed Special Assistant to Sir Henry Durand, but 'Whenever he was not specially wanted for political work he took his place in the trenches with the Bombay Artillery'. Later he joined Sir Hugh Rose's force which was making slow progress towards Delhi, taking fortified places on its way. In this manner they got as far as Chandari and invested it in the orthodox manner, but he was convinced that if they did so the country ahead of them would rise, and they would have to fight every mile on the road to Delhi:—so, for three nights running, he crept around the defences of the fortress, accompanied by his native servant, till he was able to report on a practicable point for an assault. Sir Hugh Rose said that he was responsible for Captain Keatinge's life, as he had been lent to him in a civilian capacity, and tried to persuade the servant to act as guide—the man answered that he would follow his Sahib anywhere, but he refused to lead.

The following is the only part of the story that my uncle would ever tell without strong pressure. 'As I had outgrown the uniforms that I brought out with me I led the assault in mufti, armed with a cavalry sword.' He was twice wounded earlier in the day, and in the assault received a third, very severe wound, 'and as the men stepped over my body in the breach, the band played St. Patrick's Day in the Morning.' He was carried to his tent and presently heard running footsteps and shouts, followed by a violent noise of buzzing, 'and I knew that I was up against the most dangerous enemy in India, a swarm of wild bees.' Presently he heard 'grunts from an unfortunate camel which tried to scrape the bees off its nose by rubbing it against the tent, which collapsed—fortunately not on the side on which I was lying—but leaving a gap through which a hen presently entered, hopped on to my bed and laid an egg. I was beginning to be hungry, and even a small Indian egg would be something to eat', and anyhow, he thought he was the only Bombay gunner who had seen a hen actually laying an egg!

His most painful wound was in his right hand, and he felt sure that there was something left in it, but the surgeon assured him that if anything *had* lodged in the cut he must have died of lockjaw within a very short time. So when the surgeon refused to do so, he opened the wound with his razor and extracted several pieces of the hilt of his sword. 'After which the wound healed.' He was awarded the Victoria Cross for his conduct at Chandari.

General Keatinge

As he was unfit for active service he returned to his District, where Sir Bartle Frere held a special Durbar to confer on him the Insignia of the Order of the Star of India, but shortly afterwards he was in command of irregular troops in an entirely successful attack on Sita Ram Holkar, and of Regulars with whom he finally cleared the Satpura Hills of Tantia Topi's followers. He again received the thanks of the Governor General in Council, and the medal for the war in Central India, with clasp.

Sir Richard Temple, Chief Commissioner of the Central Provinces, who was not used to be enthusiastic about the work of younger men, speaks, with what amounts to enthusiasm, of his work in the Revenue Department of the schools, and dispensaries which he founded, of his irrigation schemes, and of the start he made in mining and smelting iron. Sir Bartle Frere refers to his organizing a steam ferry over the 'impassable Nerbudda', and of his wonderful work with chiefs and people, and goes on to tell a story which so much delighted me in my youth that I think I must repeat it here. Addressing my uncle at the Durbar, Sir Bartle Frere said 'All you have done was mainly by and through the natives of the land in all their various ranks, chiefs as well as ryots; by stimulating and encouraging what was good in them and not by imposing on them the law of a wise but stern taskmaster. You upheld the same character during your tenure of office as Resident at the Court of the Maharajah of Gwalior, and won the respect as well as the personal regard of the Maharajah of Sindia. When, after many years of separation Her Highness the Begum of Bopal unexpectedly met you at Poona, there was no mistaking the great pleasure with which that great and wise ruler recognized you. She recalled you to mind not only as the British Political Officer who had been the channel of advice and criticism of the Indian Government, nor even as the gallant soldier winning the Victoria Cross in the deadly breach at Chandari, at the same period when Her Highness was proving her loyalty to the British Crown by so bravely curbing her own mutinous troops—but Her Highness recognized you as he who had several years earlier travelled hundreds of miles to add éclat to her daughter's wedding, by placing on the lake in Her Highness' capital the first steam boat which she, or the great body of her courtiers, had ever seen.'

One subject on which he often spoke to me, and in which I think he took a specially deep personal interest, was the college at Adjmir for the sons of the chiefs. He wished it to be as much as possible on the lines of a Public School 'To train men to whom responsibility will eventually come, to be ready and anxious to take it.' I suppose the Rajcott College has gone now, with the chiefs for whom it was founded. Is the world any the better for that?

One story he was always ready to tell, as illustrating the devotion of some of the native followers, was that 'when he was in command of two guns, and had his horse shot under him, his sais, hearing of the occurrence, without orders and in spite of very heavy fire, ran up to the front with a spare horse.'

I do not know precisely how it came about that in 1867 my uncle and his friend Captain Thomas Cadell of the Munsters found themselves appointed to pacify a large district in Rajputan but I feel sure that either Sir Bartle Frere or Sir Henry Durand had to do with it. Someone was heard to express the opinion that it was a tough job for two comparatively junior and inexperienced men, and to hope that they would not fail. One of the old chiefs, and again I do not know to which of them the story refers, answered 'Those are not the kind of young men who fail.'

Half a lifetime later, when Colonel Cadell of Cockenzie was my very dear friend, he told me how one day when he was riding back to his camp, he saw 'old Keatinge sitting in the door of my tent and he called out "You've got it at last, old fellow" and I wondered which of my sins had found me out. But it was Keatinge who had come to tell me that I had been awarded the Victoria Cross.' My uncle always said that it was Cadell who really deserved the Cross for extreme gallantry at the siege of Delhi, and I heard that he refused to wear his Cross until Cadell's had been awarded.

General Keatinge

Colonel Cadell told me that at this time my uncle was so weak that he asked him to tell visitors not to try to shake his hand, 'Or they'll have me out of the saddle.'

I have mentioned how my good times with him came to an end at my uncle, General Keatinge's second marriage. Shortly after their marriage they went out to India to visit some of his old friends. Before they sailed he told his wife categorically that she must not accept presents, and it was a fearful shock to him while they were there to find that she was doing so.

He told me this because he said 'I ought to know.' I never mentioned the subject to him again because it hurt him so desperately. He told his son-in-law, Dr. Butler, and I think no one else. She used to show charming little things which she had bought or had given to her while they were in India, but I do not think there was anything of money value among them.

He took a great interest in the London Hospital, which was at the time in great need of reorganization and rebuilding, and he made friends with the rather terrifying matron, who began by saying that she wouldn't have any General interfering with matters that were none of his business, and ended by eating out of his hand. They agreed that when any cases were brought in whose language they could not understand, he might be communicated with by night or day. I remember one stormy night when I was staying with them, a message came, reporting a black man said to be in a very bad way, and no one able to make out what he was saying. 'I only hope he isn't an African negro', my uncle said as I helped him with his coat. 'They seem to expect me to know the language of every man who has a brown skin.' In the morning I asked how he had got on. He said 'The patient was a Lascar from the docks, frightfully burned, poor chap. He will not recover, but I was able to take down his depositions and write a letter which I hope his father will understand. I held his hand while he made his mark.'

General Keatinge

During the last months of his life after his move to Horsham I saw him fairly often. He was cared for by two devoted nurses, who refused to leave him even when his wife held up their wages. When he died there was an obituary in the *Pioneer* and I added something about the Rajput schools in the *Homeward Mail*, but the biography which Sir Diedrick Brandis told my mother that he proposed to write was never written, and Sir Diedrick himself died not many years later. He was the original for Muller in Kipling's *In the Rukh*. I read this story to my uncle first in Edinburgh, and over and over again when he visited us in Oxford. He always lay back in his chair and chuckled, saying that he could see it all, and that Muller was a perfect picture of his old friend Brandis.

In France they judged that England would have no further trouble in South Africa because we had sent out our two most famous and successful administrators, 'Les frères Bartle', to govern the country. Upon a change of government, Sir Bartle Frere was recalled and came home 'almost in disgrace'. My uncle originated and carried out the plan to give to Sir Bartle Frere a dinner of welcome on his return from the Cape, 'The gathering to be of a social and non-political character, without public advertisement and without reporters'. He wrote to me afterwards: 'The dinner was a grand success, two hundred and thirty good men present, the Service gathering was really very remarkable, and the telegram we got during the dinner from the Prince and Princess of Wales was really nice, I "owe" the Prince one for this, and I shall cease to be a Republican for six weeks, say end of December.' It was one of our standing jokes that he insisted that he must be a Republican. Great Britain was the only satisfactory republic in the world; so of course he was a Republican.

CHAPTER VIII

Friends at Bournemouth

❖

During and after the Franco-German war there was quite a colony of Scotch people at Bournemouth—I remember Napiers, Dalrymples, Scots and Blackburns and the daughters of Lord Mure, one of the Judges. A herd of milking donkeys toured the town in the early morning, and attractive as the babies were, I was always afraid that asses milk would be ordered for me as it was for the invalid Miss Mure—but luckily I escaped that ordeal. The elder Miss Mure was a great beauty —tall, dark and rather aloof; people said that she had 'Italian eyes'. I always wanted to gaze into them! She was a friend of Mimi Abercromby, who I think came to Bournemouth chiefly to see her, when for the first time she stayed with us. Afterwards she became a great friend of my mother's. The guest I remember best at The Firs is my father's naval brother, my Uncle Jim. He was said to be 'ripe for promotion' when he went crazy about photography, and fell out with his captain, afterwards Admiral Milne, who could not stand the 'muck' he made developing his plates. They always remained good friends, and I fancy he just preferred photography to discipline. Anyhow, he came to The Firs with great plans about going out to the Argentine—a chart was produced showing land offered for sale, and eventually my father put up the price, or some of it, and Uncle Jim went out to claim his property, but it appeared that the chart had been faked—a strip of land had been inserted between properties which really marched—a degree of latitude had been shifted to make room for it—the strip did not exist at all! Uncle Jim was

88

apparently not much troubled; he wrote that 'roughing it' was the life he liked, and sent me stuffed humming birds.

After a drill class in the garden, Alfonso and Raphael Merry del Val, and some of the other children stayed on and we played brigands, Alfonso and I were captains almost every time, till Raphael complained that we never gave him a turn, so we promised to let him have one if he 'proved worthy'. We imprisoned him in a kind of den between the walls of the rockery, put him on parole and removed the sentry, after which we pelted him with fir cones. He did not try to escape but he cried, and one of the governesses heard him and quite naturally said we were bullying him. We tried to explain that it was a test, and that we had to let him be a captive for a time! He was a Cardinal in later life.

Another friend of my mother's was Lady Collier, the widow of an admiral who interested me because he was said to know more 'swear words' than anyone else in the Service—a distinction which I have heard applied to various other admirals! Her grandson, Clarence, a Public School boy, used to wangle permission for me to come from the school-room, and we had wonderful days of exploration, suggested, I think, by Stanley and Livingstone—he could tell a story thrillingly as we crouched among the rhododendron bushes. Then one wet day when my mother was going out with Lady Collier—I must have been about nine—Clarence suggested that he might come along and play in the schoolroom. My mother told me that as both she and my governess were out, she would tell her maid to bring her work down to the schoolroom and sit there, 'it would be nicer for you.' I protested that it wouldn't be nice at all, and begged that the maid should only come in and make up the fire, but my mother said she had better bring her work and sit with us, which made me definitely uncomfortable, and after a short time one of us made a joke—we were acting something with figures cut out of paper—and the maid laughed at the joke and joined in, entirely spoiling the play. Clarence saw and understood, and never suggested playing in the school-room again. Lady Collier had a cottage in the New Forest, and we sometimes stayed near her for a few days. She was a sentimental old lady and quite hurt because I did not wear a wreath, which Clarence made for me, just before he went up to Oxford. I must have been an unaccommodating child, but it seemed a silly thing to wear, and it tickled! Clarence was drowned before the end of his third year.

A rather exciting family was the Mostyn's. Looking back I think that Mrs. Mostyn must have been a keen educationalist, and she was really anxious that my parents should take an intellectual line about my education. One Christmas holiday we children were all made to learn some poetry, and to recite it to our parents, and to a very select audience of their friends. I do not remember what the Mostyn girls had prepared, but one of the boys had learned pages and pages of Hiawatha, and gave them to us with tremendous verve and theatrical gesture. It was my introduction to Longfellow, and I got some idea that reciting was not precisely the same thing as 'saying poetry'. I had been given two short pieces of Wordsworth to learn, *The Skylark* and *The Mountain Echo*. In *The Skylark*, Wordsworth writes 'Slaves of folly, love or strife, Voices of two different natures,' but my mother said 'You could not be the slave of love; love was wholly good and did not make slaves', so she amended it to 'slaves of folly, passion, strife'; I repeated it as I was told to do.

The Mountain Echo ends with the words 'True to the kindred points of Heaven and home.' I was told 'When you finish your poem you may kiss papa and mammy.' I did as I was told—I am sure that at this time many people, Lady Collier for example, would have thought this a touching gesture and 'quite charming' and would probably have said, if asked, that they believed it to be spontaneous, but I saw Mrs. Mostyn's and the boys' faces, and their expressions said unutterable things! I felt ashamed, and had to struggle hard not to cry. My mother, by the way, thought the Hiawatha recital had been 'rather shocking, exaggerated and theatrical'. It did me a very good turn, however; I asked for, and was given, a complete edition of Longfellow. At the same time I was given an anthology called *Springtime with the Poets*, in which two or three pieces were marked, and I was told not to read these until I was older. One, I remember, was Hood's *Song of the Shirt*.

Mrs. Mostyn's children's parties were very educative. At one of them we had a spelling bee. She dipped her hand into a bag and going round from one nervous child to the next, she told it to spell whatever word she had drawn from the bag; 'So you see, it is bound to be quite fair.' I got the booby-prize when I spelled 'Parliamentary' without the 'i'! The child next to me fell for 'yacht', a catch-word, which Miss Smith had carefully taught me to spell. I did not mind about the booby-prize for myself, but I had the grace to feel sorry for Miss Smith. It must be hard when your pupil lets you down before an assembly of governesses!

Of our Bournemouth friends much the most exciting were the Von Hügels. Baroness Von Hügel had been a Scotch girl 'of no family' at the Embassy in Vienna, probably, I think, a nursery governess. Baron Von Hügel fell in love with her, and to the horror of his family she married him. The Von Hügels were devout Catholics and the resolute young woman refused to be converted. He died suddenly, leaving her well off and the custody of the children. His family did not dispute the legacy, but got hold of the children and told her that, as a heretic, she would never recover custody of them.

The Embassy was unable to help her, so she bombarded the most eminent ecclesiastic of her acquaintance and insisted on being received into the Church then and there, without the usual long preliminary instruction. She got back her children and when the Von Hügels wanted to have at least some say in their education, or the custody of the eldest son, she escaped with them to England, and when I knew them she was a very strict and ardent Catholic.

But the Bournemouth friends who really mattered to me, and they were near neighbours when we left The Firs and bought the house on Richmond Hill, were the Lefroys, two sisters and a brother. Their father was a County Court Judge, and the household was presided over by a charming old aunt. They showed their French origin; Willie might have been a politician or *Littérateur*, a small courteous man with a neat brown beard; he was just a pleasant acquaintance, but the youngest of the family was for years my best girl friend. Mary Lefroy was tall and slight, brown-eyed and brown-haired, with a lovely clear brown skin, touched with sunshine. She always dressed in shades of brown, and in spite of much active exercise, was always immaculately tidy, a condition to which I early recognized it was impossible for me to attain!

Mary was a great-niece of Jane Austen and used to read *Pride and Prejudice* aloud to me, while I toiled through a compulsory portion of fine needlework. Fortunately all these young people were very popular with my parents, and I'm sure it was owing to them that we had several 'carpet dances'. For these a drugget, an enormous coarse cotton sheet, was drawn tightly over the carpet, and we danced on this. The Lefroys must have found most of the partners, for I am sure that we knew very few young men.

It must, I think, have been while we were still living at The Firs that a very disturbing family event took place. My mother's unmarried sister and her youngest brother joined the Church of Rome. It was said that Newman's *Apologia* convinced them. I got the impression from my mother that they were doing something extremely wrong, and from my father that it was something very foolish. For some time Aunt Annie did not come to visit us, though I think Uncle Willie always continued to do so, although he undertook not to talk to me about religion; and I was forbidden to question him. Then some years later Aunt Annie accepted a Papal title. This *did* upset my father! He said it was worse than marrying a cheap, German Baron! Later I heard that the uncle had a much more exalted title bestowed upon him, but that he refused to use it outside the Papal States, which they visited several times.

Many years later, when Cardinal Manning was supporting Home Rule, he met Uncle Willie at the Athenaeum, and said that he counted on his assistance 'as a fellow-Irishman'. The uncle answered 'Your Eminence forgets I am an English gentleman.' It made rather a sensation, and people he didn't know crowded up to shake his hand and wish 'More power to his elbow'; but he always alluded to it as 'only a painful incident'. It made some ill-feeling between him and his sister, though God knows she wasn't a Home Ruler, but she always behaved as if she did not think him quite her equal intellectually, which was probably true. She was a lively spirit, and completely bossed their charming flat in Duke Street, Grosvenor Square. They had lovely old furniture and very interesting Keatinge silver, which they left to the Keanes, though I think any money went to the Church.

Even after I was grown-up I was discouraged from haunting the flat when I was in London, but I always went there, and was warmly received. I have a very grateful recollection of this aunt and uncle. When I was about eighteen I persuaded him to lend me both Newman's and St. Augustine's *Confessions*, but they had no effect—in fact I was appalled with much of St. Augustine. My poor mother needn't have been anxious!

About this time, when he was staying with us on an Ash Wednesday, Uncle Willie went out breakfastless and stayed in Church all day. Coming back tired and hungry, with a cross marked in ashes on his high forehead, he lay down on the sofa beside which I was working at something with gum and brush, and sighed and fidgeted and asked whether I could not put the hour of dinner forward a little. Unsympathetically I dabbed the gum brush over the ashes—he wasn't really cross as he well might have been, only rather hurt. He wouldn't be able to wash it off till next morning he said, and he came down to dinner with a red mark upon his forehead, where he had tried to pick off the dried gum. It was evidently part of the ceremony not to wash off the ash under twenty-four hours.

As a child the text that worried me most was 'Thou God seest me'. I asked my mother about this: 'Do you think God

93

really sees us all the time?' I do not remember the answer, but it must have been to the effect that 'His loving eyes follow you everywhere; do you not understand how grateful you should be for his loving care of you?'

That wasn't my reaction. 'But God is a *man*' I said, 'Can he really see me in my bath? How horrid!' I have a sneaking feeling that, put like this, my mother though it 'rather horrid' too. She said at once that, of course, God wasn't a man. 'But He must be,' I argued, 'they always call Him "He", never She or It. He must be a man, and I wish He wasn't there!'

I don't remember what more was said, but my mother was badly shocked and pained. She said I must not let myself think such things. It left me feeling very uncomfortable.

My attitude to dogma was, on the whole, experimental. When I was a small child I had heard that the Sin against the Holy Ghost had no forgiveness. I went up to the attic in Edinburgh, and, all among the suitcases and derelict pieces of furniture, I stamped and repeated: 'I hate the Holy Ghost!' I went down the stairs into the warm nursery rather quickly. But that was all. Later on for at least a week at a time, I kneeled up in bed and prayed: 'Oh, dear God, please, please, let me wake up in the morning a boy!' But again nothing happened!

It must have been slightly before this, for they were all rather older than I, that the Woodhouselea children made their Act of Faith. The four older ones agreed to pray 'That this mountain be removed and cast into the sea.' The mountain was Allermuir and the sea was at North Berwick. They knew that their father would not like this, but they hoped that he would be so pleased at the strength of their faith that he would not be really angry at the loss of his hill. They did not let the younger sister join in their petition, either because there was some risk involved, or because she was too young to have enough faith.

In the morning the one brother in the family stole into the dining-room and opened the shutters. The view was unchanged. He reported to his sisters. 'Ah', said the eldest sister, quite logical and determined to cling to one of 'the promises'. 'We have not enough faith. If we had enough we should have known that it *had happened*. We should have waited till breakfast time and not sent anybody to look.'

I was confirmed when I was about fifteen, during one of our stays in Edinburgh. It would have been simple for me to join a Confirmation Class at Bournemouth, where the two principal Churches each held one every year, but the parish church which we attended was 'too high' to suit my parents' views, and Dr. Sandford, of St. John's Episcopal Church in Edinburgh, undertook to 'prepare' me. I went to his house a few times, and read two or three books he recommended, and asked a few questions about historical evidence, but never confessed to doctrinal doubts. I fancy that I thought taking the Sacrament might make it easier to 'be good', though what 'being good' actually was became increasingly difficult to understand, unless it just meant doing what those 'set in authority over you' wished done.

I had been confirmed all by myself by the Bishop of Edinburgh—rather a trying ceremony. It took place, I think, after afternoon service, and when we got home I was told that I should 'certainly want to go to my room and be quiet for a little', after which I was to come down to the drawing-room for tea. Altogether shy-making, and impossible to avoid being self-conscious! After tea my mother told me to write a note to a cousin to thank her for having come to St. John's for 'my' service. But why should I thank her I asked? I am sure that my mother was overtired, or had been worried, for she turned on me and said (or words to this effect) 'There now! Even today you can't feel properly. It doesn't seem to have done you any good.' I sat down and wrote the note with black anger in my heart. The cousin had come because she wanted to, or to please my grandmother. Why should I write and say that I thanked her?—I didn't! I objected to being told to write a lie.

95

Friends at Bournemouth

Dr. Daniel Sandford was afterwards the first Bishop of Tasmania. I liked and respected him, and I think many of his congregation in Edinburgh did not appreciate him or do him justice.

To return to Bournemouth. It was through the windows of 3, Richmond Gardens, the house to which we moved from The Firs, one brilliantly clear Sunday afternoon that we saw the *Eurydice* sail up the channel—a most beautiful sight—one of the largest ships in the Navy under full sail, a mass of white canvas against a blue sea and sky. We had been warned at what time to watch for her, as there was a young cousin on board. Quite suddenly the sun was blocked out by a storm of snow from a black cloud. When the light came back, beams of sunshine shone upon an empty sea.

We tried to believe that the *Eurydice* had rounded the Needles. Reports said that she had been carrying too much sail; only five or six of the crew were saved. . . .

Was it because of the disappointment about the eucalyptus that my father suddenly took it into his head to 'try Edinburgh'? Even before we moved to Richmond Gardens he had planted a row of eucalyptus, which grew surprisingly quickly into reasonably sized young trees. He was pleased with the result of the experiment, particularly as the gardeners had said that the climate and soil were quite unsuitable and prophesied disaster. We dried the leaves in the autumn and stuffed pillows for the hospitals—they were supposed to be useful to bad sleepers. Then there came a late frost, the one hard frost of the year, and all but one of the poor young trees shrivelled up and died. My father shook his head and said 'We might as well try Edinburgh'—and we did.

CHAPTER IX

Family Affairs

✤

In 1876, my uncle, Captain John Mowbray Trotter, then on leave from India, went to stay at Callender with his mother and sisters, and Mimi Abercromby visited them there. We followed and must have completely filled up the small hotel, for we all had separate sitting-rooms. The grandmother was extremely anxious for an engagement between my uncle and Mimi, and the visit cannot have been an altogether pleasant experience for her. My grandmother and my aunt were aggressively possessive people; and she used to escape from them to my mother's sitting-room, where there was a solid table at which she could sit and work up her sketches. Then my uncle and I would go for a scramble together, which I always enjoyed immensely. He gave me a complete up-to-date copy of Tennyson's poems, having ordered that it should be bound in 'subjects', which would have necessitated volumes of very diverse thickness. But this proved too much for the binder and when the six leather volumes arrived, they were identical. My uncle was indignant: 'You can't possibly put *The Passing of Arthur* and *The Princess* between the same boards', he said, and wanted to send the volume back. But I was not to be parted from the best present I had ever had!

We younger people were out nearly all day in all weathers, walking and rowing, and doing some cooking on a contraption called a 'paper cooking stove'. I have never seen another one; it cooked bacon and eggs or sausages to the expenditure of one copy of *The Scotsman*.

Family Affairs

At last they were engaged, and no girl ever thrilled to an engagement not her own as I did that day. My uncle cabled 'Taking marriage leave' and we all went our ways, I to a strenuous fortnight of lessons, before Miss Smith took her holiday: Mimi to Colinton, where her companion was awaiting her. It would have been considered 'impossible' for an unmarried girl (she was twenty-six) to have stayed for a few days in her own house without a companion.

The party reassembled at Lochearnhead. Everyone's nerves were unusually taut, their tempers constantly breaking, and I was constantly in trouble of some sort. My sailor uncle arrived unexpectedly and one day, after taking some letters to catch the mail, I joined him at the post office, and we walked down to the Loch together. It never occurred to me to ask permission to do so, and under ordinary conditions, none would have been needed. But both uncles were at pains to make up to me for the violent scolding I got on this and several other occasions.

The wedding was to be early in October at Minto. Lord Minto was Mimi's uncle; her aunt, Lady Charlotte Portal, was the wife of my father's first cousin, Melville Portal of Laverstoke. Everyone was more or less related or else the families were such old friends that it 'made no odds'. We went to Minto from Edinburgh, where at the last moment my father found he was 'too ill to travel'. I do not think for a moment there was anything special the matter; it often happened when he had made an engagement, he just didn't feel like keeping it, and for one dreadful moment I was afraid we should not go either. However, we travelled by an afternoon train, along with my father's old uncle-in-law, William Pitt Dundas, and, I think, Mr. Tytler (Woodhouselea) and Mr. Haldane, the two lawyers who were responsible for drawing up the settlements.

When we came near the Tweed, Uncle Pitt asked me 'Have you any knowledge of this country?' and I began 'Uncle, I could say to thee the words that cleft Eildon hills in three And bridled the Tweed with a curb of stone:' and on for several cantos of *The Lay of the Last Minstrel,* which gave general satisfaction. Scott was still a fetish to the old generation!

We reached Minto by teatime, and joined the big party, the men just in from shooting or fishing, eating hot scones before going to try for 'first bath', the ladies rather bored and glad of fresh arrivals to talk to. I was to be a bridesmaid, but was much younger than the other three, my Aunt Mary who was even older than the bridegroom, Adela Portal a cousin and Annie Gibson Craig of Riccarton, a friend and neighbour of Mimi's. They ignored me completely and presently the ladies went up to dress for dinner. I was thought to be too young to come to dinner and was told to 'have a rest', and then to be dressed by my mother's maid and to wait in the drawing-room till the ladies came out from dinner, but—which made it ten times worse—my mother's maid was to sit there with me!

It all happened just as I expected it would. The maid and I went down to the dimly lighted drawing-room, being shown the way by a housemaid, who giggled with delight, and we waited an hour until the footman came in to light up. Lighting was by candles in wall sockets, as far as I remember—of course the men were joking in low tones when they came in, but they fell silent when they saw the maid and me, and how amused their glances were!

At last the ladies came in, the maid escaped by another door and Lady Minto said a friendly word or two, but I was desperately self-conscious, having been made conspicuous quite against my will, and also I was dreadfully cold in a white muslin frock made especially and hastily for the occasion. I was hungry, too, having had no food since afternoon tea.

We were shown our bridesmaids' dresses of white cashmere with a red velvet panel on one side of the skirt and various red 'plastrons'. We had muslin caps, like the maids' caps, with red bows and a sprig of artificial heather.

The evening wore on and everyone seemed very ordinary and cheerful, while I felt that nothing was ordinary. I kept on repeating to myself 'It's Mimi's wedding—

Family Affairs

'Ring ye the bells, ye young men of the town—
Put up your wonted labours for this day—
This day is holy, do ye write it down
That ye for ever it remember may—'

I've not the faintest recollection of where I got the quotation,
nor was it particularly apt, but why was it in my head? I'm
sure I've never come across it since. I did not flatter myself
that any of the young men would remember, they were Elliots
and Russells, cousins, not in very sentimental mood! This all
seems quite absurd, but it seemed tremendously real and
important to me: and so to bed, and in the morning the house-
maids came and lighted the ladies' bedroom fires, and their
own maids brought up their breakfast trays. After breakfast,
we went through the saloon where the ceremony was to take
place. It was all decorated with plants and flowers and looked
lovely in the chill grey morning. Everybody talked and borrowed copies of that day's papers, and presently Lord Minto
told Mr. Sandford that it must be 'about time', and they left
the room. Mr. Sandford came back in his surplice and we
bridesmaids were marshalled to the foot of the stairs and
presently Mimi came down on Lord Minto's arm, a proper
bride with a long white train. The saloon was full of family
and friends and neighbours—in the background, the people
from the estate and old servants. The ceremony was as short
as it could possibly be, the bridegroom and his old friend
'Dan' Sandford had seen to that, and certainly he read none
of the 'exhortations' from the prayer book. And then my
uncle led Mimi round to greet all the elders; I overheard them
saying something very heartfelt of Lady Minto, to whom he
was devoted; and presently we sat down to the wedding breakfast and drank toasts and listened to speeches. After which,
Mimi went up to change, and I was terribly hurt because she
asked the other three bridesmaids and my mother and Lady
Charlotte to visit her in her room, but left me out!

We saw them off in proper form, with rice and slippers, and
just before they started, Mimi gave me a sprig of myrtle from

100

her bouquet and asked me to grow it for her, which I did with much pains and care, till someone knocked down and smashed the flowerpot.

The men went off to try for a bird or two, and we went to rest till dinner, to which I was invited on the strength of being a bridesmaid, and after dinner there was dancing, chiefly reels and strathspeys, which I had never even seen before, and of course could not dance, so I sat out with a lame cousin, Arthur Elliot, and Mr. Sandford. Most of the men were quite young, but a few of the elder ones danced better than any of them, Mr. Tytler, tall, handsome Lord Minto and tubby little Uncle Pitt; the last two, facing one another, doing their steps in precision and snapping their fingers, were a sight to remember. But Mr. Haldane sat solemnly on a sofa and seemed rather to repel any attempt at fraternising, and this was the first I ever knew of my husband's family! Mr. Haldane and Mr. Tytler were responsible for getting settlements, wills etc., signed, and this was done, I suppose, between the wedding service and the breakfast. Mr. Tytler's role cannot have been important, for my uncle had little besides his pay, but Mimi was a considerable heiress and all her business was in the hands of Mr. Haldane's firm. Some years later there were complaints that this had been mismanaged (this was after Mr. Haldane's death), and I think what happened was that the firm had allowed them to draw on their settlement without warning them that they were exceeding their income.

They started in a fairly lavish way. She immensely enjoyed giving him anything he liked—a copy of Sir Henry Yule's *Marco Polo*, a wedding present which he had specially asked for from an old aunt, was bound in vellum for him, and each volume of the *Encyclopaedia Britannica* as it came out was sent out to them, initialled and fully bound. My father once showed me a letter he was writing to them, with a sketch which represented them being carried in palanquins, followed by a row of bearers, each with a volume of the encyclopaedia on his head. But later volumes which were sent out as they were published went in ordinary cloth binding.

101

CHAPTER X

Growing-up in Edinburgh

❄

Part of our first winter in Edinburgh was spent at Gunn's Hotel in St. Colm' Street. I have only most unpleasant recollections of that dark and dreary abode.

What a pity it seemed that only six years earlier my father had owned, and sold, a house in George Square—but at that time the idea that we might settle in Edinburgh had never been mooted. George Square is no longer in a fashionable quarter of the town, but it has many advantages. The square itself is large enough to separate opposite neighbours pretty effectively, and almost at their back doors they have the Queen's Drive, Arthur's Seat and nearly unspoiled country. Before I begin to write about my more-or-less adult life in Edinburgh, I shall tell the story of the sale of this house, for it is rather curious, and characteristic of the behaviour of some members of my family!

The house in question had belonged to my grandfather's sister, known to the family as 'Aunt Kate', and had been let after her death. Early in 1876 the tenants gave up their lease, and the house was advertised for auction.

I do not know whether it was let as a 'furnished house', but it contained, to judge by the list sent to Bournemouth, quite a lot of good furniture, besides Indian rugs and brass, and quantities of china. My father said he would go to Edinburgh before the sale and see what he wanted to keep; but when the time came the weather was bad, and as he did not feel inclined for the journey, my grandmother undertook to see to everything for him. She asked, among other things, whether they wished to keep all the china? She was told not to sell any of it. 'What' she wrote, 'not cracked willow pattern'? My mother answered '*Particularly* not cracked willow pattern'! She was anxious to go north herself, as she guessed that there would be a good deal of interesting matter in the house, but it was thought that my grandmother would be 'hurt' if she were not trusted!

There was no special notice made of the sale, no catalogue was printed and everything was just 'let go', as it might be in an ordinary 'roup' of an unlet lodging house! Just at the last moment they had a piece of quite undeserved good luck. The agents sent word that there was a boarded-up cupboard in the kitchen, and asked should they break it open. It was found to contain a full dessert service in Crown Derby china! In the autumn, when my uncle was going to be married, my mother and grandmother went about Edinburgh looking for something nice for a wedding present they had been commissioned to choose for him. In the curiosity shop under the Music Hall in George Street, they came upon what I have heard described as 'magnificent' green Wedgwood flower pots. My mother exclaimed in admiration and my grandmother tried to divert her attention, but the shopman said 'Oh yes, those are very fine pieces indeed. I can show you some other very fine things which I got from the sale in George Square.' Collapse of the grandmother! My mother said she made no comment. I heard years afterwards that people went to the shop and asked whether there was still anything to be had from Miss Trotter's sale, and good prices were given for things because everyone knew they were genuine.

Aunt Kate must have been a character. When she went to London by coach to meet her brothers, she never leaned back because, she said it 'disarranged' her watch. She left a 'jewellery case' full of queer things, such as copies of the Lorne Brooch, with large cairngorms, a Queen Mary brooch in blue enamel, ropes of sham pearls, and filmy hollow gilt brooches and pendants, such as they are making copies of nowadays. There is also my one 'ornament', of which the centre consists of real diamonds, and the edges of pebble or glass with red foil behind them, to look like rubies. I feel sure that what happened was that Aunt Kate was sent diamonds by some of her brothers in India; old letters prove that her three brothers adored her. She thought that she would like an ornament. The diamonds made a good centre, and why should she not have red glass round the edges, which made it look much handsomer? No-one would have believed her if she had said they were rubies—they are much too large!

To return to my own affairs. The family (grandmother and aunts taken into consultation), decided that I should 'come out', and at the same time continue my education. I was told how nice and exciting it was for me to 'come out'. It did not apparently occur to anyone that one's first ball might be poor fun if one didn't know a single person in the ballroom!

My first ball dress was made by Mathieson in George Street, my grandmother's dressmakers. They definitely did not specialize in girls' clothes. I fancy their clients were chiefly elderly ladies, and that they had no strong views on ball gowns, for I am sure that my mother said the first and last words about that dress. It did not look very unlike most of the other girls' dresses when I saw it in company, but it certainly was not a garment likely to inspire the wearer with confidence. My mother and I both had long quilted cloaks and knitted overshoes like bedsocks, for outdoor evening wear. Mathieson's made the cloaks for us in coloured cashmere —my mother's was maroon and mine was blue. No other girl was wrapped in anything of the kind. I was told that it was 'so nice and warm', but it was pain and grief to me.

We dined before my first ball with friends of my grandmother's. She had spoken to me about 'the Walker girl', so when we got to the house I was still expecting to see someone of about my own standing, but Louisa Walker was very much my senior. I believe that she was a sensible young woman, and that we were now embarking on what she had decided should be her last 'season', for I don't remember her at a ball after that winter.

Growing-up in Edinburgh

The party at dinner consisted of Mr. and Mrs. Walker, their two 'young people', Louisa and her heavy, and not particularly young, brother, my parents and me. It had not apparently occurred to our hosts to invite anyone else. A partner for Louisa would have been a useful addition, unless she was supposed to dance all night with her brother; but presumably he had sometimes to dance with me! He did, but we had nothing to say to one another, and our steps did not suit any better than our conversation.

Of course in all the stories, the heroine gets off at her first ball with the best partner in the room, but I sat out more dances than I danced. The stewards at these very select Assembly Rooms' dances were supposed to act more or less as hosts, and to do a certain number of introductions, but I don't think they took their duties seriously. It was altogether very unlike a Jane Austen novel!

For our second winter in Edinburgh, we looked for a furnished house—nothing too permanent—we were still 'trying' Edinburgh. One morning I looked over a house which had been recommended by the agents, reported on it to my mother, and returned there with her in the afternoon. We were ushered into the dining-room of 17, Charlotte Square, where a young man lay on the hearthrug surrounded by open books. He scrambled to his feet, saying that he was 'just working'. 'No, you were fast asleep', I said. He followed us when we went round the house with his mother—not a tactful young man, as we had to enquire about sanitary arrangements and service bedrooms. This was my first sight of John Haldane, my future husband.

We took Number 17, and gradually accumulated some possessions of our own round us. There were always plenty of books, newspapers and magazines, and gradually it became home-like. We were still living there when I married some eight years later.

In our early years in Edinburgh, we had not many acquaintances in the town, but people from the country came in and out pretty constantly. My mother always preferred receiving at home to accepting invitations, and we were almost always 'at home' for luncheon, and not often without some guest or guests.

Then people came on long visits; my handsome cousin Blanche Dundas often stayed for weeks at a time, and her elder brother Harry, Lord Melville, found us a useful 'town house'.

Twice a year we had a visit from Colonel Sir Henry Yule. He wrote his great book—in which he describes himself as 'Editor of the Book of Ser Marco Polo'—in Italy, when he was detained there by an accident to his wife. They were on their way home on leave from India—she died in Italy, but it was before my time. His strange daughter Amy was about my age, but a much more impressive person than I ever was! He liked going about the country revisiting old haunts in East Lothian, and I liked to feel that he wanted to have me with him.

A very different person was Professor Robertson Smith, the victim of a heresy hunt by the Fellows of the University of Aberdeen, where the pundits were shocked by his views on the Hebrew Prophets. My mother had all his books on the Prophets, and read them to such effect that she was prepared to take on anyone who questioned his history or his theology. He was at the time co-editor of a new edition of the *Encyclopaedia Britannica,* and came to Edinburgh to discuss with my father his articles on Central Asia and the Pacific Islands. From staying with us on his last visit, Robertson Smith went to Cambridge, where he was received with honour, and, I think with affection; but he never got over the way in which his own university had hounded him out. Cambridge friends used to say that he had arrived a broken-hearted man, and that 'we could not mend it for him'.

I liked and respected Dr. Joe Bell (the original Sherlock Holmes). He knew all the family and could sum up their characteristics in a couple of scathing sentences, which were usually excruciatingly funny. He used to say that they only consulted him professionally when they were bored by their own doctors and that he usually began his treatment by making them exceedingly angry, which was at any rate stimulating! His very charming boy, Ben, was in the 72nd, and was killed in South Africa.

But of all our visitors, the one to whom I was really devoted was my father's cousin, Colonel Sir Henry Trotter, R.E. He came to stay before his adventurous mission to Kadigar and on his return, when my father helped him to compile the report on his journey. I have a few odd leaves of it, and one of the maps, by the discreet use of which one could get him to tell stories. I pinpointed the map and asked 'How did you get from here to here, Cousin Harry?' and then, if one was in luck, the story came! The account of that mission would have made a wonderful article in *Blackwood's*, but I do not think that it ever got into print except in the official Bluebook.

Colonel Sir Frederick and Lady Roberts spent a few days with us once on their way to stay at Colinton. I remember this because it is the only time I ever talked with the General.

I wish I could remember the name of the Naval Lieutenant who told stirring tales of capturing slavers in the Red Sea. We sat so late among the remains of breakfast that the butler had to ask us to move to enable him to lay the table for luncheon.

My principal recollection of real Edinburgh people in a pleasant, friendly Edinburgh home, is of the Noel Patons and their house in George Square. I liked all the Noel Patons, brothers and sisters, more than any one of them ever liked me! How pleasant it must be to be one of nine or ten brothers and sisters! When Sir Noel was painting for a friend in Australia his picture of Queen Margaret reading the Bible to Malcolm Canmore, I tried to persuade him to put in a plant of the Star of Bethlehem, but he laughed at me, said it was 'a conceit' and refused, even when I dug up the plant at Colinton and took it to him!

But of course the family at Colinton House mattered more to me than the whole of the map of Scotland, and most of all the crippled boy there—my cousin Archie, so brave and so unlucky. One of the few things that still make me happy to remember is that when Archie met with one of his many accidents, someone was sure to say 'send for Kathleen'.

In 1885, the 1st Battalion of the Seaforth Highlanders was quartered at the Castle, and life was pleasanter than usual. We knew Colonel Guinness and many of his officers, including my cousin Henry Knight, but above all Granville Egerton, who became my life-long friend. He started his career in India by arriving at Umbala to enquire for his regiment after the Field Force was well on its way. No one could give him any orders, but he heard that Roberts had passed through Alikhel, so he collected a guide, hired ponies and went in pursuit of the 72nd. He was in Kabul during the winter, and slightly wounded on the march to Kandahar; a wonderful campaign for his first taste of Active Service! Promotion followed, and for a considerable time he was the youngest Captain in the Army, but he missed the South African War (he used to say that all his friends were killed there), and for what seemed an even longer time, he was the oldest Captain on the Active Service list.

Later, in Gallipoli, he refused to obey an order to take his 'Glasgow Corner Boys' into an impossible position, and insisted on Ian Hamilton and some of the staff coming on shore to see what the men were being ordered to do. The result was that the staff supported him—one of them said that 'carrying out the order would have been plain murder'—and reported to Headquarters. The order was cancelled, but the incident did him no good, except with the few people who had been ashore and seen for themselves. Much later on he made friends with my husband, and sometimes came to stay at Cloan when we were there. He posed as a Liberal, though at heart he was an old-fashioned Whig—and he used to say things which made my Tory eyes see red! but on all Empire questions we saw eye to eye, and that was what mattered.

But besides 'coming out', the family had settled that I should 'continue my education', and how better could I do that than by attending classes at the School of Art? For some

months I went there on three mornings a week—I hated
drawing pots and pans, and even the young Augustus (the
model offered to pupils who had finished their first stage and
could shade nicely in chalk), had no attraction for me. I told
my father that rather than go to the School of Art, I would
learn to sew! This produced a crisis. He had always supported
me when I did not get on with the wonderful German darning
Miss Schweitzer taught, saying 'Why worry the child with
this—she can *draw.*' Now it appeared that she either would
not, or could not, draw! He 'was used to disappointments' he
said, 'but this one was a severe one.'

Then there came to call Miss Annie Dundas of Arniston, who
as a young girl of twenty years earlier had been rather a
friend of my mother's. I do not think she ever paid calls, either
from a sense of social or of cousinly duty. If asked she would
always produce an excellent reason for not disturbing other
people who were presumably either pleasantly or usefully
employed. This time she had come to tell my parents about
something she wished them to understand and appreciate,
something on the success of which she had set her heart—the
Edinburgh Association for the University Education of
Women, which had already established itself in a flat in
Shandwick Place. It filled such a considerable part in my life
for the next four or five years that I feel I ought to give it as
many pages, and to record my thanks to the three remarkable
women whose creation it was—Anne Dundas of Arniston;
Elizabeth Hamilton, daughter of Sir William Rowan Hamilton the astronomer; and Margaret Houldsworth. There were
usually two courses of lectures running concurrently at the
Association, one on literature or philosophy, and one on some
branch of science. The founder ladies must have been very
persuasive to have induced two busy university men to devote
each two hours a week to lecturing to us. They even took the
trouble to set us examination papers at the end of each seme-
ster, and to have them read and corrected, though the science
lecturers, at least, must have realized how little their audience
could profit from lectures on chemistry when it had never

109

seen a retort or condensed a gas. When years afterwards I went to Oxford, I was very crestfallen when told bluntly that it was useless for me to 'take' physiology till I knew some chemistry!

English literature, of course, was quite a different story. Professor Masson at any rate stimulated the desire to read 'good literature'. He had been speaking on the influence of the classics on modern poetry, and quoted *Balaustion's Adventure*. He read slowly, rather solemnly, but with beautiful distinctness. The lecture room emptied quickly that morning, and when my mother and I reached Douglas and Foulis's we found that several of our classmates had got there before us, and we secured the last available copy of *Balaustion* from the library. (Yes, my mother attended the lectures with me, and I think she enjoyed them even more than I did). While Professor Campbell Fraser talked he almost persuaded us that we had grasped Bishop Berkeley's meaning, and if a few hours later I had to confess to myself that the only philosopher I could understand was David Hume, I had still enjoyed listening to beautiful language, beautifully spoken. The most Philistine of his hearers would not have missed Professor Campbell Fraser's lectures, and what an odd audience he had! I can remember only three or four contemporaries of my own among them—they seem mainly to have been middle-aged spinster ladies. I think there was a disproportionate number of these in Edinburgh at that date.

There were so very few things to do for any except an extremely adventurous lady, but so many quite nice occupations if she cared to take them up. She might widen her education at Shandwick Place, or she might draw at the School of Art; and beside her 'social duties', her church could provide her with a Sunday-school class. She generally took her Sunday-school seriously, and made a great effort to interest and improve her pupils. There were concerts at the Music Hall, and she probably went on attending balls at the Assembly Rooms long after she got any pleasure from them, because it was easier to carry on than to change her pattern of life.

110

Growing-up in Edinburgh

Anyhow, to the rising generation, there did seem a super-fluity of maiden aunts, until some of them joined Professor Geikie's geology lectures, and he announced that we were to do 'practical geology'. Then it was most convenient to be able to affirm that there would be at least one chaperone on every party. And what fun his practical geology was! We climbed Arthur's Seat, of course, and saw how glaciers had carved out the Lion's Head, we counted Samson's Ribs! and we found trilobites at the Compensation Ponds. Fossil-collecting seems to have gone out of fashion along with the making of herbaria. (Miss Young's heroines did both—see *The Pillars of the House* and *The Trial*.)

The best of all our expeditions with the Professor was when we took the boat at Leith for Burntisland. Since then I have met more than one citizen of Edinburgh who does not know that the Binn is the remains of a volcano, half of which fell into the sea—hence Burntisland. If you climb the Bin, and lie flat on your face and look over the edge, you can see the dark streak of calcined rock where the lava from the eruption found a vent.

While we were having tea at the inn after this climb, the Professor told us of his appointment as head of the Geological Survey, and that he was leaving us to live in London. I do not remember whether he got his knighthood at the time of his appointment or later. His brother succeeded him as Professor of Geology in Edinburgh.

One of the maiden aunts, Miss Mary Jane Urquhart recovered sufficiently from the shock of the news to remind the Professor that he had once promised to give his women students a week of practical geology in Arran, as he did yearly at the end of the course with his men students. We hardly expected that he would make time to do this, but presently we all got our notices, and naturally I was wildly anxious to accept, but my mother did not feel quite sure—we should all be staying at an inn, apparently. My uncle, General Keatinge, was with us at the time, and he gave me a quiet sign, and said casually 'Geikie seems a very good fellow. I think I'll get him to take me on as a bottle-washer.' 'Oh, of course it will be all right if you join them', my mother said, and I think he enjoyed that week as much as any of the geologists—it was a most unacademic picnic! The two Raleighs (sisters of Sir Walter Raleigh, later Professor of Poetry at Oxford), persuaded me to join in some very elementary and childish acting with which we entertained the party on some of our last evenings, and I found to my surprise that I could produce any amount of gags when I had made up my mind to join in playing the fool, and that it was good fun! Quite a useful discovery, which I add to the number of things for which I have to thank the 'three remarkable women' of the Society for the Higher Education of Women!

The 'three remarkable women' each gave me a present when I joined the Association, Cousin Ann Dundas' was an excellent notebook and pencils, and one of the early fountain pens, Miss Hamilton's was a copy of *Nathan der Weise*, whose philosophy I tried for a time to think that I understood. Miss Houldsworth's was, at my own request, Mrs. Browning's *Aurora Leigh*. She said that it gave her immense pleasure to find a girl who cared for it, and was not afraid to say so. There were so many things we were afraid of saying in those far-off times!

Of course, the Porters still kept their stances at the corners of the Edinburgh squares or gardens. The Porters were super-respectable elderly men, licensed by authority to wait for custom at certain fixed corners. They wore straps over their shoulders—the badges of their trade—and were otherwise respectably dressed in garments which might be threadbare, and even patched, but which were well cut. I doubt that one of the Porters ever *bought* a suit. They were ready to carry luggage, provided it was not too heavy, to fetch and deliver parcels and letters, to call cabs, or to meet trains or horses. I have known them asked to change books at a library, or to secure a special number of an evening paper. I don't think any job which did not require extra physical strength came amiss to them—and while they waited for jobs they played draughts.

If both Porters were absent from their stance, their draughts-board would be carefully propped against a wall or railing, and he would have been a bold boy who took it away! From time to time one of the College of Justice challenged a Porter to play with him. We used to hear about these games, and I always wanted to watch one, but I never had the chance, though I believe that two of our neighbours on the north side of the Square were among the challengers. One of them had played in Paris when he was a young man, and still used the French names for anything connected with *le jeu de Dames.* 'That's a fine damier' he was heard to say to one of the Porters and he was right. The old man was nursing a thick heavy draughtboard with alternate squares of ivory (or bone) and Madrassi blackwood, such as the French used to import from Pondicheri. 'Aye, it's a fine damebrod' said the owner. And the draughtboard was such a familiar object that the word was used by the ladies when they wanted a piece of material with a check pattern. 'I'm asking you for a damebrod' the shopper was heard to repeat when, for the seventh time the shopman brought her a pattern of very wide stripes. 'That's fine, but I'm asking ye for the damebrod pattern.' 'And I am doing the best I can for you' said the exasperated, but too English young man, 'and you need not swear about it.'

One summer when we got back to Edinburgh from abroad, my mother found a letter from George MacDonald, novelist and minor poet, in which he reminded her of a talk they had had at Bournemouth after one of his lectures. He had ex-pressed a wish to lecture at Edinburgh, and she had offered him the use of the drawing-room at Number 17. He asked how soon she could be ready for him, and what arrangements she was making about advertising the lectures? The letter had not been forwarded, and was at least ten days old. He gave an address which was sure to find him up to a certain date, but this was past. My poor mother was aghast! I don't think she had ever contemplated 'making arrangements' for a lecture, though she was pleased to lend the room, and to give any private help. But to ask her to *advertise* was out of the

H 113

question! We both cared a great deal for some of George Mac-
Donald's books (*Phantastes, Robert Faulkner* and so on), and
she would willingly have invited a few friends to meet him.
But to deliver lectures at her house was a terrible idea, too
much to ask of anyone, and when I reminded her that no one
was in Edinburgh in August, she was very nearly in tears—
and yet there was no one for whom she would be more ready to
make an effort than George MacDonald! She was terribly
disappointed, but if he had had a proper address, she would
have telegraphed at once and cancelled the whole thing.

Then I began to think about it—she so seldom had a plan of
her own which she really wanted to carry out! Perhaps it was
not so impossible after all, and I said I would not try to collect
people for some sort of literary tea-party, but if she would
like me to see what I could do in the way of arranging for some
lectures, I would try. She said 'Oh, she really thought—perhaps—if I would really try . . .' so delightedly, that I thought
I must undertake to do so. (It was good practice for much that
I did in later years.) We filled the rooms and made quite a
nice little sum of money, for there were no expenses. I hand-
wrote all the notices and got MacVittie's and other shops which
we knew well, to post them in their windows, and I borrowed,
and helped to carry in chairs. I do not think that my mother
really liked this amount of publicity and advertising, but she
was delighted when the room was so full that people had to be
turned away. George MacDonald had some very curious and,
I thought, unconvincing ideas about Shakespeare's plays, but
he was a charming talker, and really devoted to my mother.
I wonder whether anyone now reads *Robert Faulkner* or *David
Elginbrod*?

Apropos of this, I went on a short visit to Ormiston, where
Charlotte Dempster, author of *Hotel du Petit Saint Jean* and
Blue Roses, and her sister, were staying with their uncle, Mr.
Dempster. Someone talked of the George MacDonald lectures
and asked about some of his views and opinions, which led me
to quote 'Have mercy on my soul, Lord God, the soul of Martin
Elginbrod, As I would have were I Lord God, and thou wert

Martin Elginbrod.' Mr. Dempster was, or pretended to be, fearfully shocked.

That visit was fairly trying! I had to make up a rubber in the evenings, and there was a young Dempster relative with whom I was supposed to go for walks (objectless walks, which I have always detested). It was better when we found our way into the kitchen garden, where the beds were red with strawberries, but after a long and weary dinner, when dessert was put on the table, only a tiny dish of the smallest strawberries appeared. Pointed remarks were made, and after dinner Charlotte Dempster took me aside and told me that the gardener had declared that the young ladies had cleared the strawberry beds! Of course I was furious, and said it was a lie, to which Charlotte answered that at any rate I was learning what happened to elderly people like her uncle when they got under the influence of their servants. 'Don't fuss, it would be useless to protest, and you had better not try to discuss it, especially after the "Martin Elginbrod" episode.'

My father found one outlet for his energies when he joined Mr. Bartholomew in founding the Scottish Geographical Society. When Colonel Cadell, V.C. gave a lantern lecture here on the Andaman Islands, of which he had been governor, he grew more irate, as each slide was put on. 'I've told you already, they are *nice* people, not in the least like that! Why this is criminal!'

'Like the Andamanese' said a voice from the back of the hall.

'What's that? I've told you they are *nice* people, and I lived among them for five years—thank God that's the last slide!' The art of making lantern slides has made great strides since those days.

My mother used to regret that my father had not 'taken seriously to botany', as he might have got charge of the Botanical Gardens, a charming garden, with a good house for the keeper. She did not realize how far removed his field botany was from the scientific side of the subject.

My father went up to England at frequent intervals, sometimes to pay a visit, more often to stay at Garland's Hotel and pass the day at the Athenaeum, with occasional excursions to the Carlton. For a long time he belonged to the Junior Carlton also.

For years it did not strike me as peculiar that my father should make these solitary expeditions to the south. I looked on all his movements and engagements as entirely his own affair and having no bearing on the family life. This applied most particularly to his solitary expeditions to London. Only as I grew older I wondered at my mother's ready acceptance of it all. She generally showed very definitely a dislike of being ignored or overlooked, but all she ever suggested was that he should take me with him—he constantly deplored that I did not know more of my Portal cousins and the sons of some of his old Indian friends, but nothing ever came of this—except that he gave invitations to all these young people to visit us, and most of them did so!

A rumour that he had a *penchant* for me might have spoiled my friendship with Jim Tytler (I suppose the aunts were responsible for the rumours), but it must soon have become obvious that when we sat in a corner together he was pouring into my sympathetic ear an account of his wooing of Christian Scott Kerr; when he was fortunate enough to win her, the family at Number 17 and at Colinton took her straight to their hearts. Our friendship was as sincere and our confidence in one another as complete at the end of fifty years as it became in our early years in Edinburgh. In all the illness and trouble at Colinton, she was the friend on whom young and old relied, and she never failed them.

When I was about fifteen, I managed to change the name— Louisa—to which I had answered up to date. My father never called me anything else, and in speaking of me to him, my mother did the same, but to everyone else I became Kathleen— it was quite an uncommon name in Scotland—in fact, Kathleen Leslie Melville and I found that we only knew one other beside ourselves—Kathleen Balfour.

Seeing how numerous they were, we seem to have known

curiously few of the young advocates and Writers to the Signet, but some of the Judges came to our rather solemn dinner parties. My mother took great pains over these parties, and discussed with my father what guests could suitably be invited to meet one another. I have often laughed over the very incongruous people I used to ask to meet at my parties, and wondered what she would have thought of them. I sometimes had as many as sixteen or eighteen guests, particularly when there were people whom I wanted to introduce to a mildly roaring lion, and I never gave them more than three courses, and the sweets were usually cold ones. It was as much as my Oxford 'staff' could manage. In the Edinburgh dining-room the staff consisted of the butler, a parlourmaid and one housemaid. Outside, there was another housemaid, and a woman who carried dishes up from the kitchen. But my mother always disliked 'ploughing with an ox and an ass', and looked back wistfully to the footmen of the household in Dublin.

While I was dressing for one of these parties, an agitated housemaid once rushed in to tell me that the kitchen chimney was on fire. I ran down and found the front door open and my uncle standing on the steps among falling smuts and bits of burnt paper. He came in to say 'Don't worry, it has been a bad blaze, but the worst is over, and a woman passing by has just whispered in my ear "The police is past, and he hasna seen it".' This was satisfactory as there was quite a considerable fine for people who allowed their chimneys to sweep themselves in this way.

Considering the height of the house, the servants did wonders. There was no hot water above the pantry floor, but the housemaid always brought up two big cans of boiling water for my bath, and mine was not by any means the only bath to fill. When my parents moved to Randolph Crescent, John and I clamoured for a bathroom. My father said 'Oh, have it if you can't be happy without it! I shall continue to take my bath in my own room before my fire, like a gentleman', and I don't believe he even once sampled the excellent new bath!

Growing-up in Edinburgh

It must have been during an election, when Home Rule was the one burning question, that I made friends with Samuel Henry Butcher and his wife. When he succeeded Blackie in the Chair of Greek at the university, Mrs. Butcher was duly called upon, and they were asked to dinner, but nothing further came of it till we (the younger generation), met on politics. Then I found that we cared intensely for the same things, and acquaintance suddenly ripened into friendship. Mrs. Butcher was a Trench, a black Protestant, of course. She was a fairly good speaker and liked canvassing, or at any rate did it as if she liked it, that is to say, well; I hated it, and felt that I produced no effect at all, so I took any clerical work that no one else wanted.

I do not think that Mr. Butcher held the Chair for long, his heart was always in politics. They had already moved to London when (was it at a by-election?) a candidate standing squarely as a Tariff Reformer was sprung upon us. He went canvassing in the Old Town and I sat in the office, polished up the leaflets we printed, and tried to make everyone who came in pledge themselves, before they went out, to 'buy British'. We had even less help than at the Home Rule Election, and I got badly pushed about in our small office; my mother did everything she could to keep me out of it, while my father hurled Free Trade arguments at me whenever we met. When I was most tired and feeling most keenly the shortcomings of my fellow Tariff Reformers (tho' not of their tenets!) I used to wonder whether I should be of more use to my cause if I had attended at Miss Mair's debating society more regularly— just because I had not faced some boredom, had I missed the chance of helping my cause? This was one of the cases of conscience with which I more than once nearly worried myself ill! Most of the members of the Debating Society were ladies of a 'certain age'. My mother was horrified when she heard that I had actually spoken—it was *de rigueur* for members to speak—and still more that I had been asked to prepare a subject for debate, which meant at least one short speech. I do not remember what the subject I chose was, but it implied reading some Herbert Spencer, who was considered a horribly advanced thinker. I never understood what on earth induced the ladies to elect me. After the first few weeks I did not attend regularly. Had I done so, I might possibly have got some idea of speaking, but the subjects for debate were very dull ones.

My mother and I only went to London when John and Ralph Abercromby lent us their little house in Chapel Street, Belgrave Square, or, later on, when he lived in London, to stay with my uncle, General Keatinge. Looking back on those visits it seems to me that we did not get much 'fun' out of them. There were always old aunts and other relatives to be visited. Aunt Margaret, Miss Trotter, was a sister of my grand-father (I never discovered why she went to live in London). She was a very tall old lady with a splendid figure. Every year she presented me with something intended to encourage my needlework. I had a whole series of little inlaid boxes, and red morocco cases fitted with the tools of the trade, growing larger and more complicated as I grew. Once, instead of the work box, she gave me a bright yellow cashmere dress trimmed with bunches of little steel beads. I liked it because it had a long grown-up skirt, but I was only allowed to wear it once to show off to Aunt Margaret. She had a number of interesting Indian things, paintings and nests of boxes, and what I was always allowed to have out of the press where she kept the treasures, a big hamper-full of brightly coloured wooden men and animals, elephants, men, peacocks and tigers all the same size, and one huge cobra. One could make up stories about these, while one ate *bisquits de Reims* (and never anything else), so visits to her were never dull, and she seemed much more human and alive than most old ladies.

Aunt Eliza, a step-sister of my grandmother's, was a very different person—there were no toys or finger biscuits, but as I grew older I liked listening to her conversation with my mother, and trying to understand what they were talking about, though they were not so full of surprises as the con-versations with old Lady Abercromby, who asked questions about anything she wanted to know, and always called a spade a spade.

I sometimes stayed with the William Trotters—kind people —where an evening at the Lyceum Theatre was the highlight of the visit, and we sometimes had an ice at Gunters. He and Cousin Isabel, his wife, and a charming little daughter are among the people I remember as always doing kind things! The Cavendish Fitzroys were kind to me too, and we went to see pictures, or possibly to the zoo, just to take a look at some new animal, or at some pet which the zoo people were looking after for its owner who was abroad—Cavendish Fitzroy did not like people to be too sentimental about animals. He was a badly crippled man and for a long time was secretary to the Charity Organization Society, and I sometimes went with him to visit an old soldier who had long tales of woe to relate. 'It's all we can do for the poor chap—just let him talk', Cavendish would say patiently. How he would have rejoiced had St. Dunstan's started in his time.

I immensely enjoyed visits to the Lefroys, who had moved to a cottage close to Aldershot, and Mary and I saw as much as we could of manoeuvres—sometimes quite close, for Mary was a good driver, and could insinuate the cart and the New Forest pony into narrow places. How horrified my parents would have been had they seen us on some occasions when the first skirl of the pipes had started the pony and, we raced along between lines of troops. My uncle in the 93rd came to remonstrate with us, but other ranks could scarce forbear to clap!

Once when I was staying with Lady Metcalfe, she told me that she was going to India for the cold weather 'To visit Metcalfe House' she said and that, if proper arrangements could be made—I must have my own ayah while we were in India, of course—she would like to take me with her. It seemed as if the dream of my life might be going to be realized, just as the chances of its coming true were becoming more remote. Both the Indian uncles had retired—and who else was likely to ask me to visit them? Hardly able to speak calmly about it, I approached my mother, told her Lady Metcalfe's plans and

asked 'Could it possibly be managed?' I'd expected sympathy
at least, but all she said was: 'My dear, *I* have never been to
India.' I don't mean to suggest that my mother was cruel, it
was just the way she saw things, but to me it meant kismet—
if I missed this chance, I was most unlikely to get another. I
would give up every other chance in the world to seize this
one. To go East was the one thing I really wanted to do. I
might want to help other people and causes—I did—but to get
to India was the one thing that I wanted *for myself.* If I gave
up that hope, there seemed to be nothing to look forward to
and I thought bitterly how young I still was.

CHAPTER XI

Country Houses

❄

Until I was well into teen-age I only once or twice stayed away from home except with my mother. I usually slept in her room and her maid kept me tidy and looked after my clothes. When we first went north in summer we stayed with Mimi Abercromby at Colinton House. The feel of that house always fascinated me. There were two Speakers' chairs—two because Mimi's grandfather, Lord Dunfermline, had been Speaker at the time of the Accession of William IV, and he had a chair for some function in connection with the Cornation as well as his Speaker's chair from the House, which in those days became the property of each Speaker when he vacated the office.

There was Grinling Gibbons' carving in the libraries, making a perfect frame for the old leather bindings and for the beautiful portrait of Sir Ralph Abercromby by Gainsborough, and there was also much interesting china, most of it European and strikingly different from the oriental china among which I had grown up.

The policies were exceptionally attractive too. They did not reach the foot of the Pentlands as those of Dreghorn did—the high road to Edinburgh cut them off—but from the terrace behind the house one looked between the famous old gean trees over farm fields to the Water of Leith, and from the edge of the little wood one could see directly down into the garden of the manse where Robert Louis Stevenson 'climbed into the cherry tree', but that feat was not chronicled in verse till years later.

Country Houses

The holly hedges were famous. I quote from Sir Herbert Maxwell's 'Scottish Gardens', who himself quotes John Sabine, F.R.S., who contributed a detailed description of them to the Horticultural Society of Scotland. He wrote 'that the hedges were planted between 1670 and 1680, certainly not later than the latter year, so that at the present time of writing (1908), they can be nothing less than 228 years old.' Their height is from thirty-five to forty feet and the depth being in some places twenty-one feet, the lower branches layering themselves and forming an impenetrable rampart.

Beyond the holly hedges are the ruins of the old house: three feet thick stone walls with the narrowest possible windows and the first flight of what must have been a very steep staircase. To quote Sir Herbert Maxwell again, 'about the end of the eighteenth century, the Colinton Estates were broken up and this portion was bought by Sir William Forbes of Edinburgh, who deliberately caused the old castle to be dismantled and built himself a commodious but unromantic mansion nearby.' On the death of Sir William Forbes, Colinton was purchased by James, third son of General Sir Ralph Abercromby, who was Mimi's grandfather. Sir Herbert Maxwell does not add that the 'castle' was so well built that Sir William Forbes had to commandeer guns from the docks at Leith to reduce the building to a ruin. Beyond the stone walls there is left just one doorway, leading nowhere. Mrs. Oliphant contributed to *Blackwood's* a ghost story called *The Open Door* and domiciled it at Colinton. We had often said that it was curious that no ghost should inhabit those broken walls, but there had never been a whisper of one.

Mrs. Oliphant did not name the place, but it was so well known, and her description was so accurate that everyone in the Lothians recognized it at once—with the result that the tenants (my uncle and aunt were then in India and the house was let) could not keep their servants, and even thought that they had sufficient grounds for breaking their lease! Mrs. Oliphant wrote to *The Scotsman* apologizing for the trouble she was causing and declaring that there was no foundation

123

for her story—which was entirely imaginary—but visual evidence for it was much stronger than her denial; there stood The Open Door.

In my time the hedges enclosed small squares of lawn with one brilliant border of flowers, startlingly bright against the dark background of holly. A perfect place for tea and talk on a summer afternoon. Hot scones, at least two sorts of jam or a honeycomb, as well as plenty of cakes, are included in a proper Scots tea. It was quite a good step from the house to the squares, but no one thought of offering a helping hand, as I think some of the young folk would almost certainly do nowadays, and the servants took it all as a matter of course.

Mimi Abercromby was the wife of my uncle, Colonel John Mowbray Trotter; on his death his crippled son Archibald could not afford to live at Colinton and among other possible purchasers he had to choose between two, Merchiston, one of the Edinburgh Hospitals (schools with endowments), and a Roman Catholic sisterhood. He asked me what I felt about it, and I said at once that I should like to think of boys climbing the trees and playing games in the park. We talked of the cricket matches of long ago, when he had scored while his brother made runs against the village. He used to score sitting in his wheelchair and one never heard a murmur of complaint. I hope there are some people still left who think of him in his stoical boyhood.

After the sale I found that his sister had been anxious for the Sisters to start another school; they had one already at Craiglockhart. Perhaps she should have had a say in the matter —but still I am glad that the boys are there.

One of our yearly visits was to Muirhouse, Davidson's Mains. It was one of the houses where whatever one expected always happened. The sun always shone, there was cherry-pie and sweet-scented geranium in the flower garden by the house, and raspberries or gooseberries in the kitchen garden; and masses of sweet red berries in the huge old yew trees which surrounded the garden walls. In Scotland, children were al-

lowed to suck the sweet pink yew berries, but warned so
solemnly of the danger of swallowing the yew berry seeds that
they never failed to spit them out. But when I encouraged
Naomi to eat them from the yews in the parks at Oxford, a
horrified gardener remonstrated with me!

Mr. Henry Davidson was a friend of my father's, and, I
think, of most people in the county. He was not a very keen
politician or churchman, but was always ready to hold out a
helping hand to any good cause or to any young person in
want of help or counsel. The Davidson children were older
than I, but not terribly remote in age. I called them by their
Christian names which was not then the universal habit as it
is now. Randall, the eldest son, was the future Archbishop of
Canterbury. He preached his first sermon after he was or-
dained at Dunira (Crieff), when he and his own family were
staying there with Sir David and Lady Lucy Dundas. A whole
family of young Davidsons, the Minister under whom most of
us had sat in the morning, the household and people from the
estate and farm were all assembled in the hall.

I can remember nothing of the sermon, but my mother
whispered to me how clever it was of Randall to preach about
the Good Shepherd when there were several shepherds present.
She wanted me to 'say something nice' to Randall about
the sermon, but I am glad to remember that on this occasion
I refused to obey.

The second Davidson son, Harry, was, in the year when I
like best to remember him, engaged to Alice Smythe, daughter
of a rather peppery old general. When I went to live in Edinburgh four or five years later, Harry and Alice were among
my few close friends. Alice's elder sister was the well-known
musician Ethel Smythe and for her date and generation, an
extremely advanced woman. She wrote what at that time was
the only English opera, 'The Wreckers'. She was distinctly
alarming, but in later years I was proud to be able to say that
I had known her before she became famous.

There had been an old house at Muirhouse which was de-
molished in the same ruthless way as was the old house at

Colinton. The new Muirhouse was really a large villa, not very suitable to the banks of the Forth. Its charm was that over the tops of the trees one looked across the Firth to Fife and, as I have said, the sun always shone at Muirhouse when I was there as a girl, so the waters of the Firth sparkled and the shores of the kingdom of Fife looked fairylike.

We went once or twice to stay at Kilconquhar, in Fife, with Lord Lindsay and his French wife and their adopted girl, whom she always introduced as 'the child of the half of my brother'. The little girl grew up to be a silly young woman who did not do the interesting things she might have done, but enthusiastically accepted the 'good' marriage provided for her. I was ready enough to be her bridesmaid, as my father would give me the dress! However, some relatives died and the wedding became a quiet one, and the bridesmaids were dispensed with. Lindsay of the Byres is a delightful title and seems to indicate that the care of cows was a family obsession, for both my daughter and I have had it.

Visits to Kilconquer were dull: Pinkie House was much livelier. We stayed there with all of the three Hope brothers, who succeeded one another at all too short intervals. Sir John was my father's chief friend, and he took me to the pony races at Musselborough, the only races I ever saw!

There was a ghost at Pinkie, and one Hogmanay I went up into the gallery to wait for her, but there was no sign of her, nor did anyone look over my shoulder when I brushed my hair before the mirror. In the morning, Harry, Lord Melville, said that he too had waited for 'Green Jean' in the gallery, but I doubt it.

There was a ghost at Woodhouselea too, and the room I usually occupied opened on to the passage which was said to be haunted. After it had roused me twice in the night, I determined to be ready for it if it came again, being fully convinced that it was being impersonated by Jim Tytler or possibly his sister Alice. When I heard the characteristic ghostly shuffle, I opened my door and launched a very wet sponge, which hit the opposite wall and made a fearful mess. In any other house

I should have got into fearful trouble, but Woodhouselea was the kindest house in the world. My elders, Mary and Annie, made me feel rather silly, but they never 'told'. Woodhouselea with its three-foot thick walls, and the basement where iron rings still hung on the walls to remind one of the days when the cattle, and sometimes the women, were tied up there, when a raid was expected, was by far the nicest house I have ever visited; and the Laird was, and is, my ideal of a perfect friend and host. How did he manage, with four daughters of his own, to find room in his heart for a stray girl? At least I like to believe that there was something more than just his normal kindness in what he gave to me.

At Archerfield, Blanche Dundas introduced me to her cousin Constance Dundas Christopher Nisbet Hamilton, whose many inheritances of property account for her string of surnames. When I first went to Archerfield, close to North Berwick, her mother, Lady Mary Hamilton, was alive, but quite childish, and used to be wheeled into the drawing-room wearing long, heavy, black silk garments held in place by diamond brooches. I at least felt that it was rude to laugh—if there was anything to laugh at—or even to talk naturally under the gaze of that silent pathetic figure.

Constance and I took long, cold walks by the sea, with her big dogs circling round us. Her great interest was in music, of which I knew nothing, so conversation was difficult. Her large house Biel, also in East Lothian, was a rather alarming place to stay at. On my first visit there I got hopelessly lost trying to find my way down to breakfast—it was perhaps not so stupid as it seems because we did not breakfast in the same room in which we had dined; and no one had warned me of this. The huge rooms were curiously devoid of books, and the newspapers and magazines were all laid out on a table as far as possible from the fire, and if one had a magazine and laid it down for a moment, it was sure to be picked up by a tidying footman and refolded on the newspaper table. But what should we not have given for one of their fires during the war years! Big blocks of coal in big steel grates which grew so

127

hot that one dared not touch them; and a log or two of apple-wood for the pleasure of the scent and crackling!

I met various quite interesting people there, notably Lionel Tennyson, son of the poet, whose wife was a cousin of Constance's, and I listened, slightly shocked, to intimate tales about the poet Laureate. Another visitor was Sir Francis Doyle, and I got so fearfully chaffed for selecting his company for a walk, that I almost made up my mind never again to try to be kind to an elderly gentleman! He gave me copies of his poems.

I remember a big house party there, twenty or more, for a ball at Yester. Besides a couple of neighbour couples the partners were people whom Constance had been asked by the ball-givers to invite. They each, of course, asked their hostess for a dance, but otherwise I think their programmes were pretty well filled up in advance. We drove in various vehicles to Yester, and the men tried as much as possible to pile in together in those which seemed likely to arrive there first. Also each man made straight for a lady with whom he was already engaged to dance the first dance. None of them asked me for it! It was a long, long evening for any girl who had only an occasional partner.

We had eaten off gold plate at dinner, a change from the good but rather uninteresting silver we generally used. Gold plate is really not nearly so decorative as the name seems to imply, and flowers do not look their best in gold vases, not even in the lovely gold plate that I have seen used at the Goldsmiths Company entertainments in London. Constance was really kind in inviting me to stay as often as she did, and I hope I was grateful, but she was an unimaginative hostess and it really wasn't much fun.

Constance on this occasion of the ball at Yester wore many diamonds, one huge star somehow fastened into her short, fluffy grey hair, and a shimmering white satin dress. I had had nothing in the way of a ball dress ready when the invitation to this party came, so my mother's maid was set hurriedly to make up something for me, with some lovely old flowered silk from one of my mother's trousseau dresses, and deep lace flounces, lovely stuff but not suitable for dancing in. Gracie Hamilton, coming in to inspect, said it was awfully pretty but 'not a real dress'. I was conscious of this all the evening, especially when someone caught his spurs in the lace.

I remember another dance: a New Year's Dance at Woodhouselea to which I went from Melville with Blanche Dundas. During the Lancers I looked up into a somehow familiar face —up because he was several inches over six foot—and then I heard someone say 'Hullo Craigie-Halkett!' Then of course I knew it was Duncan Craigie-Halkett, whose family were living at Stirling when we were at Plean during my childhood. Duncan used to take my part, taught me to climb and lent me D'Arcy Thompson's *Fun and Earnest*. I liked him immensely and I think he liked me but I found out later in Edinburgh that my mother did not approve of Mrs. Craigie-Hakett or of the girls. She considered the girls 'fast', and I suppose Duncan would have been thought an unsuitable friend for me had he been much at home. Their father, Colonel Craigie-Hakett was an old friend of my father's and sometimes lunched with us, but with the rest of the family our dealings were formal and infrequent. Now Duncan was in the 72nd home on leave from India; I decided to speak to him the moment the Lancers was finished.

Meanwhile, however, Blanche came behind me and whispered 'What's the matter with your neck, it's dirty and your dress is too!' Of course I was horrified. One of the Tytlers came and helped me to wash my neck; the dress was hopeless. Driving from Melville I had worn for the first time a fur cloak which my mother had given me. It had been bought at a sale for £5 I think, and had evidently lain about in dust and dirt for ages. When we got back after the dance I got Blanche to help me to clean it and we dirtied two towels before there was much improvement!

Meanwhile, the rest of that evening I kept out of sight as much as possible wherever there was a dark corner and felt utterly ashamed, miserable and deflated. Why should such a horrible thing have happened to me? Was it my fault? Ought

I to have expected the cloak might be dirty? The worst moment was when we joined hands for Auld Lang Syne and Duncan slipped into the ring beside Blanche who was looking magnificently handsome. When we were driving home she said 'That young Craigie-Hakett held my hand as if I had been his long-lost friend.' I said nothing. There was nothing to say. I never had any luck! Duncan was killed in Egypt shortly after that.

Gracie Hamilton always looked charming and just right. I often spent a few days at Preston Hall, with the Hamilton's, He was one of my father's Calcutta friends, and had begun life as Claud Hamilton Browne, but later dropped the Browne. It was of one of this family that Mr. Dempster, when introducing him, made the famous remark 'My brother-in-law, Mr. Browne with an "e".' Someone said that the 'e' was very important and Mr. Dempster agreed 'Yes, there'll soon be none left of the good old family of plain Brown's!'

Why, I wonder, was it that there were always snowdrops in full bloom in the wood at Preston Hall early in February? In Oxford they seem to come a month later. We acted charades in the evenings there, and I once made Mr. Hamilton exceedingly angry by going through a form of Scotch marriage with someone. He said 'Young people should avoid taking unnecessary risks.' As a magistrate he couldn't countenance this, and he left the room! Had he been present we would, in theory, have been legally married under Scots law!

My mother and I stayed with Mr. Carrick Moore at Stranraer on several occasions when we were on our way north in summer. He always promised to take us to the Giant's Causeway, but this never came off. I am not sure that my mother would have really appreciated even such a short sea-voyage!

Mr. Carrick Moore was a nephew of General Sir John Moore of Corunna, and gave my family the General's copy of Horace, bound in vellum.

Sir Henry Taylor was author of *Philip von Arteveld*; I sometimes went with my mother to listen to literary conversations with him, and when I was older I went by myself. He had been

a clerk in the Foreign Office, out of which the Colonial Office
was evolved, and if he had talked to me about the colonies,
I should have paid more attention than I did when he tried to
persuade me that I *ought* to want to read Spencer.

Nearly every summer we stayed at Dunira at the head of
Loch Earn. Sir David Dundas used to say that his house was
one of the most expensive that he knew. A few hundred yards
beyond the lodge gate at one side there was a five shilling toll
and a few hundred yards on the other there was a half-crown
one. It was a pleasant house, though not a particularly interesting one, but to me it had a fascinating thing, a curling
table, much more available to the young than billiard tables,
which people didn't like us to play on. There was a wonderful
garden. I slept in my mother's room and she used to send me
running down the garden while she finished dressing.

One day I had a desperate fright. From behind a sweet-pea
hedge Sidney, Sir David's weak-minded eldest son, jumped
out on me. I do not think he wanted to do anything except
just to kiss me, and I certainly had no idea that he might want
anything else, but that was quite terrifying enough and I
screamed and fought. Sir David came running, put his hand on
Sidney's shoulder, saying very quietly, 'You know you mustn't
do that' and to me 'Run in, my dear, Sidney won't do it
again.' I ran.

My mother very wisely tried to make me feel very sorry for
kind Sir David and not to dwell on the matter as it concerned
myself, but it gave me a shock which I never really quite got
over. There were 'not quite all right' members of several of
the families we knew best, besides the 'natural' who was
found wandering about in nearly every village in those days.

One of the loveliest of small country places that I know is
Winton, East Lothian. Constance Nisbet Hamilton took me
there once to see the place, and I saw also, and was interviewed
by, blind old Lady Ruthven, who apparently took a fancy to
me and said that I must visit her whenever I was in the
neighbourhood. These visits could be rather disconcerting as,
for example, while the footman was in the room setting tea,

she asked me to write down the names of French novels. 'I make the footman read them to me in the evening' she said. 'His pronunciation is fairly good, but he doesn't understand a word of it, so you don't need to consider his morals, just tell me the names of any you have enjoyed yourself.' This was pretty difficult as my reading of French novels was anything but wide. I remember suggesting *L'Isle des Pingouins*. She said rather doubtfully, 'Birds, I wonder whether I'd care for that. Well, one can but try'.

This reminds me of a morning at Douglas and Foulis's ten years later, when John asked me to look up a remark of the doctor's in Zola's *La Terre*. Someone had told him that it showed wonderful appreciation of some genetic problems by the old grandfather. He wanted to know how far Zola had really got in research and speculation. I went to Douglas and Foulis's and asked for the book. 'Yes, we have it' said the librarian, and he went to consult another man. Looking up from the books I was browsing among, I found they were both looking peculiarly at me, and after a few minutes the man came back with the book wrapped in paper. 'This isn't one we usually lend to the general public', he said. 'Are you quite sure of the name?'

I said 'Yes, my husband has asked me to look up a scientific point treated in it.'

'Oh, science,' he said, evidently greatly relieved, and gave me the parcel.

I have just got a note from the old shop about a book I want and can't get here. Not long ago the firm wrote and asked me whether I should like to buy one of my aunt, Mrs. Forbes, family 'trees', which had come into their hands. I hadn't been in Edinburgh for ten years, and they must have concluded that this was the reason—the only reason—which would account for my not having visited the shop, and I was touched by their remembering me in spite of my change of name. If I appear in the tree at all, it is, of course, under my maiden name.

.   .   .   .

Country Houses

It must have been after our first winter in Edinburgh that my mother and I paid a visit to Mells.

Mells Park was the plum which Little Jack Horner pulled out of his Christmas pie when Henry VIII sent him into Somersetshire to 'turn the cowls adrift'. From that time there was a Squire Horner at Mells Park, and the Squire's younger brother occupied the rectory until, in an unlucky generation, the Squire died and the rector found himself in possession of Church lands. He did not relinquish them, as he probably would have done had he been a hero of one of Charlotte M. Yonge's novels, but he shut up the big house and made the Dower House beside the Rectory into a seminary for young men training to be missionaries. When he died the old order returned. Fortescue Horner, known outside his own family as Jack, became Squire, and one of his younger twin brothers, George, was Rector. At the time of our visit Fortescue was unmarried and the park was shut up. George lived at the Rectory with several sisters, and a charming old aunt to keep house for them. It was the kind of house which seemed incompletely furnished without bowpots of flowers in old china jars, but there wasn't a rose in any of the rooms, though roses looked in at all the windows. Walking in the garden with the Reverend George, I picked myself a buttonhole, and when he and the sister who came with us exchanged awkward glances, I asked what was the matter? They answered that one of the sisters thought it so cruel to pick flowers, so would I please not do so. When I threw mine away I noticed that George buried them carefully with his spud.

After dinner he offered to show me the moon through his telescope, and the sisters objected that it was too late to go out. We were 'dressed for dinner', and the grass was damp. George, they said, must of course, 'take his observation' and meanwhile they would entertain me. But I went to look at the moon, and I think the old aunt was rather pleased though the sisters were not. The household was teetotal, though it offered wine to my mother—and vegetarian, though meat appeared for its guests and for the servants, and I think some

133

of the family ate of it sparingly when they got the chance. One of the sisters and George and his twin brother Maurice sometimes stayed with us in Edinburgh, and when I first went to Oxford, George was engaged on some research at the Bodleian; it had to do with the Hittites. He haunted the house for a couple of months and surprised my husband considerably —though goodness knows he was used to odd people! George tried to persuade me to urge him to give up 'smoking and drinking'—a pipe and an occasional glass of beer or cider! We seldom had wine except when we 'entertained', though our two earliest visitors brought us presents of champagne— Richard, my brother-in-law and, John, Lord Abercromby.

I found later that George objected to soda water too, though on what grounds I never discovered. It would all have been extremely impertinent had it not been so very funny. 'But why should I bother John with such nonsense?' I asked Maurice. 'Oh, because it hurts George so terribly—he thinks it worse than eating red meat' he answered. When they found me smoking a cigarette, both brothers were as terribly shocked and hurt as they might have been if they had found a woman they cared about in an equivocal situation! Then one evening the parlourmaid came to tell me that 'the reverend gentleman who called so often' was walking up and down in front of the house. The house was divided from the road by a narrow strip of garden. It was almost dark, but I could just see George prowling back and forwards outside our garden railings. I told the maid to go and ask him to come in, but as she got near him he walked quickly away.

The next day I got a note from Maurice in which he begged me not to misunderstand George, who had finished his work at the Bodleian and would not be back at Oxford for some time. As far as I remember I never saw him again, but Maurice used to come in from time to time, and we once from a sense of duty, which was strong in me in those days, showed some hospitality to one of the sisters.

CHAPTER XII

My Father in Polynesia

❋

About this time there happened my father's adventure in
Polynesia. It came about in an odd way. A new cure was
attracting the attention of people interested in their own
health. Ralph Abercromby talked most favourably about it
—though his mother said firmly that if he would only forget
about his symptoms, they would disappear!

My father had experimented with all the older nostrums,
and thought 'he might as well try the new man'. As far as I
remember, Dr. Playfair's cure consisted chiefly in keeping his
patients in bed, giving them large meals every few hours,
cutting all contact with the outside world and seeing that
they had nothing whatever to do or to read. As a concession,
my father was allowed to write a short note and to get a
message from my mother every second day. I'm not sure how
long the course lasted, it certainly went on for several weeks,
after which the patient was sent off on a sea voyage, starting
direct from Dr. Playfair's Nursing Home. My father, however,
insisted on coming home for a few days to collect his belong-
ings, but his passage was booked for him, and unless he wished
to forfeit it, he had to embark as arranged. We had a hectic
five days while he was in Edinburgh. My mother was desperately worried and Mr. Tytler was most helpful; and it was
arranged that she should, for the first time in her life, have her
own cheque book!

My father went first to Capetown and stayed at Government
House and from there to Sydney. I suppose the Governor

arranged for him, as he went in a cruiser 'a most enjoyable voyage', he wrote. He was to be landed at Apia, to stay with his friend Mr. Symonds, the Consul in Samoa.

When they reached Apia, Mrs. Symonds came off in an out-rigger to say that her husband was dangerously ill. A medical missionary had come over from one of the islands, but could do nothing for him, and said that they must get him to a good hospital as fast as they possibly could—but even if there had been a passage available, Mr. Symonds could not leave until he got someone to carry on for him. Could the Captain of the cruiser help? He turned to my father and said 'Your move, sir!' My father said he persisted that he knew nothing about the island, had no idea of the duties of a Consul, and so on; but the Captain told him that he was 'the only Englishman available' and he went ashore with Mrs. Symonds, and had about two hours talk with the sick man. He gathered that we were having considerable trouble with the Germans, whose Consul was stirring up strife among the islanders, and spreading false rumours about British activities. He was told that neither the Symonds' old cook, a native Samoan, nor the ex-cannibal chief, would try to poison him, but that he had better not trust anyone else! Then the poor Symonds' left in the cruiser and he found himself representing H.B.M.

It was obvious that the German Consul would attempt to take advantage of having a poor, inexperienced civilian to deal with, and my father thought that he found out rather more of what was going on because he posed as a simple invalid, travelling for his health. He could refuse insistent offers of hospitality on the score of having just left a nursing clinic and of requiring to have his food peptonized! He said the Consul was 'too blatantly Prussian to be let loose in Polynesia' and wrote very full reports on him to the Foreign Office; and he made firm friends with the old cannibal chief, who, when he left, gave him his own drinking cup in remembrance—a coconut, polished with kava.

He drew his Consular pay while he was at Apia (and sent it to me), but was rather put out because he got no acknowledgment of all his dispatches. 'Wonder whether they ever opened them?' he said.

Months later, at the Athenaeum, he got a message that the Prime Minister wanted to see him in the smoking-room. He went up and found Lord Salisbury, who shook hands and said he wished to thank him for the work he had done in Samoa. My father remarked that he had often wondered whether any-one had ever read his despatches. The Prime Minister chuckled and said 'My dear Sir, we read them with the greatest interest. They were most enlightening, but we couldn't take public cognizance of them without involving ourselves in a breach with Germany—couldn't afford that, you know. But your successor went out primed with all the information you sent us.' He also said that note had been taken of young men my father had named as loyal and useful, and they would not be forgotten. I think one was a young trader and another a missionary. For some years we suffered a good deal from missionaries he had met in the islands. They used to come to stay, and generally he left them on my hands to show them round Edinburgh.

One old gentleman simply settled down in the autumn and would not have moved till spring, only he heard Lord Melville ask, as he came in to lunch, whether there was any cold missionary left on the sideboard! However, we really were very kind to them.

From Samoa my father went on to Fiji, and from both places wrote that he was surprised to find how excellent his descriptions of them in the *Encyclopaedia Britannica* had been!

The next thing we heard of him was a cable. 'Write Shep-heard's.' So he had got back as far as Egypt, and there had been a breakdown of Dr. Playfair's cure. . . .

The most interesting of his acquaintances in the Farther East was Sir William McGregor, the first Governor of British New Guinea, who had an ingenious way of encouraging trade. A German firm sent out a shipment of tools and wanted to advertise them. 'Certainly,' said the Governor. 'We'll have a demonstration. The young men with German axes, the old men with shell or obsidian choppers. We'll see which will cut down most trees in a given time.' It was a holiday show, everyone came out to watch, and there was heavy betting. The old men won, hands down! 'Quite so', said the Governor. 'That's what I expected; those were German axes, No good at all! Now watch and see what I can do with an English axe.' He had a first-rate axe, no mere trades goods, and must have used it with skill as well as strength, for he beat hollow the champion young men with the German axes. That's how a good Governor encourages trade.

Sir William had a little girl at the Ministers' Daughters' College, in Edinburgh. I used to have the lonely child out on Sundays—but she wasn't allowed to play games, not even dominoes, on the Sabbath.

The only documentary evidence I have of the Samoa episode is an official envelope directed to my father, and his sarcastic comments under the address, and I only tell this tale as I remember its being told to me. The same about the meeting with the Prime Minister in the Athenaeum.

CHAPTER XIII

Town and Country Servants

❊

Naomi and Lois both ask about lady's maids and other servants, their work and wages. When I was young, every lady had her own lady's maid as a matter of course, and if there were grown-up daughters in the family, there was probably a young lady's maid too. How else could a girl pay a visit unless she was accompanying her mother? This was the theory anyway—in practice very often the girl fended for herself and if she travelled by rail, the footman might be sent to escort her.

I never had a maid of my own, and I remember various visits when I needed one badly. Before a ball the girl who had her own maid would promise to send her to help me to dress when she was herself ready. Then either the maid came so late that I was scarcely ready for dinner, or she failed to come at all, and in desperation I had to ring for a housemaid, who was probably not very expert at lacing a ball-dress bodice, and all the evening I had the uncomfortable feeling that my back did not look right; then when bedtime came, unless there was a friendly girl to help me to unlace, there was a long struggle to get out of my dress. Once I slept in my tightly laced bodice, having with difficulty scrambled out of the long skirt!

When I outgrew my *bonne*, my mother's French maid was supposed to look after me, and to see that I was tidy for meals, brush my hair and supervise my clothes and my methods of wearing them. With reference to gloves, one of them said on many occasions: 'Oh la la! La Francaise se gante chez elle.

139

Town and Country Servants

L'Anglaise se gante sur l'escalier, mais l'Ecossaise se gante dans la rue.' They were all Protestants, and on Sundays preferred to use a dozen pins to repair a tear in my frock rather than an already threaded needle in the pin-cushion beside them. 'Y pensez-vous Mademoiselle, c'est de l'ouvrage.'

When we were in a town, they were sometimes told to 'take me out for a walk'—an expression which offended me terribly! I think it was even used when I was well into my teens, and for a short time I attended the School of Art in Edinburgh; what a bore it was! I protested to my mother: 'Why must Julie "take" me, and must I really tell her to "fetch me home"?'

'Yes', said my mother, 'if you were alone someone in the street might speak to you.'

To which I rejoined that someone was much more likely to speak to Julie, and if I really must tell her to fetch me, she would have two walks by herself, so a mysterious 'someone' would have twice the chance of speaking to her, I gathered that this would not matter so much—but I may have got that wrong! I emancipated myself during our first winter in Edinburgh, when we lived in St. Colm's Street, by claiming that I could change the family books at Douglas and Foulis in Castle Street, without ever entering that dangerous place, Princes Street. That was the thin edge of the wedge, and a very useful wedge it was!

I have no idea what wages my parents' servants received, but they certainly took it for granted that they had plenty of work, and they stayed on year after year. There was a housemaid who had counted as 'an old servant' at the time of my marriage, who was still there when my father died. When we were emptying the house, I asked her to take some of Jack's larger toys to the children's department of a poor-house in the Old Town. She came back to say that 'the wee laddies just couldna believe the cairt and horse and the bricks were really to be played with. They'd never seen the like! I telled them about the auld maister, and we wept together.'

I am pretty sure that Agnes did not get much more than

twenty-six or twenty-eight pounds a year, and she probably
began with much less, and was 'raised' after several years'
service. The cook, of course, got more, and the rather dreadful
old butler, who waited on my father and had a parlourmaid
to help him, got quite good wages compared with the women.

After Henry, of whom I wrote in the tales of my childhood,
had gone to be butler somewhere in the Dukeries, we had a
very superior man called Digby, who distressed my mother
by wearing a beard, as his London doctor had warned him
'that he should not try to face the Scottish winter shaven'.
He went to Muirhouse when we went abroad, and there
received a letter addressed 'C. Digby Esq., c/o Mr. Davidson'.
Mr. Davidson was rather intrigued by this, and asked him
what he thought his correspondent had in mind. Digby answered that he did not think her mind had anything to do
with it. 'You see, Sir, she's a good woman, but quite un-
domesticated.'

My first cook in Oxford came for twenty pounds, and I
raised her to twenty-two before she left, most reluctantly, to
keep house for a relative from whom she had 'expectations'.
The house-parlourmaid, who came to me from the Jervis
Smiths, had eighteen pounds. Jack's little German maid got
eighteen to twenty, and Willie Ball, the laboratory boy, who
came in early mornings, to do boots and knives, got five shillings a week and his breakfast, which was considered lavish
payment; but he was very useful. A broken frame would find
its way to the laboratory and would return mended, and he
sometimes helped in the garden, or with the old bath under the
apple trees, where Jack kept tadpoles, and tried to keep water
spiders. Years later, when Willie was advanced from laboratory boy to laboratory man, and was known as Mr. Ball, he
went out to Texas University with Julian Huxley. He was
known there as Mr. Huxley's assistant, and some of the local
young ladies were heard to say that it was a great pity Mr.
Huxley didn't speak as good English as Mr. Ball did!

People living in the country changed their servants much
less often than did town dwellers, whose house room was

restricted. Most country houses gave hospitality to at least one old crone, who perhaps dealt out monthly supplies of tea, sugar, spices and curry powder, and at any rate knew the exact age of everyone of the younger generation, and could tell the history of his boyhood.

The standard of accommodation for the maids was rising rapidly. My mother was scandalized at the idea of her cook occupying a box bed which ventilated into the kitchen, and altogether refused to sanction its occasional use, even by a stop-gap kitchen maid when extra help was needed in the house. However small the household, there always used to be a kitchen maid, and in the country, where there were birds to pluck and rabbits and hares to skin, a scullery maid too was almost essential. I remember hearing my mother say that the girl who had been our kitchen maid for three years ought to be sufficiently trained to go as a 'plain cook' to anyone who 'did her own housekeeping'. Sometimes the cook and the laundry maid shared the second of two girls, and that girl worked hard!

There was a convention I think in many families—I am sure it held good in all the Trotter-Dundas houses—that on Sunday afternoons, after close inspection by the housekeeper, the girl or girls went to the dining-room and there 'read a chapter to the mistress'. My mother used to tell of a girl who had just been passed on to us by my aunt Mary Pitt Dundas. This was her first 'Sunday reading' and my mother thought it would be suitable for her to begin with the first chapter of Genesis. 'Quite a bright girl' she said 'and she could read well and clearly:—And He placed cucumbers and a flaming sword at the gate of the Garden. . . .' 'Not cucumbers' my mother said. The girl looked up and said brightly 'Aye, mem, 'tis so.' My mother then explained cherubim, and apparently gave such a glowing account of them to the girl (a gardener's daughter) that she exclaimed 'Losh, mem, it must have been an unca bonny gairden.'

I wonder my mother contemplated taking her through all the 'historic books' of the Old Testament.

Town and Country Servants

Years after this, when I was told to go and read to a maid (this might happen if she was ill, or in trouble at the loss of a parent or a near relative), it was always assumed both by my mother and by the maid herself that I had come to read her a 'chapter'. But it was usually quite impossible to get the maid to express a preference for any particular chapter, or indeed for any particular part of the Bible. I had a wide field to choose from, and was far too shy to select any chapter which might have a bearing on the girl herself or on her bereavement. I hated these readings, but did not dare suggest bringing a game to play with her, till one day I noticed a box of dominoes on her chest of drawers. After a game or two our relations became easier, though my conscience was far from clear.

I do not think my mother ever read 'family prayers'. She rarely left her bedroom till after breakfast. When he felt well enough—or, shall I say, felt inclined—my father read them. If not, he sent me a message that I was to do so. I hated this; I was never dressed in the morning till just in time for prayers, and not expecting to have to do so, I had no time to look ahead and see whether there were unpronounceable names or unmentionable incidents in the chapter following the one my father had read the previous day. I plunged desperately in wherever the large book marker was left, and the Old Testament is an unchancy book for a shy reader. When my father was laid up for any length of time, I knew beforehand that I should have to 'take prayers' and I might, of course, have come to them prepared; but I never did so, whether from pure laziness, or in the vain hope that something would happen to prevent my having to officiate. It was, of course, extremely unlikely that the telegraph boy should ring between 9 and 9.10, or that the tea-urn should boil over so violently as to require attention, but these things had happened, and might happen again.

The lamp under the big silver tea-urn was always lighted as the prayer-gong sounded, and the knob on the lid, where the hissing steam was discharged, sometimes rattled rather disturbingly, and some boiling water splashed over the table;

then the Lord's Prayer, with which we always ended, was apt to finish rather hastily. No, it may have been my fault, but to me there was nothing devotional about those prayers. In other houses it was different. Later on, at Cloan, prayers were read only on Sunday evenings, and by the eldest male member of the family present. Lord Haldane read fluently in his rather harsh voice, exactly the portion selected by his mother, and prayed extempore and at length. John, when it fell to him, selected some rather obscure passages from one of the Prophets or from Proverbs or Ecclesiastes, and read, not only just the portion, but enough for his congregation to feel the rhythm of the prose; he read the prayers, but as though they were something rather odd and surprising, which made them sound different. Jack, when he happened to be the eldest male, though he was still at Eton, took it all quite easily. I think the prayers he recited were something used in college.

My daughter remembers that Granniema and her descendants—but none of those who had only married into the family!—met by her bedside on New Year's Eve, while Uncle Richard told the Absolute, in prayer, about the doings of the Haldanes over the past year. From the window she could see across the strath to the ridge of Auchterarder, where there was a great bonfire and the 'heidyers' and 'futyers' of the village fought one another.

It was curious how the feel of the ritual varied at different houses. I can recall the difference in one's reactions. The only place where prayers moved me at all was at Colinton, where my uncle read the chapter standing more or less at attention, and remained standing while his congregation knelt for the General Confession (Episcopalian prayer-book) and gave the Blessing almost in the tones of an army order. It all meant something to him and therefore to me, which the same words did nowhere else.

CHAPTER XIV

A Young Woman's Clothes

⁂

What, I wonder, was the fetish connected with red flannel? If old Mrs. Somebody at the lodge was rheumatic, quite the best present to give her would be a red flannel petticoat, or possibly a bed-jacket, only be sure it was red flannel. As for my personal wear, my nightgowns were red flannel, and there was a sudden change when I was about nine years old and they became white cotton. Then, about five years later, I was allowed to choose the material for what must have been one of my earliest shop-made dresses and jackets, a chocolate-brown homespun. When I went to be fitted, I was told not to forget to remind the shop that the jacket must be lined with red flannel. Much against the grain, I obeyed. Other girls, when they took off their jackets, did not exhibit red flannel linings, but it couldn't be helped. However, when the suit was sent home it was discovered that the sleeves were lined with some material which made it easy to slip them on. The shop was requested to change this for red flannel—it did so, under protest—and the sleeves were always too tight for comfort!

Bathing dresses were made of thick, blue serge with patterns of white or red braid. I seem to remember that one's clothes were almost always of very thick or very thin material. My grandmother, by the way, never allowed her daughters to change into summer clothes until the 1st May, but on that day, whatever the weather, the change was made! I have seen them shivering in cotton frocks in an east-coast wind. My mother nearly always wore a shawl, or at any rate had one handy to put on if required. I think she gave up a crinoline as soon as it was possible to do so, but I certainly remember her with some sort of modified crinoline, because when I leaned against her in front, she bulged out at the sides! She always wore her very pretty hair loosely crimped at the sides over frisettes, and a lapelle of lace or embroidery over her head, instead of the usual married woman's cap, and at night a muslin night-cap, lace-trimmed and tied under her chin.

Later, in the eighties, she had very elaborate and most becoming caps. The trouble was to find anyone who could copy them; she designed her own bonnets too, and had them made up. Coming out of St. John's Church, Edinburgh, one Sunday, Henry Chancellor came up to her and said, 'Oh, Mrs. Trotter, you've got a new bonnet, and what a beautiful one!' She said this was very familiar of him, but she didn't mind in the least! In fact a new cap or a new bonnet was an event. Clothes were elaborate and meant to last, and she took a lot of trouble about both mine and her own, but after I passed the black velveteen and coloured sash stage at the age of eight or nine, I think mine must usually have been rather hideous.

It must have been just as I was into my teens that we both started wearing merino underclothes (combinations). Up till then we had linen, not cotton, chemises and drawers. Chilly, but much less uncomfortable than the terribly tickly merino! I was glad, however, of woollen stockings when they came in.

After I was about twelve, the one thing I minded about was to have my frocks lengthened to a nearly grown-up level.

What strikes me as really queer is that after I ceased to wear childish straight frocks with a large sash, we—I, my contemporaries and the older generation—scarcely ever had a dress made entirely of one material. We did not just trim our cashmere or merino with silk or poplin; we inserted panels of a different material if not of a contrasting colour, so that the 'good line' for which the dressmakers nowadays try so hard, was hopelessly lost.

A Young Woman's Clothes

Of course grown-up skirts swept the ground. One nearly always held up the back of one's skirt as one walked, and in the autumn of the year when I 'came out', skirts were provided with a *balaieuse*. We had been abroad during the summer, and with a view to giving me a good start with a dress allowance, my mother had two or three costumes made for me by her dressmaker at Aix-Les-Bains. These had a silk frill, which showed as one moved, attached to the underskirt or lining. A black dress had a scarlet *balaieuse*, a green costume a purple one. If one must sweep the streets, it is probably better to do so with something which can be removed and renewed. I rather think the *balaieuse* fashion did not catch on in Scotland, for my Tytler and Hamilton girl friends looked askance at it.

My dress allowance started at £50 a year. When I was told that I should have this, it seemed fabulous wealth, and I started giving my friends presents. Of course I was soon bankrupt, and after a year or two my allowance was increased to £60. My mother's French maid was supposed to do a good deal of plain dressmaking for both of us, and I do not think it ever occurred to me to do any sewing for myself, though I did trim my hats with the help of many pins.

The fashion in hats seems to move in circles even more than that of other clothes. I have just (1956) seen a modern advertisement for a 'sailor'. It is a stiff straw hat with a flat crown and a straight brim (we called them 'boaters'), and it carries a bunch of flowers on the brim behind the crown. In 1877 I had just such a 'boater' with a bunch of buttercups on the brim in front of the crown. Two years later the buttercups were removed by a more sophisticated cousin, who assured me that 'we have quite given up trimming boaters'. After that as long as I wore them, my 'boaters' had a plain black or white band. Once I wanted to substitute a Hunting Stewart ribbon, but this was not approved of.

We bought our artificial flowers, of which it seems to me we used a great many, from some woman who ran a tiny business far up in the Lothian Road. I made friends with her, and used

147

to take her real flowers of which she made surprisingly life-like copies. My grandmother gave me my first wreath—wild roses, I think it was—but somehow I got into disgrace about the first one I ordered for myself. It was of moss with tiny scarlet and yellow 'puddock stools' and drosera embedded in it, and sprays of cotton grass and bog asphodel. The moss was really quite beautifully made—several sorts of it. I got quite a lot of fun out of that wreath, though it was rather hot and heavy.

My impression is that it was *de rigueur* to wear wreaths at evening parties as well as at balls. All unmarried women wore them, as did the younger married ones, even those who had taken to caps for morning wear at home. Caps like my mother's were made of lace, tatting or slightly frilled muslin, and about the size of penwipers. It seemed such a pity when a young aunt by marriage adopted this fashion, for she had a beautifully shaped head, and masses of hair drawn into a big bun. But my grandmother said: 'The sweet girl! So suitable.'

Whenever we were in London together, my mother and I always paid a visit to her French corsetière. I ought to remember Madame's name, but I have not written or heard it for sixty years. She and her friend, both rather more than middle-aged French women, lived in what would now be called a basement flat. It was the first dwelling of the kind I had ever visited, and there seemed something extremely adventurous about descending the area stairs into the tiny, beautifully kept little garden in which grew magnificent carnations, a border perhaps eighteen inches wide, and a central bed with three beautiful Gloire de Dijon rose bushes. We always called by appointment, and Mademoiselle was always on the lookout for us and began on business as soon as we entered. We were seated at a tiny table and offered coffee (my mother had warned me that I *must* drink at least one cup of coffee, though I hated it) and Madame said firmly 'C'est pour l'estomac'. I was to be very careful not to make faces over it, or Madame would be shocked. So I kept a smiling face and added an extra lump of sugar when I could.

A Young Woman's Clothes

Then Mademoiselle poured me a little glass of delicious Sirop, and when my mother began to worry her for opening the window, 'à cause de la petite', she handed to Madame a chenille scarf which she wrapped round me. Then my mother went into the next room to be fitted and I asked to look at a big illustrated book of fairy stories and always astonished Mademoiselle by being able to read it. In our earlier visits I doubt that I could read anything at all well, but French was not more difficult to read than English—in fact, sometimes the accents helped me to guess at a word if I did not know it. There was no such help in English!

Soon I was promoted to wearing a corset of my own; later they made me a 'corset de mariée'. It was a beautiful one, most elaborate, and after Jack was born I wrote and asked for another, But alas, the little assistant told me 'Dear Madame has just died and I am going back to Paris.' I have never been comfortable in my stays since.

CHAPTER XV
From Edinburgh to Oxford

❉

I did not marry till I was twenty-seven. I had refused John twice before I got engaged. I always liked his mother, no one could help doing so, and I now deeply regret that I was not kinder and more sympathetic in my dealings with her, though Naomi made up for all my shortcomings. It was Mrs. Haldane's constant insistence that I should 'appreciate' her eldest son, Richard Haldane, that made the difficulty between us. I disliked him personally, quite apart from his politics. Mrs. Haldane used to ask me to try to forget these, and I couldn't explain to her that his omniscience, his self-satisfaction and his sneers at the ideas and loyalties of people who disagreed with him, were enough to account for my dislike. Nothing, however, but realization of the harm that he and his party were doing to the country would have accounted for and justified the strength of my antagonism. But for his politics he would not have been interesting or important enough to command such intense dislike! If only the topic of R.B.H. could have been eliminated, all would have been well between his mother and me.

The Haldane family history was very different from my own. Mrs. Haldane came of a well-known Northumbrian family of Burdon. Her father was deeply involved in the religious revival of the time, and persuaded his devoted daughter not only to break off what promised to be a brilliant and happy marriage, for the sake of her soul, but that it was her duty to marry a dry Scotch widower with five children. Mr. Haldane was the son of James Haldane of Gleneagles, who, with his elder brother, Robert, had sold a considerable amount of their property in Perthshire to raise funds for a Mission to convert the population of Bengal. He was refused leave by Pitt's Government to embark on this enterprise, and the brothers turned their attention to Switzerland, where, until the beginning of this century, there was still a remnant of the sect of Haldanit es. The elder brother wrote a commentary on the Epistle to the Romans, and was known to the younger generation as 'Robert the Romans'. His brother James had served in the East India Company's Navy and had fought a duel. My husband and his brothers were very anxious to get particulars about the duel, but I do not think they were ever given any.

Fortunately 'Robert the Romans' did not sell the family home, Gleneagles. It lies at the foot of Glendevon, one of the passes between the Lowlands and Highlands. I gather that, apart from the two evangelists, the Haldanes were 'douce' folk who tried to keep on good terms with all their neighbours. They were hospitable, and expended much good beef and brose on fugitives from both Highlands and Lowlands. They were elders of the established Church until Robert and James joined the Baptist community. My husband's father belonged to it, and as far as I know, all the children of his first marriage had been 'accepted by the congregation', but when it came to the turn of Mrs. Haldane's eldest son (the future War Minister and Lord Chancellor) Richard refused to have any profession of faith made in his name, though for the sake of peace he agreed to let his father 'present him to the congregation'. Apparently in what he said, Mr. Haldane did not keep strictly to his side of the agreement, and Richard protested.

Haldanes and Trotters had very different ideas of education. At sixteen Richard Haldane was already attending classes at Edinburgh University. He obtained his father's leave to go to Göttingen to study German philosophy. His mother and his old nurse saw him off from the docks at Leith, where they must have made a pathetic little group!

From Edinburgh to Oxford

Before we were engaged, after months of correspondence and some rather agitated interviews, I made John understand, as clearly as I could do, that I could not and would not alter my political faith. For the moment, Home Rule was the burning question. Other things might follow into the limelight, but allegiance to the United Kingdom was a fundamental tenet with which there could be no tampering.

I could not, even had I wanted to, drop politics and become absorbed in the theory of vitalism—it did not interest me, particularly. For his part John said that he was not really actively interested in politics, that he would certainly never take an active part in them, and never try to interfere in any way with anything I felt called upon to do. This I understood to be a definite pledge.

Of course the family expected me to have an Episcopalian wedding service, but among other things I strongly objected to the farce of being 'given away'. So we settled to be married according to the Presbyterian custom, not Free or U.P., but the Church by Law established in the Country. St. Georges Church, Charlotte Square, next door to No. 17, was the most convenient and natural place for the ceremony, though Mrs. Haldane and, oddly enough, my mother, would have liked it to be in the drawing-room of No. 17, where John's half-sister, Lady Makgill, had been married twenty or more years earlier.

A friend of John's, the Minister of Glen Devon, a young Hegelian with a German wife, was asked to perform the ceremony. He drew up a short form of service and sent it to us to look over. I heard that he complained afterwards that I had put my blue pencil through most of it! I believe we were scarcely twenty minutes in the church, which John and I reached by a side door through the lane next to No. 17, after the congregation had trooped in by the main entrance. The only stipulation I made was that four of my young cousins at Colinton should have the front seats.

We were a trifle late, for John had forgotten his umbrella and had to go back for it, and in the narrow passage inside the church we came face to face with Lady Glasgow and her

brother Jock, Lord Abercromby. Lord Glasgow had died quite
recently and she had refused to attend the wedding in her
weeds. I had protested that she must come, and here she was,
saying that she had tried to get in by the back way, un-
observed, and she was trying now to slip out again. I said
'Nonsense, Cousin Monty, we'll go in together.' And we did,
hand in hand. Jock and John followed with the umbrella,
under which John and I walked to the Caledonian Station
when the ceremony was over.

When we were well away my mother asked Granville
Egerton to open the large doors of the church and herd the
congregation into the house next door, where they found the
cake ready for Daisy to cut.

Some friends who had not been invited to the church—
scarcely anyone was except relatives—watched us from Val-
lence's shop window making our way to the station; but all
they saw under the umbrella were the heels of my thick shoes
splashing on the pavement.

My grand-daughters always ask about clothes. For the wedding I had a dress, jacket and muff in fine grey cloth with a
deep belt and revers of pinkish velvet—not pink, about the
colour of plum juice mixed with milk! Some grey fur I had was
used on the muff and on a matching three-cornered grey felt
hat. I think the whole costume probably looked very nice indeed. Mrs. Kerr in London, who made it, was a charming
woman, and some sort of far away cousin, who was running a
shop to keep her home going. She was first and foremost a
milliner. I got all my hats from her and I do not think she
ever let me buy anything unbecoming! All I can remember
of my trousseau is a summer dress in lavender-coloured Indian
cashmere with silk embroidery trimming, and a long dark-grey
coat with astrakhan collar and cuffs. Afterwards Mrs. Kerr
made my dress for the Drawing-room, a grey satin train with
a pattern of purple thistles, and a complete white evening
dress underneath with lace flounces which my mother gave
me as a wedding present. They were old Limerick lace, lovely
but very fragile.

From Edinburgh to Oxford

In 1942, when Lady Fortescue was collecting lace for a Red Cross sale in the U.S.A. I sent it to her. I believe her helpers made up the lace sent to them into scarves and head-dresses which sold wonderfully well in Boston. Apropos of lace, my grandmother gave me a small but lovely Brussels appliqué square which had been her wedding veil. When she heard that I was not going to be a 'proper bride' she rather wanted to ask for its return, but never quite came to the point of doing so. I once wore it as a scarf when I presented Naomi at a Drawing-room, but had forgotten its existence till ten days before Lois' marriage, when it was hastily washed by the bridegroom on the advice of the Victoria and Albert Museum and made a charming addition to her wedding dress, which had been her sister's—Valentine Arnold-Forster's. She looked quite charming in it. It made a better contrast with her dark hair than it had ever done among fair-haired Lowland Scots.

My father's wedding present was an enamel and diamond brooch which is interesting because it is the same pattern which Sir Henry Yule selected for my twenty-first birthday present, made by Juliano: a copy of an old Greek jewel.

At Christmas the year we were married, John and I spent about ten days at Cloan. After dinner we went up to our room, and John dictated to me the first of the many drafts of his book on Vitalism. He thought that dictating helped him, and he was obsessed by the theory, and spoke as if nothing else in the world was of so much importance and interest. If accepted, it would revolutionize the teaching of physiology, and explain much which perplexed men of science more and more as knowledge of the life and growth of cells increased. He was groping for words in which to clothe his ideas, and the dictation was very slow indeed—words or half a sentence would stand for a time and then be deleted, and we looked for a new starting point some pages further back. The pauses were so long that I tried to read, gripping my pen at the right angle to start writing immediately if he began to dictate. But he didn't like that. He wanted me to follow his thoughts and tried to make me feel how important it was and to say things

154

which would show that I was not only interested, but convinced and in complete sympathy. I was not convinced and could only answer 'I understand that you mean so and so. Had I not better write it down?' Mrs. Haldane sometimes came in to say goodnight, rather worried because she thought I was cold, which was certainly the case.

I went back to Edinburgh by train and John walked. We had a big reception to show the wedding presents and to drink healths. I tried to make it something of a festive occasion for my cousins, the children at Colinton, but it was no good; they were as depressed as I was.

We went up to Oxford in time for the beginning of Term, to 11 Crick Road, a little house which John had taken for himself about a year previously. The sanitary arrangements were rather primitive, but there were two Burne-Jones lights in the drawing-room bay window, and the dining-room opened into a perfectly charming little garden, which must have been carved out of an old orchard. It was half-filled with the best bearing apple trees I have ever had to deal with.

We took with us from Edinburgh a highly recommended house-parlourmaid, and got a very good local cook, as well as Willie Ball, who came in the mornings to do the boots and knives. This was a small household from my point of view, but in those days ample for an Oxford one. I was told that with it I ought to have got more sewing and washing done at home!

John had a whole cupboard full of clothes, which, when the drawers were opened, crawled and flew out to meet me. I have never seen such a flight of moths. He also had several unpaid bills and some unfinished papers dealing with experimental work, but he was so absorbed in writing his book that I doubt whether these papers would ever have seen the light if his nephew, Rob Makgill, and I had not nagged him about publication.

Meanwhile he was worried about his position in Oxford. His being there at all was rather fortuitous. His uncle, Sir John

Burdon-Sanderson, his mother's brother, Professor of Physiology, had asked him to help with some elementary teaching, and he had just carried on doing it. Of course he had the use of the laboratory, but no influence on its running, and not even a workroom of his own. I think his uncle paid him about a hundred a year.

Lady Burdon-Sanderson, Aunt Ghetal, was the sister of Lord Herschel, then Lord Chancellor. Of course they were Liberals, but they never seemed keen on politics. She asked all the 'right people' to call on me, but the university society was very limited, and a queer thing happened. The parlourmaid hid in a back of a drawer in the hall table the cards of several people I should have liked to know. I found them more than a year later, and heard from the other servant that the parlourmaid had told her she would not show them to me as I had far more visitors than was good for me! The callers must have come when the poor woman's religious mania was more than usually active, as it was upon the day when she ran into the drawing-room exclaiming, 'You've got a book on the table there by a woman who doesn't believe in the Divinity of Christ.' I think it was Mrs. Humphry Ward's *Helbeck of Bannisdale*.

I dismissed the parlourmaid before we went to Scotland for the summer vacation, after rather a frightening morning with her, while I packed the plate to go to the bank. We—I at least —still looked on sending the plate to the bank as a normal reaction when the house was left empty, but I don't think we ever did it again! The maid stood behind me, handing the things to be packed and bombarding me with portions of scripture, and I was really afraid what she would do next. I wrote to the doctor who had recommended her, and said I thought it would be sensible to have her met at the station in Edinburgh. He replied that he would have that done. He was not in the least surprised to have my letter, he had sent the woman to me because he had thought a change of scene might do her good!

This made me see red, and I wrote and told him that he had

taken a considerable risk and given quite an untrue reference. The odd thing was that John was not at all put out, even when he heard that the poor woman had been sent to an asylum straight from Edinburgh station, and reported dangerous. Mrs. Haldane, however, agreed with me!

One of my earliest visitors said that he was our clergyman, the incumbent, I suppose, of our parish. He had not seen us in his church and remarked that this was sad for him. I don't like parsons who speak about 'my church" but I offered him tea. He then hoped that if I was in any spiritual difficulty, I would 'open my heart' to him. This must have made me look rather savage, because he said hastily that he hoped we had found some church where we 'could be happy'. I still didn't want a fuss, so I said we hadn't settled anything yet. He said, 'Dear, dear, oh dear, really', and asked to which branch of the church did we belong? If he had been anything like Mr. Sandford or Mr. Lockhart of Colinton, I should have remained courteous to the end, but he was fat and familiar and I said, 'My husband is an Original Seceder and I am an Anti-Burgher.' He did not call again.

To return to the Burdon-Sandersons. They asked us fairly often to dinner. Their parties were the least sociable that it has ever been my lot to attend. The dinners were long and solid, the room got fearfully hot and stuffy, and their dogs were often not in the best of health. I usually had 'Uncle John' on one side of me and on the other some elderly scientist who tried to produce light conversation. If either of them said anything which made me laugh, everybody looked up and someone said hopefully, 'Oh, do tell us what that was', and the poor joke fell dead. After dinner we women were arranged carefully in pairs round the drawing-room. You never got the chance of picking your partner, and if by good luck you started a conversation with your neighbour, it was sure to be interrupted—not by the men! (they sat on endlessly and John used to come in yawning and looking a picture of misery)— but Aunt Ghetal conscientiously broke up the couples she had arranged so that one had sometimes started the same subject

157

with six or seven different ladies by the end of the evening. I was sorry for her, because she so obviously worked hard, but if she had been less conscientious about it, she would have done better even with her very unpromising material. I am sure her one feeling was that she must run Sir John's house to his satisfaction. She was a blindly devoted wife.

The two houses which I enjoyed going to were the Diceys' and the Romanes'. My first dinner party was at the Romanes', and he was quite definitely Romanes of Nigg, not an unfamiliar Oxford professor. I saw a good deal of him during his last illness. The excuse was that he liked to hear about some experimental work of John's and we talked at large about people and things, and on the last few visits rather tentatively about religion. He spoke very restrainedly of the many visits he had from the clergy his wife believed in. 'They mean well,' he said, but they tired him terribly, and would try to make him answer questions. On my last visit, he held on to my hands and said, 'Don't go, don't go,' but what can one do when a man's devoted wife almost pushes one out of the room? I am quite confident that his death-bed confession was merely the result of being too exhausted to argue. It was not meant as acquiescence to Anglican doctrines.

Early in his illness I lent him my little grey paper-covered first edition of the early Kipling's, published in Calcutta. They would have been valuable possessions, but I foolishly gave them away. Before Jack was born, when I was at a loss for light literature, John went to the University Union and returned triumphantly with *Tom Jones*. He was very despondent when I didn't appreciate it! Mrs. Dicey brought me more pleasant literature and was extremely solicitous and kind. I cannot understand why at that time we had no library subscription, and I do not remember when I first got one. Probably it was a present from my mother. My library subscription, and my subscription to *Blackwood's*, have been the things I have stuck to during both wars, whatever else I dropped.

The Diceys' was a really interesting house to go to and I

loved their Sunday lunches. When John was engaged or going on a 'Sunday walk', they asked me to come, saying that I should like to meet so and so, and I did! Professor Dicey was a marvellously plain old gentleman, a skeleton with a red nose, and so short-sighted that he was always knocking over things even in his own house, where he might have been expected to know his way. They were building a wooden balcony outside the dining-room, and I said something to Mrs. Dicey about the grain in the wood. 'Has wood grains?' he asked, and went to examine a new door. I said, 'The curious thing about this door is that the grain runs in the same way in the panel as it does in the uprights. Usually one would see the grain in the panels running cross-wise, if it ran up and down on the rest of the door.' 'Do you see?' Mrs. Dicey asked. He answered tentatively: 'I think so, Eleanor, but I am constantly surprised at the number of things that you and Mrs. Haldane see about this balcony.' He was author of *The Case Against Home Rule*, which brought many wanderers into the fold, and interested people in Unionist work. In his queer cracked voice he could be very eloquent in argument; I never could understand how little effect anything he said had on John.

Miss Thackeray was living with the Diceys when I first knew them and like Professor Dicey she too was a good talker. Afterwards she became a member of the Oxford Corporation. I'm not sure that she wasn't the first woman alderman, in Oxford at least. Of course we talked about the franchise for women. There I think John agreed, but his point of view was that it wouldn't really make much difference, and he didn't think it was a question of justice, of right and wrong, as his sister and I did. Both Professor Romanes and Professor Dicey belonged to what my uncle Willie Keatinge used to call 'the Athenaeum Gang', and it was through my father that we knew the Diceys. They were certainly not friends of the Burdon-Sandersons. I should be inclined to say that the Burdon-Sandersons knew everyone in the university except the Fellows of All Souls—but this is certainly not strictly

159

accurate! Just after we were married, my father put down John's name for the Athenaeum and he asked to have the date when he should come up for election put forward as he felt that he would never really use a London club. When finally he was elected, we really couldn't afford the entrance fee and the yearly subscription, so he retired. I was sorry, but I knew him well enough by that time to understand that he really wasn't a clubable person. He became much more so after he got his Fellowship at New College, and I used sometimes to think that he would have found a London club quite helpful, but the Athenaeum is not a gregarious place and what he needed was a club where he could take a Danish or Japanese professor or a mine manager to a meal!

Just before Jack was born, T. H. Huxley and his wife came to stay with the Burdon-Sandersons. I wasn't feeling inclined to face a dinner party there, so John brought Professor Huxley to see me, or rather for me to see him. But I can't remember anything about him, nor whether I felt the thrill I was expected to feel! What I do remember is a visit from Mrs. Huxley, a charming old lady with a cap tied under her chin like an early Raeburn portrait, who talked encouragingly about the unpleasant aspects of child-bearing. She was a dear.

When I first arrived at Oxford, there was only one woman doctor there, an Irish lady of uncertain age. I don't think she had more than five or six patients, but I enrolled myself among them.

A general vaccination campaign was started because a man who had pustules was told in the morning to keep to his bed till seen again by the doctor, but 'thought he'd better get up and go to church'—which he did! A doctor noticed the pustules on his neck, got a colleague to help him to keep the man back in his pew, and himself went into the church porch and stopped everyone whom he had seen sitting near the patient, and got their addresses. My mother insisted that I must be vaccinated, so John got some tubes of lymph, used one on me, and gave me the rest to use on our maids (one of whom had never been

COLONEL RICHARD HARTE KEATINGE V.C. C.S.I.
POLITICAL AGENT IN KATHIAWAR from 1862 to 1867
THE CHIEFS OF KATHIAWAR HAVE CONTRIBUTED THE FUND
FOR THIS PORTRAIT IN GRATEFUL REMEMBRANCE OF THE MANY
BENEFITS CONFERRED ON THE PROVINCE NOT THE LEAST OF
WHICH WAS THE INCEPTION OF THIS COLLEGE FOR THE
EDUCATION OF THEIR SONS (?)

My uncle, then Col. Keatinge

Mr Tytler of Woodhouselea

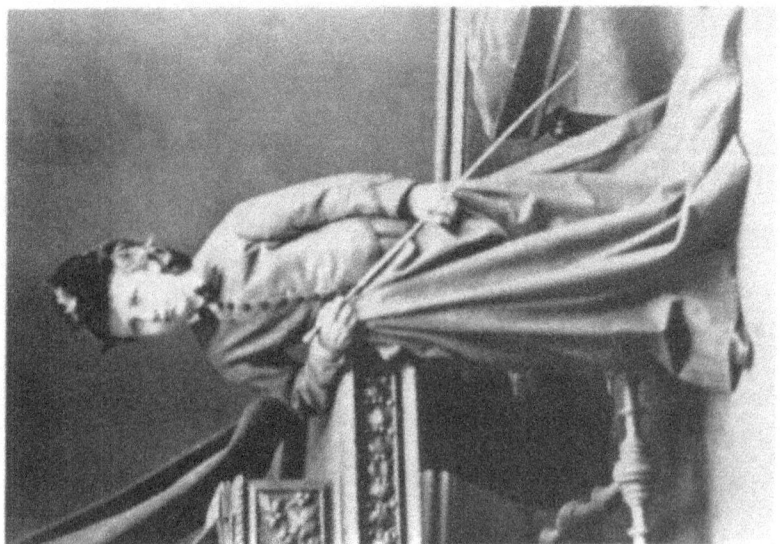

L.K.T. ten years old

vaccinated) and I thought it was time that I stirred up my
Edinburgh doctor, who had promised to try to find some suitable person ready to try her luck in Oxford.

Dr. Jessie MacGregor who was later with the Scottish
Women's Hospital Unit with the Serbian Retreat wrote about
a student who wanted to start in practice; she was very young
and socially inexperienced, but perhaps I could help her. Miss
B. was an uncompromising Scotch lassie. She might have had
a better chance with a different type of practice, but how does
a young, strange doctor begin to get a practice, unless some
lucky accident gives her a chance of showing her skill?

She and her mother, who came to visit her, talked it over
with me, and when her brother, who was starting a practice
in the Outer Isles, offered to take her into partnership, we
could do nothing but urge her to accept.

I hadn't got a step nearer to providing Oxford or myself
with a woman doctor, so I went to Edinburgh for Naomi's
birth.

We always went to Cloan in summer, and usually in the
other academic holidays. It was on a hilly road in Perthshire
in the early years of this century that I saw one of the first
private motor-cars to be driven in Scotland. I was out with
Mrs. Haldane and we looked at one another in annoyance and
surprise when sounds reached us, which suggested machinery
being forced into use for which it was not intended. They
came from beyond the brow of the hill, and to the mechanical
sounds were added curt orders, spoken with much authority
and accompanied by some fairly strong language, and there
appeared a man walking backwards and making complicated
gestures with both arms.

Our horses were by this time fairly excited, though not
nearly so upset as the coachman. In answer to Mrs. Haldane's
inquiry as to whether he could not pass 'the obstruction', he
said, 'No horses of yours will stand for it, Mem. It will be the
new machine with the Macdonalds. What gars them take it on
the public roads? You could have the law on him, Mem.'

Then one of the horses backed, and the other made an

attempt to rear, and the coachman's language sounded much like a milder version of what he had just heard from the backward walking man. The carriage crashed into the bank of the roadside, dislodging a small fall of earth and stone, and almost unseating the coachman. The walking man whipped round, and was at our horses' heads at the moment the car came into view. His exclamation of extreme annoyance changed into a mixture of apology and orders. 'Mrs. Haldane—I much regret —don't be alarmed! I apologize most deeply. I never thought of meeting you on this road. I hope you are not shaken. Here stand, you brutes!' The horses were settling down, and Mrs. Haldane spoke in the comparative quiet. 'I consider that you. are making illegitimate use of the public thoroughfare, Lord Kingsborough.' The Lord Justice Clerk made the universal gesture of the male reprimanded by the female in authority. He rubbed his forehead, leaving a slightly muddy mark—or was it oil?—and continued to stand at the horses' heads while he expressed his regrets and Mrs. Haldane sat in monumental silence.

The coachman asked suddenly, 'Shall I drive on, Mem?' It was obvious that a move of some sort had to be made. Lord Kingsborough said, 'I could easily turn the car into the bank and make room for you to pass, but I fear the engine is bound to make some noise, and the horses. . . . You would not do me the honour of driving you home? I assure you the car is perfectly safe.' Mrs. Haldane replied that she was not easily alarmed. 'Then you accept?' 'Oh, do,' I interjected. 'I should be so much honoured to have you as my first passenger!' But Mrs. Haldane put his offer away with one wave of her hand, and said to the coachman, 'Home. There is room for the carriage to turn if Lord Kingsborough will leave the horses' heads.'

Lord Kingsborough looked very downcast, but I thought I detected a faint flicker of a smile as he said to me: 'Perhaps you will let me take you for a drive soon, Mistress John? I will ask my daughter-in-law to arrange it.' 'Delighted' I said, adding 'your grandson has told Jack so much about the car.'

'Oh, you had better let him come and spend a day with Donald. They can sit in the garage and gaze at the car the whole day long.' 'Provided they don't touch it,' said the voice of a very superior-looking mechanic, in a superior English voice. 'All very well, but how can you expect boys to learn about machinery which they are not allowed to touch?' Here spoke the grandfather, and the man who loved machinery, but not the car owner or the Law Lord! He opened the carriage door for me, and I slipped out and round the corner to have a glimpse of the car—an ugly thing compared with our pair of horses! While I got in, he looked at the damage to the back of the carriage, some scratches only. Mrs. Haldane noticed my muddy shoes, 'I am afraid you got your feet wet, Kathleen' was all she said, and we had rather a silent drive home. I think she almost wished that the carriage should show clearer signs of the encounter to give her still more legitimate cause for disapproval of the illegitimate use of the public highway, more especially by one who certainly should be an upholder of any law about the use of the road—supposing there was one.

CHAPTER XVI

John's Early Oxford Career

✳

After about this time the troubles at the Physiological Laboratory came to a head. The other demonstrators were, I think, being paid a little—very little—more than John was, and were not helped or encouraged to do original work or to publish their results if they got any. Everything appeared 'under the auspices of' or 'under the direction of the Professor', and was the product of his laboratory. This was not fair to young men who had their way to make, and John felt this acutely on their behalf. We talked things over, and I was quite prepared that he should resign and try for a job elsewhere. This would have made it necessary for the position of the other demonstrators to be improved—and when he talked with him, Sir John wasn't pleased. A lectureship was open at Belfast University; I said that if we went there I should be bound to take an active part in politics, and that John might find things difficult at the university if he made friends with Home Rulers. It would have been an impossible situation and, though I longed to join the fight, I was relieved when the idea was given up. There were other vacancies, of course, but nothing at all well-paid or attractive.

Then Sir John suddenly took on the role of an aggrieved old man, and told John that if he deserted him he would resign; and the aunt who evidently thought me responsible for the 'unpleasantness', came and begged me to get John to 'withdraw his threat', as his uncle was offering him much increased pay! I was not enthusiastic and said that the other demonstrators had to be considered. She said that his uncle did not consider John as 'just a demonstrator', and that he, John, had nothing to do with them and their appointments. Primed by him I explained that this was not the way in which he could look at the question. A memorandum asking for university recognition and better pay and positions was being drawn up, and John would sign it with the others. He not only signed it, but drafted it; and I do not think that the professor had much difficulty in getting the necessary funds for paying the demonstrators, voted by the university. The difficulty had been to make him ask for the money: he preferred to run the laboratory as his own show and 'no questions asked'.

John and his uncle were both 'hurt' and lost their appetites, and our good cook had to go into hospital just when she was most badly needed. Knowing the state of affairs I thought that the aunt might have lessened the nervous tension by asking John to a good dinner—he could not eat our stop-gap cooking—but the idea did not occur to her. My excellent 'monthly' fed me extravagantly on Brand's Essences.

I suppose there is still a definite taboo against canvassing, however remotely, for anyone who has been proposed for election to the Royal Society. Anyhow, after the incident of the demonstrators, John told me in the strictest confidence, with directions not to let anyone guess I knew it, that his uncle had put him up for election. He said that it was desirable that the proposal should be endorsed by ten or twelve really 'good names', but undesirable to have a long list of less distinguished supporters. When, on a visit to Burlington House a few days before the day of the election, Mr. Jervis-Smith found John had been proposed, he was extremely indignant because he had not been told of it. Why hadn't I told him? I explained. Why had Sir John put him up if he didn't intend to see that he was properly supported? That I couldn't explain. 'It is now too late', said Mr. Jervis-Smith, 'to do more than speak to a couple of people at the meeting, and not time to get at Cambridge.'

John's Early Oxford Career

John wasn't elected; very few people are, I believe, on the occasions when they are proposed for the first time. A year later he had very influential support, especially from scientists at Cambridge. On Sir John's return from London after the election, he came to announce the news to us. John was in the middle of an experiment, and had gone down to work at the laboratory, and I was delighted to be able to tell his uncle, 'Thank you for coming to tell us, but we've heard already. A telegram from Cambridge, of course, and Mr. Jervis-Smith wired too.' In honour of the occasion, the Jervis-Smiths gave Jack a clockwork engine, which was the pride of his life for many years. They left Oxford when Mr. Jervis-Smith was superannuated, and very tragically the family died out.

It was not very long after this that the professor announced that he was resigning the Chair of Physiology to become Regius Professor of Medicine. John at once became a candidate for the Chair, and as far as I recollect, there were only two other candidates, Professor Langley of Cambridge and Mr. Gotch, the latter a friend and, I think, a one-time assistant of Sir John's. At any rate those two were the only ones that counted.

Mr. Langley wrote that if he were elected, he would at once divide the work of the Chair, keeping the anatomical side for himself and handing over to John the chemical side of the teaching—'in equal partnership'. He said that the Chair gave opportunities for far more work than any one man could do if he were interested in research as well as in teaching. Mr. Langley was considerably senior to John and was much more used to the business side of university life. He was editor of the *Journal of Physiology*, and I believe, an outstanding scientist as well as a very pleasant, courteous gentleman. That he should get the Chair seemed to me a very happy solution for all the people concerned, as John would have resented the amount of routine work which he would still have felt a professor ought to do, and all committee work would have been shared.

John's Early Oxford Career

The electors to the Chair are reported to have said that they were not convened as an election committee, but had 'come to do what Burdon-Sanderson told them'. One of them remarked that of course Sir John would support his nephew, to which he replied that if he did so, he would be accused of nepotism. 'But', said the elector, 'if you don't support your nephew everyone will think that you have something very serious against him.' As far as I remember, Sir John's final answer to everything was, 'If I don't support Gotch, it may go to a Cambridge man!' It went to Professor Gotch.

John was terribly disappointed and sick of the whole business. He was not connected with any college, except as a member of the common-room of Jesus, to which his friend, Professor Ritchie of Dundee, had introduced him, and he had no feeling of belonging to Oxford, no roots in it. He did not know most of the 'nice' and important people, and his college means much more to the Oxford man than does that abstraction the university—and it was not even John's own university!

Sir John came in person to announce the result of the election. He said that he had come to see *me*, that he counted on *me* to induce John 'to take a reasonable view of the position' and would I make him promise to give his 'full support to Gotch, and to carry on at the laboratory exactly as he was now doing?' I was glad to be able to say that John had already written resigning the demonstratorship. The old gentleman was very angry indeed. Striding about our little drawing-room with clenched fists, he declared that there was 'nothing further' *he* could do for John, so what did he propose to do now? I longed to say that John had never had so much backing from him that he would miss it. Afterwards I rather wished that I had said so, but he was Mrs. Haldane's brother and I did not want to make bad blood in the family. To the end, she never quite believed that her brother had not John's 'best interests at heart'!

One of the first letters we got after the election was announced, was from Professor Michael Foster, of Trinity College, Cambridge. I cannot remember whether it was addressed to John or to me. Michael Foster said that if they had anything going at Cambridge which would be worth John's acceptance, he should have it at once. This pleased him and delighted my father, and we settled down to low living and high thinking till something should turn up. I should have liked to try for a Chair in the Dominions, but I knew that my mother would be miserable if we left the country. While we were living in Crick Road, where there was not room for her and a maid, she used to take a lodging for a month in spring somewhere close by, and Fanny Keane usually accompanied her. Twice she had Miss Poynter's little house in Park Terrace, where all the walls were hung with etchings and reproductions of Poynter's pictures.

We made the best of our financial difficulties and before very long a Grocers' Scholarship of four hundred a year fell vacant, and the 'Cambridge interest' secured it for John, so we were very well off for the period of its duration. Naomi was born in Edinburgh, and we found the Crick Road house impossibly small, and began looking out for a dwelling large enough to house the increased family.

We walked for many weary miles and saw several very attractive places; but were sensible and refused to be tempted by the Alms Houses in Cowley Road. There was a rumour that these were to be sold, solid little grey stone buildings, out of which a really charming house could be made, and what mattered most of all to me, a large walled garden at the back, but the situation was very much against this. Above all I wanted to be fairly close to the Dragon School, as I was already planning that Naomi should go there!

A yet more interesting house was recommended to us, Paradise House in Paradise Square. This was a fascinating place. The front door opened into a tiny courtyard, with a stone basin of water in the middle of it. Inside the courtyard, a door at each end led into a passage with several fair-sized rooms which looked out on to a pleasant large garden. Upstairs there were on the right and left of the courtyard several smaller rooms, and what I have never seen anywhere else, a couple of complete rooms surrounded by the passage into which their windows and doors opened. An enormous pear tree was trained over the back of the house, 'an excellent fruiter', the house agent assured us. Of course I fell in love with the house, even the distance from school did not seem at the moment to damn it completely. Then John said quietly 'no bathroom and water only laid on to the kitchen' and besides, we found there was a public house next door at each side!

We ended by buying No. 4 St. Margaret's Road. We put in a second bathroom and cut off the end of the drawing-room to make a study, and it held us quite adequately. It was indeed 'a superior villa-residence'—but I had seen two buildings in Oxford which might have been made into *homes*!

John was elected to a fellowship *honoris causa* at New College. He was the first Fellow to be elected under a new statute and the Fellowship had no teaching attached to it. I do not know who, besides the Warden, was chiefly responsible for the appointment. Nor do I remember how well we knew the Spooners before our connection with the college began, but we became firm friends, and I loved 'the Spoo' and liked and admired Mrs. Spooner.

Most of the desperate dullness at Oxford parties was due to the fact that on Guest Nights men asked their friends to dine with them at High Table, till the only people whom no Don wanted to talk to or to entertain were left over (with their wives) 'to meet a few friends at a very quiet dinner', or else at a stiff tea party, at which the host appeared for just as long as it took him to bolt his tea, and then remembered that he had a letter which must catch the post, leaving a solitary undergraduate to hand the bread and butter—they were probably not worse than tea parties in other places, but they were my first experience of the species. On two occasions we met the same couple dining with the same hosts two years running, and John had to escort the same lady on both occasions. Even in these little parties the men still armed us in to dinner, as they had done at the big parties which I remember to have watched in my childhood.

Often in later years, when I wanted John to preside at a Victoria League Sunday supper, he would say with *schadenfreude* that he was dining in college, but he always thought that we 'ought' to accept private invitations, though even when he had not had trouble with his razor we generally arrived late, and I did not feel that we made up for this by being the last to leave. He couldn't bear to interrupt an argument with his host, even when the hostess and I began in desperation to blow out the candles! We were (as usual) the last to leave one very unusual dinner party. It was at the Warden's house in New College, when I met Lord Milner for the first and only time—one of the meetings one likes to remember. The rest of the guests had walked out through the quad, we were the only people with a carriage waiting in Queen's Lane—and the Warden came with me to the top of the stairs, saying: 'Be careful, they're very slippery, I'll turn the light on for you.' The light was on and he turned it off. I stood still, having a proper respect for that flight of stairs, till one of his daughters looked out of the drawing-room saying, 'Ah, he does that sometimes', and turned the switch on again.

So many stories have been invented as well as told about the Warden. This one I believe is true, and it is certainly characteristic. On a fifth of November, he noticed a figure huddled up against the wall in Queen's Lane, close to the Lodge. He called the porter and told him, 'A gentleman who seems to have been overtaken is outside—would the porter go and investigate the case, as it might be a very serious matter for the gentleman if he were found by the Warden.' The porter went —the gentleman was a guy!

CHAPTER XVII

Science

❊

It was John's nephew, Rob Makgill, who nagged him into publishing the unfinished papers he and I found in our house at 11 Crick Road. Rob had just taken his medical degree in Edinburgh, and was exceedingly capable about all kinds of laboratory work. He and I were inclined to think that John insisted on a series of experiments being done over again because that postponed the day when he would no longer be able to put off 'licking the stuff into shape' for the *Journal of Physiology*, or some other scientific publication. Rob undertook all revision, never grudged writing and rewriting the papers until the author was satisfied with them, and the way was clear to start the next set of experiments to which the published ones obviously led.

Years afterwards I found it was a source of great satisfaction to Rob, and to contemporary colleagues such as Gillies Priestley, to have been associated with this early work. They called John the Senior Partner, and the name was handed down by many generations of young physiologists. His early experimental work was the foundation on which his later work on respiration grew, and led up to all that he did for ventilation of mines and factories, for diving apparatus and eventually, in 1915, for gas masks.

If he had dropped this experimental and practical work, other people would almost certainly have carried it out in course of time, but would they have grasped the full significance of their results, and been able to act on them as promptly as he did in 1915? It was probably essentially a one man job.

Science

After Rob left to return with his parents, Sir John and Lady Makgill, to New Zealand, John became interested in the function of the air bladders of fish, and as usual upset the commonly held explanation of their use. This led to work on ventilation of factories, for which he did some research for the Board of Trade, and to questions of respiration at high altitudes. He had no competent or permanent assistant, though there were usually young men with jobs of their own, such as Ted Boycott, Mr. Ramsden, Mr. Pembrey and Dr. Douglas of St. John's associated with him in the publication of all the papers. They were all most devoted colleagues; but some found it frustrating never to know when the Senior Partner would be ready to start work, and without warning to find that their day might begin after tea-time, or even after other people were preparing for bed. In her delightful autobiography Mrs. Gielgud gives some idea of the hours we kept! One result of this was that I was sometimes called in to do things for which by training and nature I was totally unfitted. There was the occasion when the Italian professor, Senor Mosso, was said to have died as the result of an experiment in the Alps (roughly speaking inhaling at a high altitude air deficient in oxygen), because he trusted in the correctness of the data in one of the *Journal of Physiology* papers. I had been left to read the proofs while the Senior Partner was in Denmark, but I had carefully noted for the editor's attention that I would not be responsible for the position of the decimal dots in the tables!

But if I was inefficient, Jack was not. His father took him down a coal mine when he was ten or eleven, and by way of demonstrating that asphyxia may result from trying to move or work at the top of a gallery, though the lower levels are quite safe, he hoisted him up to the ceiling, told him to say something. Jack began with 'Friends, Romans, country-men', but before he got to 'your ears' he had passed out.

I do not think that he did any tests with Peter Fraser-Tytler who, he said, was the only other boy he would take down a mine. Besides going underground they had the experience of dinner and a concert given by the mine managers, and came back very much pleased with the entertainment and with the company they had met, as well as with their experiences underground. I agreed with them about the miners, one or two of whom used to come here sometimes to discuss modifications of the miners' lamp. The only mine I ever went down was clear of gas, and we carried naked candles; that was at Arniston, Midlothian, years earlier, before I knew that I should ever have anything to do with mining.

Jack had a marvellous summer with his father when the Admiralty wanted the results of all the experimental work that had been done in Germany and elsewhere, prepared for publication as 'New Instructions in Deep Diving'. There were a few more experiments to be made, and tests repeated under service conditions, so the Admiralty sent up H.M.S. *Spanker*, commander and crew, and put them at the Senior Partner's disposal in the Kyles of Bute, where there is deep water, close inshore. The work they did put the finishing touches to an entirely new system of diving. Instead of bringing a diver up from the bottom as quickly as possible, they found that he should be brought up slowly, stage by stage, and made tables of the time which should be allowed for decompression on each stage.

Naomi and I stayed in an abominably uncomfortable inn on the mainland with Arthur Makgill, a younger brother of Rob's, but our men folk lived chiefly on board the *Spanker*, and soon we made friends with officers and ratings, and they gave us a wonderful picnic, where they managed in pouring rain to get a fire going and to boil a kettle, on one of the vitrified forts. They also ran into an uncharted rock and instead of the reprimand which they expected for this, they got a very good chit, and I felt that entertaining us had not resulted in bad luck for anyone!

Jack was allowed to dive. The diving dress was for a full-grown man and before he had been down any length of time, water began to soak in at his ankles and wrists, but he understood the working of the valves of the suit, kept the water down to breast level, and refused to come up until he had had his full time submerged. When he was brought to the surface he was naturally very cold, so they gave him a big enough dose of whisky to induce a long sleep and put him into Lieutenant Guy Damant's bunk. Guy is one of the people who for years came very much into our lives. As a very junior naval officer he had written and asked John to let him join in the diving experiments. John handed me the letter saying he would not think of taking on a boy of that age for experiments in which there was bound to be some element of risk. Meanwhile Guy had followed on his letter and when John came in he found him having a lively time with Naomi and her pet duck, and any question of his not being taken on was shelved. Much of their work was done with goats, as these were the largest animals which could be introduced into the diving bells with which they were working, and they both became attached to their experimental animals. One special favourite, a goat which had swallowed buttons from their coats (and, it was said, a watch and several tobacco pouches), was sent to the Isle of Wight, where it had its horns gilded by Guy's classically-minded brother, and lived to a disreputable old age.

The goats remind me of a much earlier occasion. One of our first visitors in Oxford was my cousin Jock, Lord Abercromby, who, like others in the family, had been bombarded at the time of my marriage, with publications of the R.S.P.C.A. I said something to John about taking food to the laboratory 'for your cat in the bottle'. 'Oh, you don't really put cats into bottles, do you?' Jock asked in rather horrified tones. I said, 'Come and see. We'll take our tea down to the lab.' We found the cat curled up comfortably asleep in a big beaker. When it heard or smelt preparations for tea, it partially roused up. John poured some milk into a saucer and set it down near the neck of the beaker. The cat lazily uncurled and put out its forepaws, stretched its neck, and when it had finished its milk, went back to sleep again in the bottle. If that didn't satisfy Jock, he had a further proof of the relationship between vivisectors and their animals, when in the evening the cat insisted on following John home, stalking him from behind the park railings most of the way, and finally having to be let into the house, for one could not leave the poor thing out in the wet and cold. I don't like cats in my kitchen!

The first time Jack was put on to speak at the boys' Scientific Society at Eton, a fatherly diver was sent down to help him to demonstrate the working of a diving helmet and respirator which Siebe Gormann's, the makers, lent for the evening.

After the *Diving Manual* had come out, the Admiralty asked John to call to receive its thanks. They were very cordial (I wish I had been invited!), and presented him with a huge silver salver as a token. He said the salver would have required a robust footman to carry it. I imagine he looked rather aghast for (as I heard the tale), one of the Admirals took him by the elbow and said, 'we quite understand; have you got a wife'? John said that he had. 'Well, you bet she knows what you want,' said the Admiral. 'Go together, and let her choose; they'll know how much you have to spend.' We followed the Admiral's directions, and found a paunchy elderly man who looked as if he might have been a naval purser. He had obviously done this sort of job for the Admiralty before. He held in the palm of one hand what was evidently the amount of the Admiralty grant, and whatever we settled to buy he made a note of, and his lips moved in calculations. I have always wanted a silver ship, it would be such a delightful thing to play with. I want one still, for the suggestion met with no approval. 'The Admiralty likes to give things on which an inscription can be engraved', our guide said. Then John thought that we really *did* want a mustard pot, and in the end we had candlesticks, a coffee pot, a salver, a big tankard which had room on the lid for a long inscription and our arms —luckily I had had these matriculated some years earlier— and finally a large useful tea urn—less useful nowadays when one turns on current if one wants to replenish the tea pot.

Of course John was tremendously interested in the ventilation of submarines, and delighted when the request came from the Admiralty that he should advise on this. They suggested that he should go in one which was on her trial run. We talked it over. One difficulty, he said, was that this was secret work, and he would need someone to look after the soda-lime. 'I can't just take any laboratory man.' Jack was standing on one foot, then on the other, as he did when he got really excited. I kept frowning, putting my finger to my lips. Then when John had got thoroughly worried about the laboratory man, I said casually, 'Why not take Boy?' Jack behaved with admirable restraint; his father said, 'Eh, what? Is he old enough?' and then suddenly, 'What's the formula for soda-lime?' Jack drew a deep breath and rapped out the formula. His father said, 'Well, that would simplify matters, but remember, you mustn't even *look* as if you knew anything about it.'

One more tale of the submarines. John often recommended the use of mice or small birds for detecting carbon monoxide content in the air. They had been in use for a good while in mines before they were taken on board submarines. He was being shown over a new submarine, and in the absence of senior officers, a quite young one was doing the honours. He saw John glance at a cage of canaries and said, 'Oh, not just pets, sir! I am told they give valuable information. When the atmosphere gets dangerously polluted they begin to sing very loudly and flap their wings.'

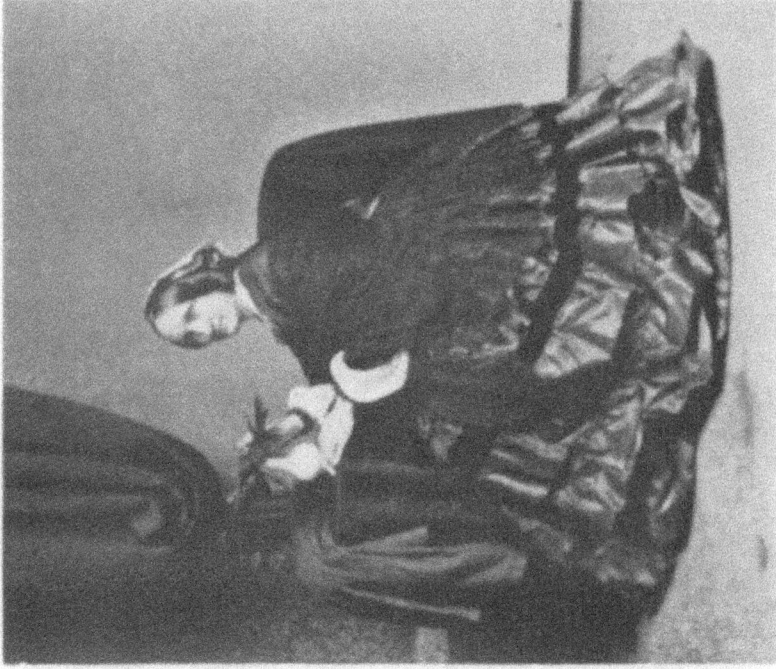

Mrs Davidson of Muirhouse

L.K.T. twelve years old

L.K.T. about eighteen years old

CHAPTER XVIII

My Political Interests

✤

Everyone is born—or, to the end of the last century, every-one *was* born 'Either a little Liberal or else a little Conserva-tive.' Nowadays there are so many cross-currents in the political sky, that a child might very well get a slant on life without feeling that it necessarily belonged to the Right or Left Wing in politics. Of course the Left Wing steals that thunder which appeals most to a child; it poses as the party of the under-dog.

Then, as to the first part of the question, in an obituary notice of the late Lord Altrincham (Sir Edward Grigg), he is stated to have had 'Imperial Service in his blood, a key to his life was his almost fanatical devotion to the Empire.' The author of the obituary notice makes two statements about his sub-ject and leaves it at that. I claim permission, in a very humble way, to make the same statement about my subject.

Of course there were times when I found everything very puzzling. When we were staying in London I went to tea with children who lived in Cromwell Road, and was apparently very gloomy after the party, and my father asked me what the matter was. I said I was sorry for those children, it must be horrid to live in Cromwell Road, you would always be thinking about King Charles. My mother said that I mustn't feel un-happy about King Charles. It all happened so long ago. My father talked about the shortcomings of the House of Stuart, and the high respect in which Cromwell and the Common-wealth—which I insisted upon calling the Interregnum—were held in Europe.

M

My Political Interests

It must have been much later that I began to feel very strongly about the Empire. It was before Sir George Parkin published *Round the Empire*, or I should have supposed that his hand had sown the seed. Anyhow, it was a long while ago, when I listened to my father discussing with a stranger the relations of Canada and the United States. For some time the papers had made references to these relations, and I think my father had either met or corresponded with Goldwin-Smith, and had been much impressed with his ideas, and inclined to think of him as a practical politician, who represented the people on the spot and understood local conditions. He held that the absorption of Canada by her more prosperous and populous neighbour, was only a matter of time. The rising generation of Canadians (a mere handful compared with their neighbours), had far more in common, much closer relations with them than with Europe, of which we were an integral part. 'They will profit from every point of view if of their own free will, they join the larger community. If they did this, they might make some good bargains which they would not be able to do if they waited till their economic condition worsened, and they had to appeal to the States *in forma pauperis*.' Their absurd frontier beyond the Great Lakes, a 'geographical abstraction' for hundreds of miles, showed the artificiality of the resistance to Union. 'Let them go with a goodwill—I wouldn't raise a finger to stop them,' he said.

I had been sitting on the floor, listening, and the last sentence had been my father's, so I jumped up and said, 'You can't do that! You can't let them go! Remember the United Empire Loyalists.' My father was cross, perhaps not unjustifiably—he said, 'Don't talk about what you don't understand, child. You'd better go away.' His companion laughed and asked, 'What do you know about the United Empire Loyalists?' 'Only that they gave up the homes their fathers had built and went to take up new lands and start all over again under the Flag,' I said. This sounds like a quotation, but I haven't an idea what it came from. 'All over again from scratch', the stranger nodded. I didn't like his voice or his looks, but possibly he might take my side, so I said, 'We can't fail people like these. We are all part of the Empire and the States are not!' My father said again, 'Go away and do not be silly', and the stranger said, with what I recognized as a sneer in his tone, 'Oh, the Empire!' I went out quickly enough to shed my tears in the passage, and I think it was from that day I felt my strongest loyalty was to the Empire. The Stuarts and Scotland were things to dream about, but the Empire was here and now; what could one do for it?

There are two things which I expected and which I meant to happen. I don't think I ever doubted that some day I should go to India, and that some day, somehow, I should be able to 'do something for the Empire'. A clear case of making dreams your master.

The Suez Canal was opened in 1869, when I was just old enough to take in that it was a very important occasion, and to ask more or less intelligent questions about it, but we had a cabinet full of Egyptian curios, which my father had brought home twenty years earlier, and I rather fancy that I visualized the great Monsieur de Lesseps surrounded by bird-headed figures like those on sarcophagus' lids, until from continual hearing of people going out or coming home via the Canal, the interest faded and it became the name for a journey, no more interesting and exotic than going north by the east coast.

Then in 1875 came Disraeli's purchase of the Canal Shares. 'Our way to the East safe for all time', my father said, adding after a while, 'you must not be surprised if France finds it hard to forgive England for acquiring a predominant interest in a great commercial concern created by a Frenchman, and at least partially financed by French money. They would naturally look askance at their own government's management of the problem, but to have this most outstanding national achievement filched away by an English Jew is really damnable luck.' I do not remember ever to have heard that our position on the Canal was secure only to the end of its hundred years' charter. It certainly was not till seventy-five of those hundred years had passed that the man in the street looked at the situation or, if he ever did so, his impulse was to look hurriedly away.

Surely even the Foreign Secretary must have murmured, 'Thank God, nothing like Fashoda!'

I only once saw de Lesseps, when he was in Edinburgh receiving an Honorary Degree from the university, which was celebrating its tercentenary by bestowing degrees on people whom it delighted to honour. He was a short man, looking squarer and broader on account of the palms of the French Academy embroidered on the lapels of his green coat. Clinging to his hand, or dancing round him, was an excited little French girl, in a Paris frock, a child of his third marriage. They said that he could not bear to be separated from the child, and I hope he got some happiness from her. The hauling down of his statue by the Egyptians in 1951 seems almost more revolting than their sabotaging of the canal. Has the present generation in Egypt never heard of that Dr. de Lesseps who lived there and fought an epidemic of bubonic plague almost single-handed?

Our cabinet of Egyptian curios was collected in the years 1850 and 1860 and was full of interest for adults as well as children. There were many cases of painted wood, and clay jars, containing a mummy bird or beast, a woman's hand with gilded finger-nails, children's feet (which my mother insisted should be 'decently buried') and above all, one large scarab with a piece of mummy-cloth still adhering to it, which my father believed to be of the same date as some of the earliest in the British Museum. One of the few writings he did not attempt to read was hieroglyphics, and he asked me to take it to Oxford and have it read for him. I had, unfortunately, to report that though the scarab was 'quite a good one' it was of a much later date than he believed, and he lost interest in the collection, but he did not doubt the genuineness of the clay jars. He had seen them unearthed by Egyptian workmen and had carried them straight to his dahabiah on the Nile. He said we might open them if we liked, and an Eton friend of Jack's, who had learned to read hieroglyphics, was sure that he could make a translation of any parchment that might be in them. Naomi was very keen to investigate, and they arranged to write a joint paper on what they might find. With great care and caution they opened a large jar and unrolled many yards of tape-like brown canvas, till they came on the parchment which wrapped the mummy, and found that it was a Coptic newspaper of the year 1886!

Some time, as a young woman, I listened to two 'old Indians' talking. They were talking over the dining-room fire after lunch. My father said, 'It was murder—a particularly brutal murder, too—but you say you wouldn't have hanged him?' 'Certainly not, as you say he was convicted against all the evidence.' 'Ah well, you're a Competition Wallah', my father said. The old gentleman looked aggrieved. He had earned a 'K' before he retired, and looked older than my father although he belonged to a more recent vintage of Indian Civilians. 'Of course you hold that against me,' he said, almost plaintively. 'Not in the least,' my father answered, 'but you remember the story—how S. said that within a week of the hanging he had enough evidence to justify the action twice over.' 'Nothing could have justified it—well, what did he find out?' 'It was not a case of finding out,' my father said, 'the evidence was shouted in the market place for all men to hear. The murderer's family complained that the money they had spent on providing witnesses for the defence had been wasted, for the fellow was hanged in spite of it all. S. had hopes that one of them, a Mahajhan, might try to recover some of his donation to the defence fund. If S. could have got him into court we would have had some fun.' 'Fun', said a sarcastic voice. 'Oh yes, *fun*,' my father repeated. 'When the family found that it could not recover the bribes it had given to witnesses, it proposed to sue them for giving false information—which the Collector Sahib had been too clever to believe. According to the murderer's family, the only person who got any kudos out of the affair was the Collector.' 'Well, put yourself in S's place. What would you have done?' My father pulled his moustache, considering his answer. 'I've often wondered,' he said, after a pause. 'I think I should probably have ended by letting him off on a plea of insufficient evidence for hanging, but I should have had him shadowed and on the slightest sign of—' 'It's not fair to have an innocent man shadowed,' the old gentleman said firmly. Then the door opened and Sir John's carriage was announced. My father stood talking to his guest while the old gentleman was helped into his coat. Then he came back to the fire murmuring, 'Competition Wallah'.

Of course Edinburgh went mad when Gladstone stood for the County.

I went to a packed meeting in the Music Hall, rather in fear and trembling, for we had all been told so much about his 'marvellous oratory' and 'compelling personality' that I feared that listening to him might put the answers to his arguments out of my mind! To my relief there was no argument, only an enormous amount of sound and fury. This must have been in the election when Gladstone was put up for Leith Burghs as well as for the County, so as to ensure his being returned to Parliament in the event of his losing the County election. His opponent at Leith was a Mr. Jacks, and the electors sang:

> '*The Scots of Leith their wits are nil,*
> *Their principles are lax,*
> *For they've returned dis—Union Bill,*
> *Instead of Union Jacks.*'

On the Sunday following the 1886 election, after which Gladstone became Premier for the third time, everyone was very much worked up, either belligerently triumphant, or beyond measure depressed, looking forward prophetically to the disasters which were before us. His party was hailing Gladstone as the G.O.M. To us he was the M.O.G.—Gordon had been murdered in January of the previous year.

In the West Kirk we, in the congregation, stood while 'wee MacGregor', the little minister, prayed for the church at home, for foreign missions, for the High Court of Parliament, for the Queen and all the Royal family, and for Her Majesty's Government. 'And especially, O Lord, for the old man at the head of that government. Give him grace, wisdom and discernment in his thoughts, his words, and his deeds. Especially, O Lord, give him wisdom, for sorely—sorely—he needs it.' The minister's hands fell heavily on the cushion in front of him. I think the whole congregation was moved. Looking up I saw round me upturned faces waiting motionless till the minister should raise his own from his cupped hands.

It was in the election of 1892 that Colonel Wauchope of Niddry opposed Gladstone in the County. My uncle was just starting to canvass a village street when an old Forty-second man stopped him to say: 'Ye needna fash yoursel wi' these houses, Colonel. We're a' Black Watch men, barring two-three, and I'll sort them.'

I think that Andy Wauchope would have been returned had he stood again—certainly if he had stood against any opponent less formidable than Gladstone himself. But the tragedy of Magersfontein intervened.

A radical of the name of Balfour was to stand (in Fife) against Beton of Balfour. The rhyme here ran:

> '*If Balfour of Beton*
> *Be beaten of Balfour*
> *He'll Beton of Balfour remain.*
> *But if Balfour be beaten*
> *By Beton of Balfour*
> *He's beaten of Balfour—that's plain.*'

When I moved to Oxford Mr. and Mrs. Jervis-Smith were among the first of the few people who made me feel at all at home there. It must have been Mrs. Jervis-Smith who took

183

me to a party of the local Women's Conservative Association, and told them that I was ready to work. I was coldly received. General Sir George Chesney had represented the City of Oxford since 1887 and I think it must have been when arrangements were being discussed about a meeting of his that I came up against the President of the Women's organization, Mrs. Max Muller. She gave me to understand that my presence at the party, to which I had been invited by a member, was really not welcome, and that my services would most certainly not be accepted.

I had already found my change of name irritating and inconvenient, but no-one had been directly rude to me till this German woman. She was said by her friends to be a favourite of the Queen's, and Oxford stood rather in awe of her. I was furious—too angry to think of anything adequate to say—and I started to walk out. Mrs. Jervis-Smith said various things, and came with me. Then the door opened, and our member was announced. I took a chance of his having a good memory for faces, and said, 'How do you do, General.' For once Providence was kind. He stared for a moment, and then said (or words to that effect): 'Miss Trotter! Bless my soul! What on earth are you doing in Oxford? How is Archie?' Archie was my beloved crippled cousin at Colinton, to whose father many politicians were in those days much beholden.

Afterwards the committee asked me to distribute notices and to do some canvassing, but I found the villa residents in the new roads north of Park Town even less easy to get on with than the people in the Old Town of Edinburgh, with whom I had failed before. I have always been a hopelessly bad canvasser.

I probably spoke inadvisedly with my tongue about Mrs. Max Muller. Anyhow Aunt Ghetal (Lady Burdon-Sanderson) thought so! But I only said what many people thought, and what really needed saying.

I was never actively engaged in local politics till Sir John Marriott's time. John called *him* an exemplary member! I think he even voted for him on at least one occasion, because he tried to get the late evening pillar box clearance in North

184

My Political Interests

Oxford restored after the war. We had had one until 1918, and it enabled anyone who had to go to London before the first delivery of letters to answer his morning correspondence on the same day—otherwise it might well take forty-eight hours. That service has not yet been resumed (in 1959). As far as I am personally concerned, though Sir John often disapproved of things I did or wanted to do, I remember that he gave me my only opportunity of meeting Sir Edward Carson, and for that I am grateful to him.

I cared a great deal for Lady Marriott, and when they moved up from Holywell to be among our nearest neighbours, we saw one another constantly. I cared even more for her daughter Cicely, and for her husband, the Bishop of Newfoundland, I had a very warm regard. Cicely agrees with me that we are firm friends, though there are scarcely a dozen subjects on which we see eye to eye.

During the early years of the century there was a very definite spirit of Imperialism moving over the face of the Empire. We found that what some of us had been told was an eccentricity of ours, was really the common faith of the common man, only he had not given his faith a name. The citizen who had Tariff Reform explained to him was heard to murmur, 'That is what I've always thought.' If he had served with Colonial troops in South Africa he might add, 'You are talking about Empire trade, are you not, sir?'

More people began to write and to talk about it. Mr. Amery published his leaflet 'Policy for Progress', Sir Hugo Cunliffe Owen addressed manufacturers, and a party of undergraduates, English and Colonial, calling themselves the Imperial Pioneers, spoke at small meetings in the industrial towns. These meetings and the keen young speakers did not get half the support they should have had. A few years later I should have known to whom to apply to get backing for them, but up to date I had always thought that the Conservative Central Office was the place to which to go for help and advice, and in this case there was 'nothing doing'.

My Political Interests

Quite the most valuable among these young speakers known to me personally was a Canadian who had lost both eyes in a skirmish on the veldt, and was known among his own people as 'Blind Trooper Mulloy'. We made friends when he came up to Balliol with a minute scholarship. I asked him once to join the children and me at Sennen Cove, and he insisted on coming with us to the Longships lighthouse. It was risky and I was rather scared, but the fishermen in the boat and the lighthouse keepers on the rock took him to their hearts, and he was shown everything up to the topmost reflector. He gave me some lessons in revolver shooting on the shore, rather to the alarm of the coastguards, till he protested to them that the weapon was much safer in his hands than in mine—which was possibly true. He was an easy guest to entertain, for there is always at least one unemployed fisherman ready for a gossip in any Cornish village street.

Lorne died in 1932 and I wrote his obituary notice for *The Oxford Magazine*. I quote this because what I say of him might stand as the confession of faith of the Imperial Pioneers. 'There was no St. Dunstan's then to help blinded men to preserve their independence . . . but Lorne Mulloy could fend for himself to a wonderful extent . . . and he at once started that strenuous campaign for Imperial Preference, which was the main interest of his life, and only interrupted by his recruiting work during the Great War. There must be many old Oxford friends who remember how the questions of Empire defence, Empire solidarity and Empire trade crept into his every conversation, and he had the fluent and persuasive eloquence of his Irish ancestry.

'He has said his *Nunc Dimittis* just when at long last there seems hope that the policy for which he worked during all the lean years may be implemented. It would have rejoiced his Canadian heart to know that the next Imperial conference is to meet at Ottawa.'

It was, alas, a false hope, but at least we never gave up.

Late in 1903 Joseph Chamberlain published a small book of his speeches on *Imperial Union and Tariff Reform*, and

almost for the first time we had in cold print and in plain
English, arguments by which 'the man in the street' might be
led to feel it his duty to ignore lesser subjects of disagreement
and to join any party which was ready to make a reality of the
dream Empire. Even if they only spoke on Tariff Reform, and
ignored the goal to which it was leading, it was an immense
step towards Empire Preference.

This is not a treatise on economics, and I will not write on
Tariff Reform, but I never ceased to work for it, though in a
very small and ineffectual way. I insisted that shops with
which I dealt should supply Empire goods, and I gave shoppers
lists of what to ask for in the shops. When a scare about dear
bread was started, I wrote a leaflet on the subject, and nearly
got into trouble by distributing it too near the date of a local
election, when my private printing of it might have had to
count as election expenses! And we founded the Imperialists'
Club, the existence of which I had entirely forgotten until I
came upon a copy of its constitution and rules a few days ago.
Here are its constitution and rules:

1. That this club be called the Imperialists' Club.
2. That there shall be an equal number of English and
   Colonial members, and that at no time shall more than
   a third of the Colonial members come from one Colony,
   or a third of the English members from one college.
3. That for the purpose of these rules no-one shall be considered an Englishman except a person born of English
   parents, or a Colonial unless he was born in a Colony,
   or been resident there for at least ten years.
4. That the host at each meeting shall act as President,
   and that the business of the Club be transacted by a
   provisional committee to consist of the secretary, and
   three advisory members, one of whom shall be a senior
   member of the University, one a Colonial and one an
   English undergraduate.

I believe I have seen somewhere the minutes of our first
informal meeting and a list of members. I was very anxious

not to be secretary, for I wanted it to be a really undergraduate society, but they said no other member would be acceptable to *all* the members, and the meetings would degenerate into general talk, whereas what we had planned was to have a paper which would arouse general discussion and, most important of all, I was the only club member who would not shortly be 'going down'.

The three advisory members were Charles ffoulkes (senior member of the university), William Grant (Colonial member) and Cecil Stollery (English undergraduate).

We sat on in the dining-room, talking, and one of the Colonial members and I took diametrically opposed views on a burning question of the hour—whether the Colonies should contribute to one Imperial navy, or whether each part of the Empire should raise and pay for its own independent navy. I was very strongly for the former plan, and fine as is the record of the Dominion's navies, I still see a great deal to be said for my point of view. But the question of the use to which the navies are to be dedicated, and still more the financial question, really settles this matter, as it does so many others. Then someone said, 'I move that the secretary speak on the naval situation.' 'And we'll all polish up our arguments against her,' said someone else. So I found myself let in for reading the club's first paper.

We met in Cecil Stollery's room in Tom Quad and talked for three hours, and the porter at Peckwater gate tried to refuse to let me out, though both Cecil and I had secured special permission from the Dean for me to remain after visiting hours, and the carriage was waiting outside Corpus, so that it was evident that I meant to get away before midnight!

Cecil Stollery's father, known as Colonel Stollery, was a business man, colonel of the London Territorials, in whom he took a passionate interest. Once when they were having some celebration—I think it had to do with his fifty years' service with the regiment—he invited me to a dinner with them, and I met a number of well-intentioned young business men, who somehow were not as easy to get on with as young Regulars would have been, but I have the impression that they were very much in earnest. Cecil certainly was so, and whatever profession he had followed, Empire politics would have occupied a large part of his thoughts. In 1914 he got his commission and was killed in action.

I suppose everyone who receives the announcement that he has been awarded a decoration receives along with the announcement an intimation of where and when he should go to receive it, and he is told also that if he is unable to 'attend', the insignia of the Order will be sent to him. I certainly was going to 'attend'. I had not seen the King since his coronation day, and not at close quarters since we met in the Black Forest.

I was staying with my sister-in-law in Westminster when the day came, and the question arose, how I was to reach Buckingham Palace. We cannot have had a car at the time, or it would have been quite simple. I thought John might have offered to walk there with me—this is the sort of occasion when I think one needs a man!—but it did not occur to him. Then Esmé happened to be in town, and she said she would drive me. Personally I should have found it embarrassing, having dropped my fare, to park among all those big cars and chauffeurs, and to wait till my fare reappeared; but Esmé is like Naomi in this respect; she gets fun out of what I should find an awkward situation. She drove me there in her queer little car which had been a joke among her Oxford friends for years, and after the ceremony she was ready at once when 'Mrs. Haldane's carriage' was called for. It looked comic emerging from among all the big cars!

Meanwhile I had had a most interesting time. Among the crowd I only saw one person I knew, Professor d'Arcy Thompson of Dundee. His beard would have been unmistakable anywhere, but he evidently did not recognize me. To speak to him I should have had to break through a double row of men and it did not seem worthwhile to disturb the march of the procession, so I engaged the good offices of two women in front of me, and they kept my place in the queue when from time to time I sat down for a rest on the raised wainscot of the gallery. From the remarks which they made to one another I gathered that they thought my 'nerve was failing', and they assured me that I need not be flurried! The idea that one might be 'leg-weary' apparently did not occur to them, though I gathered that they were there on account of their work for hospitals. They became agitated, and began to fidget with their clothes when we got near the front of the queue, and I watched to see what I should have to do when my turn came. It was obvious that one was piloted in, and when one's moment with the King was over, a courteous hand pointed the way out to seats that were ready for us. It was beautifully stage-managed.

Then, as I was being piloted in, the wretched woman in front of me ignored the guiding hand which was showing her out, turned round and ran full tilt towards the place from which she had come! We might easily have collided.

Now did I, or did I not, catch the King's eye? I think I did, and that we were both smiling. I stood to have my badge pinned on, and—I do not know whether other people did it, I had not noticed—I held out my hand and the King shook it. I said 'Thank you, sir', and made way for the next comer. Whether it was correct for me to speak or not I am not sure, but I have no doubt that the handshake was not a recognized part of the ceremony. It would have been too much to ask the King to shake hands with perhaps several hundred people whenever a presentation of this kind occurred. I know what my right hand felt like when John gave a dinner to two hundred members of the mining profession and I 'received' for him!

Just after I wrote the above I opened a packet of old letters, most of them from overseas friends. I should like to have shown some of them to whoever was responsible for the wording of my 'award', which read 'For work among Colonial students'. It had irritated me. I hoped that my friends overseas did not feel that I looked on our contacts as 'work'—in the sense that one speaks of working in an institution or for a society. One man wrote, 'It made me glad, as it must have made countless others in all parts of the world this morning, to see that the King had honoured you. It seemed in a way an acknowledgment on our behalf of the friendship and enjoyment offered to us at Cherwell.' Another letter touched me deeply. It was from Mrs. William Grant, daughter of my old friends Sir George and Lady Parkin. She writes, 'My congratulations on the honour done you by the King. I am one who knows the immense value of your work for the Empire, and for all human kindness and friendship, a work which because of these qualities goes far beyond any royal recognition, but we rejoice in that too! I think of my father and mother, and of William, and of what pleasure it would have given them.' A young one writes, 'I know I am writing as one of a very large number of Dominion boys whose time at Oxford was made much happier by knowing you.'

So the wording was obviously quite right!

CHAPTER XIX

South Africa

※

We were spending most of the Christmas vacation in Scotland, as we usually did till after my father's death. My father spoke across the breakfast table, continuing a somewhat acrimonious conversation of the previous evening—'I don't know why you are always harping on Imperial preference and Empire this, that and the other. You might be a German woman boosting her new Reich, which she believes to be a survival of the Holy Roman Empire. The good old United Kingdom was good enough for me—we kept the nations more or less in order till Dizzy got talking, and called the Queen 'Empress', aping the Germans. That fellow Rhodes is capable of doing something of the same sort, and you'll call it Empire building,' he growled as the butler came in with the morning papers, and I got up and read the news over my father's shoulder. It was 30th December, 1895, and what we read was the first full report of the Jameson Raid.

Looking back on what I heard said, and on the comments of some of the papers in the early weeks of 1896, I remember that the blame for the fiasco was laid far more heavily on the Uitlanders than on Jameson. Unless he was assured of quite reliable support from the citizens, what sane man would attempt to take a town with a force of 600 horse? It was not even as if a surprise attack had been intended! It was felt that the Uitlanders *must have* let Jameson down. It was presently asserted that they *had done so*, and that Jameson, an Edinburgh man and popular, was being made a scapegoat for the

failure of the 'aggressive policy' of the South African Government. If the whole government was not involved, at least
Rhodes, the Premier, had planned and instigated the raid, and
he was now trying to pass on the odium for its failure to his
friend. It was this apparent meanness which roused most of
the indignant comments. It is easier to blame a man for falling
short in the first of the domestic virtues than to attempt to
grasp the ethics of his policy! When Rhodes resigned from the
Cabinet, the man in the street said self-righteously, 'You see
that even South African millionaries cannot stand for that
kind of thing. They have chucked Rhodes, and high time too!'

Meanwhile my father was growling over the breakfast table,
'Those bastard Englishmen! What can you expect?' and I
was asserting that we must learn more before we turned
against our own side, even though it included such an unfortunately large number of bastard Scots and Jews.

Then Granville Egerton, with an hour to spare on his way
to the West coast, came in, and my father said to him, 'These
women! *She* thinks there is justification for this scandalous
performance.' Granville said, 'You don't really? I should not
have believed it of you.' 'You would have thought differently
about it if it had been successful,' I answered. 'But it could
not possibly be successful. It was too utterly silly. It is the
silliness of the thing which gets my goat.' 'Then it is the way
the thing was done, not the intent at the back of the action
to which you object,' I said. This was unfair criticism, but
Granville was being superior and irritating. 'I object to the
whole damned silly business,' he growled, adding, 'and so
will you when you have had time to think about it.'

When Cecil Rhodes resigned as Premier he kept his seat and
continued actively to support every scheme for the good of the
country, and much of his most brilliant work for South Africa
was accomplished during the years of his political eclipse. He
also carried on quietly taking Oxford examinations one after
the other, until he had accumulated enough Passes to sit for a
degree, and Oxford heard nothing more of him which concerned her more than it did every part of the Empire, till in

1899 the Vice-chancellor, Sir William Anson, proposed that an Honorary Degree should be conferred on him; and I cannot help thinking that Sir William must have rather enjoyed the storm which the proposal raised in the university dovecote. Some of the older generation were genuinely hurt and shocked, and others thought it desirable to appear to be so, and one heard of rifts in senior common rooms.

At the Encaenia (the ceremony at which Honorary Degrees are conferred), I looked from my humble position among the the crowding and whispering occupants of the ladies gallery and was interested to see empty seats among those of the mighty. Balliol, for instance, was unrepresented among the Heads of Colleges. It was pretty obvious that Caird would have no inclination to join in paying honour to Rhodes, but he was not at all typical of Balliol Fellows, and one wondered what line Jowett would have taken in the case, still more, perhaps, if we could have looked into the future, would we have speculated about the reactions of Lindsay, or A. L. Smith, or that most delightful of Masters, Strachan Davidson. I am glad that I once met Jowett, though I cannot record that he made a *bon mot* for my benefit!

At the Encaenia Rhodes had a triumphant reception. His project of a transcontinental railway could hardly fail to strike the imagination of the young, however little politically-minded they might be, and he was greeted with shouts from the gallery of 'Cape to Cairo', 'through trains', 'reserved seat for me, please', 'we are all coming, sir', 'all red route from Cape to Cairo'—it did one's heart good to listen to them!

Recipients of Honorary Degrees are, as a matter of course, invited to dine at the Christ Church gaudy on the eve of the Encaenia, and all Fellows have the right of dining with them. The Prince of Wales had been a student, and was now a Fellow of Christ Church, and he, it was reported, asked Dean Paget to seat Rhodes next to him at dinner. This made it more difficult for the 'unco guid' to voice their protests if they had planned to do so.

I do not remember whether it was on this, or on some other

festive occasion when good order was required, that it was thought well for undergraduates to be prevented from crowding into the Christ Church quad and demonstrating. The porter was instructed to admit by Tom Gate only persons arriving by carriage, as it was thought the diners would be. The undergraduates heard of this, and hired a vehicle which was drawn up at the gate. They opened both its doors and entered by one and left by the other. The quad became somewhat congested and lively, but not dangerously so. The porter had attended to his orders, and the well-trained Oxford police had smiled.

The Haldane family was, in the parlance of the day, 'pro-Boer', that is to say, it greeted our disasters with 'serve them right' or 'what else did you expect?' When the troubles in the concentration camps were reported, John refused to listen to reasons why the camps were created. It seemed as if he were deliberately closing his mind to any reasoning on that matter, and could only talk about 'inhumanity' and 'starving women and children'. Emily Hobhouse was a heroine, and when Lord Roberts asked Lady Knox (Alice Dundas of Arniston, wife of Colonel Knox, who commanded the guns at Ladysmith), to investigate and report on the conditions in the camps, he thought this entirely unnecessary, and merely an effort to discredit Miss Hobhouse's report. He wrote to the papers with advice about the number of calories each woman and child ought to receive, and said that he was quite ready to go out to South Africa to see that his advice was followed. I do not know, but I rather think that his brother deprecated his doing this.

Lois tells me that she knows nothing of this phase of the South African War. Has it not yet reached the history books, or have the two 'Great Wars' entirely overshadowed the events of the South African War? The concentration camps were started when it was found that so long as the Boer women remained on the farms we should not bring the war to an end. The women were able to signal to their men any movements of our troops, besides keeping them supplied with food and ammunition. Farms which had asked for protection, and had hoisted the white flag, were responsible for so many tragedies that the removal of their inhabitants was the only way of dealing with them which commended itself to our army. Most other armies would have adopted a less civilized method, and would probably have met with less criticism than did our very 'Christian' method of conducting a war.

The army supplied the concentration camps with much which it could well have used itself in the matter of food and equipment, of tents, doctors and nurses. It could not prevent an epidemic of measles spreading among children from the Bush Veldt, who had never before been subjected to even the everyday contacts of school life.

Afterwards Lady Knox's flat in London was full of South African relics—a Boer flag taken by her husband, and curious pieces of violently coloured needlework given to her by some of the Boer women—I believe she was very popular among them for she could be wonderfully understanding and kind—but she never let a 'pro-Boer' criticism pass unchallenged, or a carping reference to our soldiers go unanswered.

I missed her very much when she died. Her little flat had been a refuge for me as it was for lonely South Africans. One never knew whom one might meet there, but she never moved the captured Boer flag from its place by the Colonel's photograph.

Shortly after the Kaiser's war there had been a meeting of Empire politicians in London. General Herzog was in Oxford for a day or two, visiting his son, and had been talking to John in the study—quite possibly they had had a private tea there, as occasionally happened on Sundays when there was a special crowd round the hall tea table, and the Senior Partner thought us noisy and frivolous. They came out of the study together, and he said General Herzog had come to say good-bye. I got up to shake hands. He seized mine and stuffed it as nearly as possible into his waistcoat pocket, saying that his stay in England had modified many of his views—changed them in fact. 'I can assure you that my government will never now pass legislation which will grieve your heart,' he said. I answered, 'I shall believe that when I see it, General Herzog.' His cab for the station was waiting, and the parlourmaid with his coat held ready to help him into it. The Senior Partner who never seemed inclined to hurry himself to catch a train, hurried General Herzog off, and came back to the hall to say indignantly to me, 'How can you be so rude!'

The first thing that happened after Herzog's return to the Cape was one of the constantly recurring filibusters about the Flag. Herzog's son had gone to study in Holland and removed to Oxford partly, at least, because the Dutch made fun of his pronunciation of their language. Here he joined the Unattached Students, and I heard that he was gathering an admiring circle who listened to the political utterances of the only South African they knew. I talked to John about this, and he agreed that young Herzog would be in more wholesome and suitable company, and see more of the kind of English with whom we hoped he would work when he returned to South Africa, if he became an ordinary undergraduate. The Warden agreed and offered to take him at New College. Pressure was brought to bear on him and he moved in, but he told me later that this had been 'a bad mistake', he was happier as a non-collegiate!

CHAPTER XX

Esk and Polly

❊

Harry, Lord Melville, bred small Scotch terriers, said to be lineal descendants of the little dogs which appear in most of the pictures of the Scottish kings at Holyrood, and when I married he promised to give me one when I was ready for it. When Jack was about two years old I thought it was time for him to have a dog living with him, and I reminded Harry Melville of his promise. Shortly afterwards a beautiful puppy arrived. He was escorted by a highly superior man from whom I found it impossible to gather whether his full fare had been paid and what kind of tip he had the right to expect. I went to consult John, and begged him to come, just for five minutes, to settle the matter, but John was busy. 'It's your dog. Oh, give the man a glass of whisky and get rid of him', was all the help I got from him!

I forget on what terms I parted with Esk's escort, but John took to the little dog just as warmly as Jack did, and never spoke of him as 'your dog' except when he got lost, or misbehaved in some other silly way, and he did not eat more slippers or do more serious gardening than the average puppy—while I had to take severe measures with Jack who, though he might have refused his own breakfast, was always ready to share Esk's bread and milk. After I had had him for three years, we went to Scotland for Naomi's birth, and had to leave him with our cook, and Lady Burdon-Sanderson's coachman, who promised to keep an eye on him. When we came home I thought he looked thin and unbrushed, but he welcomed

Esk and Polly

Jack joyfully and at once wanted to sit on my lap, where there was not much room for a small dog as well as for a large baby, and he refused to accept the biscuit around which I folded her tiny fingers, and made her hand out to him, and the next morning he sat watching while I dressed her. I started to feed her and he growled—I spoke severely to him—probably too angrily, for I was frightened. He went on growling, showing his teeth and trying to get onto my lap. I pushed him away with my foot, and spoke harshly, but he continued to growl, his eyes fixed on the baby. I sent for the vet, who knew Esk. He had looked after him for me once when he had cut a foot, and was a kindly old man, said to be the best vet in the neighbourhood. 'You can't let this go on,' he said at once. 'Shall I take him away?' Then, when I suppose I looked horrified, he added, 'There is one thing which I should certainly try if he—or they—' he smiled, 'were mine. I should draw his big carnivors. Look at his mouth. He can do well without them.' 'You could give him chloroform?' 'I'd not dream of doing it without having him well under,' he answered. 'Then do it,' I said. 'Could you take him with you at once? It will be worse for both of us the longer we put it off.' That evening I got a note from the vet to say that Esk had died under the anaesthetic.

When John came home he was very angry. Someone at the laboratory had got hold of a highly coloured version of the story, and he accused me of having Esk sacrificed 'in a foolish panic'. I'd had no business to let such a thing be done without consulting him. He did not believe in any danger to the baby. 'Nonsense! You don't understand dogs, and as to that old woman who says he is a veterinary surgeon! You said you were fond of Esk, but you have been cruel to him.'

Anyhow, I ought not to have done it without his sanction! 'You always said that he was *my* dog' is the only answer I remember to have made.

Shortly after Esk's tragic death I agreed when Jack asked to be allowed to accept a more or less fox terrier puppy which someone offered him. I stipulated that it should be thoroughly house-trained, and was of course assured that this was so.

199

Esk and Polly

Jack was devoted to 'Spot', but he never wanted to wash or brush or dose him. John highly approved of Spot, but he also declined to take any share in looking after him, and to the end he always urged me to 'make nurse see to that'—and supposing nurse demurred, as she generally did, what next?

Even out of doors I can do better without a dog than with one. If it doesn't bark at strangers opening the front gate it is not a watchdog; if it does it makes a horrid noise—and a large dog, a beautiful golden setter for example, or an Irish wolfhound, which licks a child's face as it sits in its perambulator, is obeying a natural and kindly instinct, but do you really like it to be done?

Polly, however, was a large-size Macaw, green, with shades of red on his chest, and an eighteen inch tail, of deep blue and red. He had lived for some years with Alec and Alys Trotter, and had been given to them by people who had had him for over thirty years, so he must have been at least forty when I had him. When they moved to a London house where the only convenient place for Polly to perch was in the hall opposite the front door, and he screamed every time that the door was opened, he became too much for the neighbourhoood. 'But you can't send him to the zoo, I'm sure he'd hate it.' 'Oh, couldn't we?' said Naomi. So I begged them to bear with him a little longer, and I would see what I could do.

Meanwhile we had moved into Cherwell, and Naomi had the bad accident which kept her in bed for weeks, and on the sofa for months. Then Polly was a god-send. Jack and Gordon Stark brought him back with them after a visit to London. He had no cage and they carried him 'just like that'. What the rest of the third-class carriage thought of it I don't know; it must have been a noisy journey—but he was perfect with Naomi. He could walk about on her bed without shaking it, and he sat beside her pillow saying 'Ka-wa-ka waka' quite gently, but he screamed when her father came in to see her, and indeed at most other visitors, so that he often had to be banished to his perch in the dining-room. The worst of it was that he could climb down quite easily from his perch and then always made

200

for the highest point he could reach—usually the top of a door; and I was afraid that he would be killed if the door shut itself, or was shut by someone who did not realize that he was there, or trusted to his getting down quickly. Polly's movements were usually very deliberate, and he was always at his crossest and noisest with John. When he was alone in a room he expected anyone coming in to speak to him. Then he would answer and possibly ask to be taken off his perch, or climb down and come and sit on the floor near his visitor. But John never spoke to him, so, after waiting for a while, and waltzing about on his perch asking for attention, Polly would give a loud 'Ka-wa-ka waka' or two and John would throw a slipper at him. Then there was a row: Polly could scold! Or John threw *The Times* at him, and was indignant if Polly tore it up. He and Jack both got bitten once or twice, but he never hurt Naomi or me, except once, when I was going up the road with him on my shoulder, and he slipped and took hold of my arm to stop himself falling. I had on a muslin blouse and he drew blood! The funniest thing I ever saw was one morning when shouts for help brought me to the dining-room and I found John in his socks at the top of a step-ladder, trying to rescue a bird which had come in and was bashing itself against the window; and two steps below him was Polly, very talkative and pleased with himself, pecking at his heels, and if he could fit his beak into the wool, hauling at a sock. John, kicking feebly, could only beg, 'Will someone come and take away this ferocious bird?'

People who dined with us, the Poet Laureate for instance, admired the way Polly behaved at dinner. He knew that he must keep quiet until finger bowls were put on, then he began to climb from his perch and came and stood on the floor beside me, regurgitating little balls of partially digested food. This was most unpleasant to watch, and I used to scold him for it, until I learned that it was an offering of love. Presently I took him on my lap and he had a long drink from my finger-bowl, after which he dipped in his head and had a good splash over my next-door neighbour, but, this being a man, it didn't matter.

Esk and Polly

In summer we sometimes took him into the garden, but he was never really happy out of doors. Small birds terrified him —they were apt to mob him—and he made frantic efforts to catch butterflies, but of course never succeeded. I once put him on a branch of one of the walnut trees, and true to form he climbed to the highest point he could reach, but instead of coming down sensibly, he screamed till someone had to risk his neck among the small branches and go up to help him.

I felt sure that Polly would not be properly looked after if I died, so I left in my will that he should be cremated with me, but he died first, of some kind of fit. I heard him screaming in the dining room, and found him running about on the floor, dragging one wing. I picked him up and held him close, and after a bit he quieted down. A few days afterwards the same thing happened and he died in my hands.

The war was then a few weeks old and I found with surprise that no-one in the household seemed to be even aware that Polly was missing; but for a long time men back on leave would look into the dining-room and say, 'Hullo! Where's Polly?'

In those days, whenever we went to the zoo—the Burdon-Sandersons used to give us their Sunday admission tickets— Naomi used to make for the macaws' quarters and begin to talk to them. One of the attendants nearby came up to caution her —'Don't go near that bird, missy, he is a savage one', but after she had talked to him for a while she would hold out her arm and the macaw would step down onto it and stay contentedly, answering her in different forms of 'Ka-wa-ka waka', to the astonishment of the keepers.

CHAPTER XXI

Building Cherwell

❄

After my father's death my mother startled me by saying she expected us to come to live in Edinburgh. 10 Randolph Crescent was now *my* house—why should we not live in it? We had taken it for granted that, unless she preferred to have a small establishment of her own, with perhaps a Keane niece to live with her, she would come to live with us, and the idea of migrating to Edinburgh certainly never occurred to us. It would have upset John's life altogether; I certainly had no such fond recollections of living there that I should wish to renew them; and when it came to the point, we found that what my mother really cared for at the moment was to live where she would see most of the children. She even suggested that there were good preparatory schools near Edinburgh to which Jack might be transferred! Anyhow the period of consideration did not last long, and she and her maid came up to Oxford with me, and we did our best to make her happy during the last years of her life. She was quite devoted to John, and would have liked him to come to her room for a 'nice, quiet, comfortable talk' at a definite hour every day. That would have been impossible to arrange in any busy man's life, but she expected less of him than she did of me, so he disappointed her less. She adored Jack but was intensely critical of him, and still more of his school and of Naomi's attendance at it ('a rough school for boys'). This was 'a constant source of deep concern' to her.

It was quite obvious that 4 St. Margaret's Road was not a

large enough house for three generations, ourselves, the children and my mother, but I was sorry for John who had all he wanted there, and was most disinclined to waste time once again house-hunting.

I should have liked to move into the country, and there was a small country place available beyond Besselsleigh, with a fairly roomy house, and, as far as I remember, a little copse and a few fields and a cottage for the gardener and chauffeur. But John said it was much too far from the laboratory and from the station (his work took him more and more to London), so we didn't even consider it seriously, though I felt reasonably aggrieved when at last we got a hundred-year lease of land from St. John's and built Cherwell that this should cost more than the little freehold country place! We only heard of this land through a local builder. It wasn't really 'ready for development' and I don't know how Mr. Gardner got a lien on it—but as he had done so, it appeared obvious that he should be given the job of building on it.

When he heard that we were not having any other architect, my cousin Charlie ffoulkes expressed his horror at our simplicity. John wasn't really so simple, but he thought he had had enough trouble about it already and said, 'Well, well, well, the man got you the land—you have to let him build on it,' and building was begun before he had really taken in all the implications. And Mr. Gardner felt no qualms about his own qualifications.

One change we made as we saw the walls go up. In about half the house the height of the rooms was reduced by twenty inches, which saved us £200 on the building, but it necessitated steps on two bedroom floors where the higher and lower levels joined.

Another and more serious trouble faced me later. I knew nothing about electric light, and our wiring was all tidily hidden behind the wainscotting and looked a neat job. Then one day I smelt singeing, and found a piece of wainscot in the hall to be very hot. I sent for the City Engineer, who condemned the layout. He had nothing against 'concealed wiring' provided it was 'properly insulated'. However I consulted Alec Trotter about this, and he said emphatically that for safety, electric wires should be carried in a metal tube and not packed in sawdust behind a wooden board. So I demanded this, and the City Engineer said I had a perfect right to do so. By this time I could with the greatest pleasure have made things disagreeable for Mr. Gardner! It was long past the date he had promised to have the house ready. John was at Cloan, but saying that the study *must* be ready for him as he had work to do. Jack was at Cloan with him, Naomi with her grandmother at Felixstowe, and I was inhabiting one of the maids' rooms at the top of the house, and trying each day to get the workmen moved out of one room more. Also the furniture was due to arrive from Scotland. There were still workmen in the house when it did so in three railway vans, which so tore up Blackhall Farm Lane that the authorities were bound to agree that a properly engineered road was needed. Our horse and carriages had arrived before this was finished, but in our own interests we had to keep within our gates for what seemed a long time.

Jenner's, the Edinburgh firm, made a splendid job of moving the furniture. It was practically the whole contents of No. 10 Randolph Crescent, and only one wineglass was cracked in the whole consignment, and they offered eloquent apologies for that! I had difficulty about siteing the furniture. We had a grandfather clock, a wedding present from the Burdon-Sandersons, which I destined for the hall, and the one from Edinburgh was put in the corner of the drawing-room, where it looked very nice, but the man from Jenners said, 'And what will Mistress Trotter say when she sees the hall clock in the drawing-room?' What she *did* say was, 'My dear, what is the hall clock doing in the drawing-room?'

At Cherwell there had been stables in part of the land we turned into a garden, and various curios came to light there— old coins which the workmen annexed, and some very early clay tobacco pipes. Rob Makgill managed to rescue several of these unbroken or only partially broken, and took them to the Pitt-Rivers Museum to get them dated. He sent one in by the porter, and waited for a verdict. Presently the Curator came out, brimming over with enthusiasm, and said the pipes were Elizabethan and exactly what they required to fill in a gap in their historical series of pipes. He was immensely obliged! Rob didn't like to say that he hadn't intended to donate them, and he had to be content with the next best one, which he took out to New Zealand. I have only the fragments that remained.

The actual position of Cherwell depended on three splendid old walnut trees. The architect said that the ground sank to the north, 'But it will be quite easy to take down one of those trees. We don't want to have to raise the ground level for our foundations.' He was quite surprised to find that we minded about those trees, which made all the difference to the house, more especially because the oak and two horse chestnuts which we planted were still only nursery garden specimens. I really cared for those trees. We always had walnuts for ourselves and our friends—perhaps not quite so good as the best specimens from a London shop (it was sometimes hard to get enough sun to dry them properly, and of course they stained my hands and clothes) but they were our own home-grown walnuts! Then in 1918 we had the most phenomenal crop. Tired of stooping and picking up, I once counted how many I could drop into my basket while standing still on one spot. It came to over a hundred. During the war there was a general invitation to the patients at Somerville military hospital to walk in and have a rest; and that autumn, walnuts, salt and crackers were always on the hall table for them. The following spring I began to feel worried about the trees, especially the one nearest the house. There was very little bloom on it and in the autumn I scarcely had a basketful of nuts, and they were small, and either dried up or slimy. I got one of the workmen from the School of Forestry, and asked whether anything could be done for the trees. 'You'll be asking me to cut them trees down next summer, Mum', was all he would say. It was two years before the first one had to go, and the two others

followed the same course a year later. By that time the School
of Forestry was in action again, and they told us that walnuts
were not long-lived trees under the best of circumstances.
Cultivating them, no-one could feel that he was planting for
posterity, as in the case of oaks or elms. They said that walnuts began to go as soon as the roots reached water level, and
water level in Oxford is not very deep. They guessed the age
of the three trees to be about 250 years, and offered to cut
them down and cart the wood away for us without charge.
When we saw how rotten the trunks were, I asked if they
wanted to stick to their offer, and they said that they did, they
wanted specimens of walnut wood, and also to do some experiments on the rotten parts. I planted several nuts, and when I
last saw them they seemed to be growing into quite satisfactory young trees.

Within a few weeks of our move into Cherwell, on her tenth
birthday, Naomi met with a very bad accident. Her pony,
which the coachman was supposed to be holding, shied and
threw her. She never loosened her hold on the reins, but the
safety stirrup did not act, she was dragged and had a com-
pound fracture of the leg. From then for many months she
was of necessity the centre of my thoughts and activities.
The twenty-four hours of the day were not enough for me to be
able to devote to my mother as many hours as she wished!
She had been used to running her house on very different lines
to any which I had been able to adopt, and she found it very
difficult to 'make allowances'. The fact that many of John's
actions and opinions were passed with a resigned, 'Well, I
hope he knows best' did not help me much!

During the months when the surgeon could not give me any
at all sanguine hope that Naomi would not always be lame, my
friend Miss Josephine Phelps was an enormous help and
standby. My mother admired her and took her advice about
all health problems both for herself and Naomi, and she was
indefatigably kind. She told me afterwards that Mr. Symonds,
the surgeon, told her that she might 'have a try' at loosening
the child's joints, which seemed to be permanently stiff, but

he 'gave her six hours before Mrs. Haldane shows you the door, she's never satisfied'. This last was true. I never was satisfied with the nursing. We had two nurses, so that one alone should never try to move the child, but I caught them gossiping in her room when they changed over during the night, and making up a good fire quite regardless of the patient, who ought to be asleep; and she would lie waiting for anything she wanted until Miss Phelps or I came to do it for her, rather than let either of the nurses touch her.

My mother-in-law, Mrs Haldane

My mother

My husband

CHAPTER XXII

Cherwell River before 1914

❄

There is one thing about the Burdon-Saundersons which I shall always remember unto them for good—they lent us their share of a boat on the Cherwell. For its size the little Cher seems to have occupied an inordinately large place in our lives. At the end of the century there were no boats on hire above the Rollers, and only one private boathouse containing nine boats, each of which was shared by two households, so that even if all the boats were out on the same afternoon, you could not encounter more than eight families on the river. It was not till quite ten years later that the Tims' family built its wharf, and started hiring out boats and punts. When this happened, we all felt much aggrieved. Small boys at Lynam's made exciting plans to scuttle or blow up the boats! When I was told about this I said that unfortunately Mr. Tims was a very rich man and would be able to replace each fleet, however often they managed to scuttle it. About the same time Lady Margaret Hall built their boathouse, and the ladies' bathing place was started.

During summer term, a few undergraduates used to come up over the Rollers, but this was not a common custom till much later. On an evening in June, when we heard songs and bugle calls coming up the river, we knew that B.N.C. was having its annual picnic. Later the same night the same sounds, with a couple of gramophones added, came down again, and someone would say, 'There will be plenty of gating at B.N.C. tonight.'

Cherwell River before 1914

The Town never appeared during term, and only very occasionally in vacation. Until Tims put numbers of punts on the river, everyone rowed. There seemed to be plenty of room for rowing, though the channel was in places much narrower than it is now, and navigation was much more exciting, when there were interesting snags and rather deceptive backwaters, into which the cox who knew his business could inveigle an unsuspicious crew which was pressing him. It was quite possible to steer round 'the great seven-pronged snag' while your adversary rushed madly into its branches and had his rudder unshipped! The first thing which the Thames Conservancy Board did when it took charge of the Cher was to lop all the 'dangerous' willow branches that made cool, shady places in hot weather, and to straighten the channel and drag up the snags. Its management of the weirs has saved us from a great deal of flooding, but like many other modern improvements, it has made life less adventurous.

John really enjoyed rowing and we constantly borrowed the Burdon-Sanderson's boathouse key. At first it was returned to them as soon as we landed, but after a time it tended to remain in John's pocket, till one day an agitated maid came to retrieve it. After a frantic search I felt sure that it must be in John's pocket, and he was at the laboratory. I could run in those days, and the key was returned not very much too late.

It was another story when, many years later, the key of New College Tower could not be found. Only Fellows and people on business were ever entrusted with that key, and this time the bellringers wanted it to get in to practise. Someone remembered that John had been seen on the tower and they sent to me for help—but John was at Cloan and the bellringers could not practice!

When the punts began to crowd the Cher John almost gave up going on it, but in the children's early years, 'tea up the river' was a constant entertainment. I took one kettleful of tap water, but by the time we came to our second cups, it had always been refilled from the Cher. I minded this the less as Jack and Naomi always drank milk! I was not allowed to take a spirit lamp, or a bit of dry wood to start the fire, and when John had once lighted it with the damp sticks which everyone else said were useless, he shooed them away to collect branches, and woe betide anyone who carelessly threw one on to the flame he was cherishing!

When Jack came up from Eton, and later, when he was at college, we often took several boatloads up the river for tea or supper, but his father did not really like these evenings, and stuck to the ritual of the fire, and I doubt whether he was ever happy in a punt. My mother gave us our punt 'The Grandmother', and Jack and Naomi each had their own canoe. I very well remember a Sunday when a young Canadian, who had lunched with us, offered to teach Naomi to paddle; I dare say the 'Ship of Fools' was lighter than he expected, but he was scornful when warned that the wind was high—and they upset. I was in the punt close behind them and heard him say, 'I'll rescue you', and Naomi's curt, 'No you won't'. A moment later she had swum to the punt and was untying the strings of her hat and handing it to me, saying: 'It's my Sunday hat. Now I'll get the cushions.' The poor young man was much upset.

I also remember another Sunday afternoon, when she and I were out alone in her canoe and were chased by some Lynam boys, friends of hers, probably. She said, 'We won't be caught, we won't be bumped', and pulled into the bank, rather too hard and suddenly. The bows of the canoe went up as she jumped ashore and the stern went under water. I walked ashore too muddy and wet to start afresh, but paddling home we met three or four parties of friends. I remember saying to the slightly censorious Lane Pooles, 'For goodness sake don't tell my mother!' Granny always foretold disaster if Naomi and I went out by ourselves, and she was sitting out on the tennis court bank, from whence she could see the boathouse. I landed at the back of the stables, by my newly-planted willow saplings, and Naomi took the canoe home, and in answer to her grandmother's question, replied truthfully that I had been in a hurry and had gone in by the back door. The episode made me feel pleasantly young!

Cherwell River before 1914

When I think of the Cher in its old days, several well-remembered faces come back to me. Lord and Lady Russell were as keen about the river as John was. I liked him, but was not to be persuaded into a boat on a foggy October Sunday morning, though he called me 'a soft sybarite'. John, who liked Lady Russell, went!

Above 'the rapids' there was a gravelly shelf on which we often stranded, and where Hilaire Belloc once stepped out into a few inches of water, shoved the boat off and took a long stride into a deep pool. He came up talking fluent French, to the children's immense admiration.

Then there was the young demonstrator, Mr. Pembrey, who often came with us. His father had been a reader at the Clarendon Press, and could correct the proofs of a Chinese book though he had no knowledge of the language. Mr Pembrey was devoted to my little dog Esk. The first time that Esk was stolen and sold in Cambridge, Mr. Pembrey found him and brought him back. It happened several times afterwards. The police were always able to retrieve him within a couple of days, and he came back beautifully groomed, and on one occasion wearing a fine new collar. Esk committed one crime, the murder of a white kitten, for which the Charles children wished to have him executed, but John took all four of them up the river and talked to them so wisely that they told me afterwards that they understood that it wasn't Esk's fault, in the same way that it would have been a boy's fault. They adored John from that day onwards.

Lily Charles was a cousin of the Horners. She married a dour little North Ireland parson, who had adopted his brother's orphan children, and did not allow his wife any say in their upbringing, which was obviously a system on which he himself had been reared, and was most unhygienic. I enjoyed feeding those children on cakes and bananas.

Except, of course, Mr. Joseph of New College (to whom we were very deeply attached), Professor Alexander is the only Jew I have ever really liked. He seemed to have all the good qualities attributed to his race, and if he had any of its failings, they were superficial ones. Dressed in 'decent blacks', like a country minister, and, however hot the sun shone, in a thick vest and heavy flannel shirt, he rowed with great intenseness and, like John, despised punts and paddles. They had long and heated philosophical arguments, and were great friends. He introduced me to the rhyme 'How odd of God to choose the Jews' and to Claude Montefiore's most interesting 'Bible for Home Reading', on the strength of which Jack won his divinity prizes. When Naomi was born, we asked Mr. Alexander to be godfather. He was unhappy at the time, and I think it gave him great pleasure. She grew up to be a most firm, loyal and helpful friend to him.

Another of John's friends was Professor Nettleship, and people of whom we saw a great deal were the Walkers of Queen's. He was Senior Fellow for years, while old Provost Lefroy still hung on. The university had no superannuation rules at the time, and the undergraduates, who only saw him on his afternoon drives, declared that he was stuffed.

I made friends with Mrs. Walker, an emotional little Irish woman, whose son by a first marriage had been killed in South Africa. We met in a house where the atmosphere was pro-Boer, and walked out of it together. During the very short time that Dr. Walker was Provost of Queens', she made their rooms in college look perfectly charming, and was full of unconventional hospitality.

Mr. and Mrs. Walker's son, known as 'J.D.' went up the Dragon School with Jack, usually as the smallest boy in any form while Jack was the largest. They went up to New College together too, and had rooms high up in new buildings where his mother would occasionally try to bring a little order into their possessions. As she said, they had everything in common except their clothes, and fortunately this was impossible.

For some time J.D. had been trying to induce their Scout to take the pledge, but so far the man had always evaded him. Then one morning he woke J.D. to say that he had 'got 'em so bad he'd take the pledge and no mistake.' J.D. rather suspected what might have happened, but he got up at once and went with the Scout, leaving a note for Jack telling him to be sure to 'clear out his pigs' before the Scout was due to visit his room again. There had been a meeting of the Junior Scientific Society on the previous evening and Jack had illustrated his paper with the guinea pigs about which it was written and deposited them for the night in his chest of drawers. I asked whether seeing them had had a permanent effect on the Scout? 'Yes,' said J.D., 'and the best day's work the little beasts ever did.'

CHAPTER XXIII

My Son

❄

Jack was a beautiful child. In those days it was not done to cut small boys' hair short, so I kept his long lint-white locks until he went to school. I taught him to read quite early—partly in self-defence, for when he became absorbed in a book he ceased to ask questions. Just before his fifth birthday my father made him read to him the newspaper reports of the meeting of the British Association. He said the pace of the reading was 'deliberate, but not exasperatingly slow, until the child sees a long and unknown word ahead of him—then he approaches it cautiously and seldom mispronounces it—but after that we come to a full stop while I try to explain the meaning of the word in words most of which themselves need explanation.'

He had a prodigious memory for anything which interested him and also for verse. I used to send him out to run a given number of times up and down Crick Road while I dressed the baby and prepared for our morning walk. He was stopped by a neighbour, who asked to whom he was talking. He said, 'To nobody. I'm the overland mail.' 'What is that?' she inquired. He answered gravely, 'It's quite true—it's in a book—'Let the robber retreat, let the tiger turn tail, in the name of the Empress the overland mail.' Don't you know *that*?' The lady fled!

When he first went to school the lowest form was learning 'The Battle of Lake Regillus', and on his morning walks or runs he repeated long pieces of it to the road men whom he found breakfasting in their little tent round a pail of burning

215

coke. Crick Road was getting its first asphalt footpath, at the same time as the water mains were lowered from six to eighteen inches. During my first winter there we had a series of geysers along our garden paths when the ground thawed, after having to buy our supply from a water-cart during the frost.

There was no 'Baby school' at the Oxford Preparatory School (now the Dragon School) till after both my children's times. Mr. Lynam, the headmaster (hereinafter referred to as 'the Skipper'), asked Miss Baggaley, the wonderful teacher of the lowest form, whether Jack knew enough of 'The Battle of Lake Regillus' to be put up to recite. He was so much the youngest boy that it would be rather a joke to have him on the programme of a concert. Miss Baggaley said that she was sure he knew more than enough, so during the concert the Skipper gave him a 'leg-up' on to the platform, and started him off with 'Ho trumpets sound a war note'—'Now you go on.' Jack did so, and took the hand which the Skipper presently raised to check the flow, as an encouragement to continue. The Skipper tried again, saying that it was very nice, but that was enough for this time. 'Don't you really like it?' Jack asked. 'I can tell you lots more if you'd like me to.' This, of course, raised a roar of laughter, but the Skipper made it all right by explaining that it was getting late, and that some of the others wanted a turn!

Miss Baggaley had agreed with me that Jack had better not begin Latin until next term, particularly as his writing was 'shocking' and he ought to write more copy-books than the older boys had time for. When the Latin exam papers were being given round, Jack held out his hand for one. 'You can't do this, Jack,' Miss Baggaley said, but he answered, 'I can. I know you did not *teach* it to me, but I heard you all the same.' His paper was 'quite up to the average of the Form'.

For the first few weeks Ned and Austin Lane Poole, his elders by two and three years, picked him up on their way to school. After that he trotted off quite happily by himself—of course there was not any heavy traffic to cross.

There was not much traffic of any kind in St. Margaret's

Road at that time. It was then the most northerly of the cuts connecting the two Oxford thoroughfares leading to Banbury and Woodstock. It was not till long after this that it was extended past Woodstock Road and changed its character. From my bedroom window I often heard snatches of conversation in the road below. For instance, Jack coming back from school would address the old monthly nurse walking about in the sun with the last local baby: 'Good morning. Why do you cover its face with a veil? If I flop the flies off for you, she will like to look about. Is he a he or a she?' To which the nurse would express her surprise that 'the young gentleman' should take so much interest in babies. 'Oh well, you see, I have got one of my own,' Jack answered and came in to tell me that he couldn't understand why the baby's mother let its nurse wrap it up so 'chokingly'.

A few years later John was doing a series of blood counts for people of different ages and professions. Any number of boys all of school age and under fourteen could be collected at school. Mr. Lynam was quite ready to allow samples from the bottom form to school leavers to run up to St Margaret's Road to have a finger pricked and a drop of blood collected. Usually if it got the chance a whole form would volunteer and the lucky ones were directed to *walk* there and *run* back and Jack got the credit of being the son of a father who provided such an unusual break during morning school. But the 'Professor' wanted girls' blood too. Dr. Collier's two little girls arrived one day but when one of them saw the 'operation' on her sister she turned faint. 'What did she do that for?' asked Naomi, by then herself at the Dragon School. She was a couple of years younger than the others and not yet even attempting to be tactful. Presently I heard her stopping a contemporary with the words, 'You come in here. My father wants your blood.' The frightened child was removed by her nurse and the undaunted schoolgirl came in saying, 'No-one seems ready to have their finger pricked. Silly, isn't it?'

Jack had a terrifying accident while we were living in St. Margaret's Road. His father was 'stepping him' on his bicycle, having forgotten that the size of the steps had been reduced by taking clips for a luggage carrier. Jack slipped off the inadequate step and came down on the edge of the pavement, fracturing his skull. Someone produced a car and they were driven to the infirmary to find a surgeon, John explaining who he wanted; 'My son has a fracture of the base.' Jack had been unconscious but at this point he asked in a firm voice, 'Base of what?'. I had hardly got him undressed before the surgeon arrived and he found us a very efficient nurse, one of the very few really good nurses I have come across during many years' experience of them. We had a desperately anxious time but there were no complications and after about ten days Jack demanded a proper breakfast. 'Well, what would you like?' he was asked by the doctor standing with the surgeon at the foot of the bed. I can see them quite plainly exchanging glances, evidently expecting to be asked to allow something very unwholesome. 'Porridge', said Jack firmly. They looked at one another and said in one breath, 'Nothing could be better', and the surgeon added a suggestion from the pharmacopoeia, 'I should give him five drops to start with—'

'But you are the mechanical chap,' said Jack. 'Leave that to the chemical chap.'

The 'chaps' said he was a very satisfactory patient. Later they said that he must be kept as quiet as possible for some time. No school this term. Summer term—bad luck!—but I did my best to find interesting things to do in our back garden and was always on call for any entertainment I could provide. One day I had to go out for a short time. I left him with a new hook and very strict injunctions not to go into the road. When I came back he was not in either the garden or the house and I had scarcely ever felt more at a loss what to do. Desperately I took one further look round the garden and on hands and knees on the end wall I saw Jack. He was crawling quite slowly and deliberately along towards his own boundary wall. Should I go and try to help him down? I had a horrid vision of his letting himself down with a bump. If I got there in time I might prevent that happening but he would be bound to see my hurrying down the garden and if I called out he would be startled and might lose his hold. While I hesitated he turned over on his stomach and I heard the toes of his shoes scraping on the brick of the wall. He had been quite obedient he told me, he had not gone out into the road, but he wanted to borrow something from friends who lived next door but one and when he got there they were all out—he felt aggrieved and so did I but for different reasons! 'I really think he'd be safer at school,' John said. So he was allowed to go back and the Skipper spoke seriously to his contemporaries about going easy with Jack for the rest of the term.

Jack did not start epidemics at school, but when a boarder arrived at the beginning of term carrying some infection Jack managed to sit beside him on the first morning of term and was his first victim! This, as far as I remember, happened both with measles and with chickenpox. In the case of measles Naomi took the infection from him after such a long interval that I thought she must be immune. I took it from her after the shortest possible incubation period. John was away at the time and I had to get in a nurse to look after both Naomi and me, Jack being practically well and having been given a chemical set by Uncle Richard. It was a wonderful box which contained enough ingredients to make a long series of explosions and 'stinks' which kept him and Austin Lane Poole (now President of St. John's) happy and wonderfully out of mischief during my short season in bed. It was after I was up that they made an explosive substance which jumped downstairs and made for the front door—finally going off on the gravel outside—we were never able to get such a lively mixture again and I should not believe in it if I had not seen it!

It was at this time that (as Naomi put it) the mouse happened. There is surely a mouse story in every respectable book of memoirs. Ours is a tragic tale. John always had a cake and a plate of biscuits left on his writing table in the study at night and he told us of a mouse which used to climb up the leg of the table, eat some biscuit and push a large piece over on to the floor, jumping down after it. The housemaid confirmed the story but she thought that the doctor himself dropped the biscuit and would I warn him that the crumbs were very hard to get out of the black sheepskin hearthrug?

When Naomi and I had the measles the Senior Partner was away. Lying in bed half blind and feeling horribly ill I was kept awake by a mouse which ran about the room, squeaking and scratching and presently it got up on the bed. I must have been drowsing or I should have flung it off, but before I realized what was happening it ran across my face and hair and before I could do anything to get rid of it it ran back again, leaving its quite appalling smell behind it. I sat up trying to protect myself from another attack till I could get a maid up and have a trap set. I suppose the mouse must have been hungry, for the trap was scarcely baited before it fulfilled its purpose. I got up and washed my hair—but it was days before I had got rid thoroughly of the smell. When the Senior Partner came back he inquired for his mouse. I was still hoping that my assailant might not have been the study mouse—why should it have found its way to my room, there was plenty of food for it in other parts of the house? But I suppose I must have looked guilty for the Senior Partner just said: 'You killed my mouse', and made me feel a murderer!

People interested in the doings of preparatory schools had come to expect that Summerfields would take at least one Eton scholarship every year, just as the Dragons were expected to take one at Winchester. Jack's name was down for Charterhouse, where he had several cousins, so he was sure of a place at a public school whatever happened. And the Skipper was not enthusiastic when I told him that I wanted him to go to Eton. He said, however, that if he failed for Eton this year, he was still so young that he would be able to try for Winchester next summer. Then he looked at specimens of Eton scholarship examination papers, after which he made a bet with Dr. Williams, headmaster of Summerfields, that his boy —and mine—would be elected. Shortly afterwards we heard that he had betted that his boy would do better than Dr. Williams' boy, and finally he went one better, and ran his entry for the first place among the King's Scholars! I met Dr. Williams later at a college dinner party, and he told me that my son had made last term an extremely expensive one for him! Both he and the headmaster of Charterhouse were exceedingly kindly and warm in their congratulations.

Mr. A. E. Lynam, the Skipper's brother, known as Hum, took Jack up to Eton and stayed with him there during the four days of the examination for the King's Scholarships, and I am sure that this made a great difference to him. If I had gone with him I should have let him feel my anxiety and worried him about inessentials. I went to see them one afternoon. It was very hot weather, and in their lodgings the rooms were like ovens, so Hum suggested that we should take a boat —he would do all the rowing. On the river we met another scholarship candidate being rowed by his father, who called out to Jack, 'How are you getting on?' 'Don't give anything away,' cautioned Hum. Jack barely nodded, and in answer to the query said that the paper had been 'beastly long'. 'Ah, you found that too,' said the father with evident satisfaction. 'What about the maths paper?' 'Stiff and much too long.' Jack answered. 'Did you finish it?' 'No fear! It was much too long,' Jack repeated. When the other boat had pulled away, Hum said rather anxiously, 'I thought you told me you had done the last question?' 'Yes,' said Jack. 'But you say you did not finish the paper?' 'No more I did. It was much too long. Oh I did not touch the first questions. They were marked too low to be worth doing. I began with the last.' Hum beamed with satisfaction.

Jack won the top scholarship. He would have got the special mathematical scholarship had his classics not been good too. As it was, the boy next to him in mathematics took the special scholarship, and every year as they went up the school together, Jack was always first, the other boy keeping his place as second. It seemed hard luck on the mathematical scholar!

In his last year at Eton Jack cut his foot bathing, and came home for some weeks. He was worried because he was going

My Son

in for a mathematical scholarship at New College, so I asked
Mr. Campbell to give him a little coaching. After his second
visit he said that he enjoyed talking to Jack, but that there
was really nothing he could teach him and he eventually won
the scholarship and took Maths. Mods. successfully, after
which he rather irritated the mathematicians by going over
to Greats. He took a term off Greats to read zoology and got
a first in Greats after three years' residence. Dick Mitchison
took his at the same time. They were travelling up to Scotland
together, and had their 'results' telegraphed to meet them at a
station on the way! Dick's main interest had been in the
historical side of Greats, Jack's in the philosophical side. He
took after his father in this. John was apt to look down on
people who were 'mere mathematicians'.

Of course it was a terrible disappointment to me that Jack
should never seem to be happy at Eton. In his second half,
when he came home for a couple of nights for Sir John
Burdon-Sanderson's funeral, he seemed so miserable that I
said if his father agreed he might perhaps be allowed to leave.
He did not want that 'exactly', he just cried and said that he
'couldn't bear the place'. I got John to talk to him, but he
could not get anything more out of him, and we always hoped
that as he got up the school he would be at least contented.
He certainly was happier when he changed his classical tutor
for Mr. Hill the science master. The former told him one day,
in a fit of irritation I imagine, that if he passed Smalls he
could drop doing Latin verse. On this I got a wire from Jack
'Long leave (date) please arrange for me to see the pageant and
pass Smalls.'

He and Naomi went to the pageant. It was at the time when
every place in the country desired to have its pageant, and the
reasons which were alleged for holding some of them certainly
showed that we had not run out of imagination.

Eton trousers were considered sufficiently subfusc to wear
in the Schools, we borrowed jacket, waistcoat and gown from
the smallest don of our acquaintance, and Jack got off doing
Latin verses!

My Son

Dr. Alington, the Master in College, and Trev Huxley (grandson of Thomas Henry), Jack's fagmaster, were both consstently kind and friendly to him, and he was active in the Volunteers and went to every camp for which he was eligible. Naomi and I once visited him at Tidworth Pennings, which was great fun for us, and, I hope, for him—we took a large cake with us—and when, as Captain of the School he had, along with the Captain of the Oppidans, to receive the King on his first visit to Eton after his accession, he acquitted himself excellently, in spite of a gashed chin due to using a borrowed razor too vigorously. He said his piece as if it had some meaning, and was ready to shake when the King extended his hand. Naomi and I took the Skipper with us to this function and he was more than satisfied with his boy. The Captain of the Oppidans who followed Jack was Dick Mitchison, afterwards to become my son-in-law.

The Captain of the School has various more or less social duties. He visits the Eton Mission, and this and other activities take him up to London and he has the chance of meeting people of note who visit the college, but Jack got little fun, or as he would have said 'kick' out of these things. It seemed such a waste—to so many boys it would have meant a great deal, but whether he enjoyed it or not, it was very educative for Jack, and his father felt this as I did.

I am sure that Henry Dundas, Naomi's contemporary, son of Nevil and Cecil Dundas, who was Captain of the Oppidans five years after Jack was Captain of the School, got much more out of Eton than Jack ever did. Some of my pleasantest days during those years were at the Eton and Harrow matches when the Wet Bob, Jack, greeted Gerald Boswell's feats in the cricket match with, 'Well rowed Boswell', to the delight of all the other Wet Bobs; and Henry suggested to his father that he and Naomi had had only two 'goes' of strawberries and cream, and Cecil advised caution, but Nevil said he would have no opinion at all of boys who could not 'go one better' than that, and he would have one with them.

In 1916 when Henry came up to Oxford to sit for a Christ-

223

Church scholarship, he was dining with us, and someone said that no only sons should be allowed to go to the front, it was too bad for the country. Henry had already got his commission in the Scots Guards. He said, 'Oh don't say that sir, you would rule me out.' Jack had already got out again after his wound in 1915—this time to the 2nd battalion in Mesopotamia commanded by Colonel Andy Wauchope.

Jack wrote very little about personal experiences at the front, but I know that in the spring of 1915 he was once knocked down by shell blast and walked out of the smoke having lost his bonnet for the third time, and with his haversack hanging on his chest—but what he thought interesting about the occurrence was that he walked past people who wanted to contact him *talking Greek*. He found his way to his own platoon with the message which he was taking when the shell blast 'knocked him silly', and wished to carry on, but the officer in command said that he was much too seriously wounded to do so, and was wondering how he would get him to the dressing station when the Prince of Wales came in, as usual driving his own car and getting into the most interesting and dangerous parts of the front line. The Black Watch officer asked if he would drive a wounded officer to the nearest dressing station— they had sent off their walking wounded, but had no transport. The Prince looked at Jack, 'Oh, it's you,' he said. 'Yes, I'll take him, he looks fit for nothing but hospital,' and in spite of his opposition he was helped into the car. They passed a couple of walking wounded, and then came on a man too bad to walk, being hoisted along by two other unsteady hirpling comrades. The Prince stopped the car. 'We must give this chap and certainly one of the others a lift,' he said, and they got the two worst cases 'tucked away among our feet'. The car was the best on the front, though not built for the use to which the Prince put it, but he was a splendid driver. 'Anyone else would have smashed the car, to say nothing of killing the wounded,' Jack said, but at the dressing station he helped them out carefully and skilfully, and then drove away —'back to the front line' Jack noticed, calling out to him, 'see

Professor Burdon-Sanderson

L.K.H.

Naomi

Jack

you again soon I hope', and some joke about the O.T.C. camp. When the Black Watch privates heard who had been their chauffeur they agreed that it was a great honour 'but a fearsome ride'!

Just before the declaration of Hitler's war the terrible tragedy of the submarine *Thetis* shocked the country. Jack at once started an experiment in which he reproduced the conditions on board the *Thetis* and had himself sealed in so that the atmosphere he breathed should be exactly the same as that breathed by the crew of the submarine. He said that it would be some comfort to the friends of the crew when he was able to report that his sensations were never painful: that he 'quickly lost consciousness' and would have passed away without any pain or fright.

CHAPTER XXIV

The Jubilees and the Queen's Funeral

Anyone who loves a tamasha as much as I do must count themselves fortunate to have seen both the old Queen's Jubilees. That in 1887 was a great gathering of royalties, as well as of our own army and navy and other services, and many wearers of strange uniforms. On the second occasion there were fewer crowned heads, and more of the family of the Empire—magnificent among them, of course, those lost sons from India. I am glad to remember that the Queen did not know how soon they were to be lost to the Empire. They will always live with us as part of a glorious tradition.

In the earlier Jubilee procession, apart from the Queen herself, the individual who impressed us most was the Crown Prince of Prussia. It was known that he was terribly ill, and that the Crown Princess, our own Princess Royal, was trying against pressure which would have been overwhelming to a weaker woman, to get him into the hands of an English specialist. He was seen by the man who might possibly have prolonged his very useful life, and would certainly have saved him unnecessary agony—but the orders came from Prussia that they must return the hour the Jubilee gathering was over. She looked heartbroken and the tragedy threw a gloom over all the splendour.

I saw both the processions from a stand built out from the windows of the Athenaeum Club in Pall Mall. A little before we started to walk home, while Lady Metcalfe was waiting for the crowds to thin out, someone came in and said, 'Gladstone

and Harcourt are in the writing-room.' Somebody heard
Gladdy ask Harcourt how he spelt Jubilee? 'Naturally I spell
it J-U-B-I-L-E-E,' the 'aughty one answered. 'Well I don't,'
said Gladdy. 'You'd get through your work much quicker if
you shortened it.' 'Wish to God I could; I'm sick of the
word,' Harcourt answered. 'Oh hush, hush,' said Mr. Gladstone
holding up a reproving finger. 'I always spell it J-B-L-E-E,
because U and I are both out of it!'

On the evening of the day in 1887, Blanche Dundas came to
ask me to go with her to see the illuminations. Lady Metcalfe,
who had a horror of crowds, thought this a most risky performance, and could not be persuaded that we should not come
to grief in half-a-dozen different ways, till Blanche introduced
several very stalwart cousins, among them Sir Brooke Booth-
by, after seeing whom my hostess was reconciled to our going.
The crowds were absolutely quiet, good-natured and orderly
in Trafalgar Square and in any of the other centres which we
visited.

In 1897 I did something far more interesting. I was again
staying with Lady Metcalfe and met her nieces, the Clive
Bayleys. Lady Bayley asked me to stay the night with them in
Windsor. After dinner we had coffee with an Eton master, then
Teresa, my contemporary, and I, fell in at the tail of the procession of boys going up to the castle. A small gate clicked
behind us, the torch-bearers among the boys stepped forward
and formed themselves into a V.R. under the castle window,
and the boys sang to her till the Queen came out on to the
balcony. Then the singing passed into a roar of treble cheering.
I do not remember what the Queen said—probably at the
back of the crowd we did not hear distinctly. I have never seen
any reference to this incident, but among the crowd of singing
boys there must have been several whose lives have been
interesting enough to demand an autobiography, and it seems
rather surprising that a devoted reader of memoirs, such as I
am, should never have come across an account of Eton's part
in the second Jubilee. When the Queen said goodnight and
went in, there was another roar of cheering, and we all trooped

out and the little gate again clicked behind us. Teresa found her sisters, and we all went home to bed. I remember sitting up, too tired to sleep, and wondering whether I should ever find words to express, even dimly, my thanks to my hostess, whose hospitality had given me the chance of such a wonderful evening.

In 1901 the Queen died at Osborne, and the first part of her funeral was in the hands of the navy and must have been a wonderful sight. The army took over when the coffin came to London.

We were given two seats by friends of John's family. I cannot remember who they were now, or where their house was, but it was at a corner, and from the stand built out over their area, one could see for a good distance to right and left. Just at the corner there was a small open space on which a few people began to collect from an early hour. All traffic had been stopped along the streets through which the funeral would pass, and the stillness and·silence were uncanny, because one feels that noise, movement and speech are all part of the atmosphere of London. Jack and I were among the first to take our seats on the staging outside the dining-room; it was cold, but I wanted to get away from the gathering crowd inside. I knew none of them, and they persisted in chaffing Jack, who was in his usual Sunday suit (a Royal Stuart kilt). Somebody said he was 'dressed up for the occasion' which luckily offended him, so that he was not at all forthcoming, and was ready to listen quietly to me when I read him a few things about the Queen that I had brought for the purpose. However as the stand filled up he had to read to himself. We heard reports that the fog had been too thick for the royal yacht with the coffin to be more than glimpsed as she came in at Portsmouth.

There was no fog in London, only an absolute dearth of sunlight. Presently we saw the crowd opposite us stirred by something which was not yet in our line of vision and very clearly through the astounding stillness came words of command. A pause and then again words of command, the sound of horses' hooves, and the Commander-in-Chief and his staff came in sight. The little crowd on the opposite side of the street stirred, and there was the beginning of a cheer. Lord Roberts reined up sharply, and raised his hand. Many of the crowd evidently thought that he was acknowledging its reception. They were quickly undeceived. He just said 'Silence' and sat like a statue, looking straight before him. There was an audible 'hush' from some of the crowd, but it was scarcely needed. After a minute or two the general loosened his reins and the troop moved forward. That was the last time I saw the beloved little general. He died as he would have wished when on a visit to the troops in Flanders in the bitter winter of 1914. As he could not serve with the army, he at least died 'in harness'. 'Fortunate to the last', as one said who loved him, and would gladly have shared his last adventure.

I was offered a seat at a window from which to watch his funeral procession passing through London, but I liked better to see it from the street.

When King Edward's Coronation had to be postponed on account of his illness, there were contingents from many parts of the Empire assembled for the occasion. I do not know what was arranged for other contingents, but for part of the time anyhow, the Indian contingent was brought up to Scotland, and they were taken sightseeing. I was in Edinburgh with the children, and I do not think I have ever seen anything more beautiful than the Indian Cavalry on the Queen's Drive. We watched from Holyrood as they came down round Arthur's Seat. It was what was known as 'Queen's weather', that is to say, brilliant sunshine. Once and once only had the weather failed the old Queen, and a review had to be held in a downpour. We felt that there was something uncanny about it.

One afternoon the Indian contingent was given the option of going to Fife to inspect factories, or of accepting an invitation from Colonel and Mrs. Trotter to tea at Colinton House. The larger number accepted the invitation, and Mimi invited the County to meet them. At very short notice she had perfect arrangements made. Tables spread with cakes and relays of teapots on the terrace above the Burn, and everyone free to wander along the banks to the gardens and to look over the house.

Quite half the other guests could talk to some of the men in their own language, and Elshie and a couple of other schoolboys started hide and seek with the Ghurkas. Jack, a good deal younger than the rest, and in a kilt as usual, joined them and the soldiers insisted that he must belong to some regiment, and called him the 'Ghota Major'.

Colonel Cadell took me by the arm and said, 'There is a man here who knew my boy. Come with me.' And went up to one of the native officers in the Central Indian Horse; I couldn't understand what they said, but both had tears in their eyes, and presently the officer asked something, obviously thinking me to be one of the family. The Colonel said 'No', but that I belonged to one whose name was well-known to them, General Keatinge. That indeed was another Burra Sahib, the old officer said as we shook hands.

I have often thought about that party, it was so obviously right—a success worth taking trouble for. After tea my uncle made short speeches in two or three of the languages native to his guests. One of the speeches produced roars of laughter, over which Sir Robert Murdoch-Smith shook his head, and said he hoped none of the ladies present were able to follow it!— I think all the guests, Scotch and Indian, went away regretfully. The children from the village had been assembled at the lodge gate and as the carriages and charabancs slowed down in the crowd, they thrust little bunches of flowers into the soldiers' hands. That I think pleased our guests as much as anything. The Ghurkas were wonderful people at hide and seek, and compared with the rest of our guests seemed such *boys* and were tremendously popular with our young ones!

At the time of King George's Coronation we saw one curious incident when we were watching the departure of the guests

230

after one of the entertainments at Windsor. Open carriages with two or three of the guests followed one another down the uncompromising gradient—surely one of the least successfully engineered approaches to a royal gateway—I had just said to Naomi, 'That must be King Alfonso of Spain, I wonder what he is laughing at,' when there was a scream from a woman on the pavement opposite our window and we saw a man jump on to the step of the King's carriage and thrust something into his face. He did not move. The civilian beside him shrank back on his seat, or he appeared to do so; at any rate he did nothing to protect the King, who went on laughing. Then a policeman and a boy seized the man on the step and as he was pinioned he threw at the King what he had been offering to him. I suppose most people thought that it was a bomb, and held their breath while the King turned it over in his hands, then shook his head and put it down on the seat opposite to him, and turning to his companion laughed again, and said something to the policeman who now needed the assistance of several other constables to get their prisoner safely through an angry crowd. The King's companion had recovered his wits and was obviously congratulating and condoling in one breath. We could not hear a word, but his gestures were as eloquent as speech, and still the King only laughed. Later we heard that it was a petition which had been thrown at him.

CHAPTER XXV

Sennen Cove

❄

I found to my great amusement that some of our Oxford acquaintances thought it very strange that I never took 'a trip abroad', which they seemed to find necessary for their health and culture. I could have if I had wished to do so, and John would have quite understood that it was a natural desire and if possible to be gratified—but that kind of travel had no attraction for me. I know that some people expressed wonder as to whether we really could not afford that little 'change' which most people found almost essential!

I once took Jack and Naomi to Calais, and we visited the 'Field of the Cloth of Gold'.

For several years, however we did go to Cornwall for a fortnight or three weeks at Easter. John was doing experiments at Dolcoath mine, Penzance, where they had a mysterious disease that baffled all the doctors. They agreed that it appeared to be a form of a tropical complaint, but, if it were one, how could it have started and taken firm root in Cornwall? It did not occur to anyone except John that the temperature of the hottest part of Dolcoath was at least subtropical. On further investigation, and a long series of tests, it was finally established that the disease was ankylostomyasis, a fairly common complaint in some of the Rand mines. My cousin, Alec Trotter, was helping with the investigations, and produced the lighter touch which was badly needed after months of investigation, during all of which his wife and I fully expected that at least one of our men would be infected!

Sennen Cove

They escaped, but the third partner in the team, John's old pupil and friend, Ted Boycott, was infected. His wife was a St. Thomas' Hospital Sister who had done wonderfully good work both in hospital and in a concentration camp in South Africa —she came down to Sennen with her two baby boys, and it seemed specially hard that she should be involved in this unpleasant research just when she badly needed a restful interval in life.

The mysterious disease at Dolcoath was the reason for our first visit to Cornwall. We went to a place specially recommended for the wonderful view of St. Michael's Mount from the hotel windows. The view was the only point in favour of the place, however, and when John had a day off on Easter Monday, we took a 'jingle' and went to look for some more attractive place to stay at. After we had visited Land's End our driver said he would take us 'to Sennen Churchtown, but we couldn't go to Cove because the road was lost.' This sounded mysterious and attractive. Looking down 'over cliff' to the Cove, the children and I made up our minds that this was the place for us. We walked down past the lost road—a crater at the road's most acute angle. The village said the landlord should mend the road, the landlord thought it was the business of the County Council, and the County Council said firmly that the village had always got on quite well with a footpath. There was need for the road while the Atlantic cable was being laid, and all the stuff for it had to be carted down, but now that this was accomplished the village 'didn't need none of this greatness'.

Where the Altantic cable plunged into the sea there were big baulks of timber good for sitting on, and piles of huge stones among which an occasional freak wave found its way, came up in a water-spout, and drenched the unwary. Beyond the cable there were miles of beautiful sand till close on Cape Cornwall. In the middle of Sennen Bay was the Brissons, the great rock over which all day long the cormorants and gulls flew screaming. There was also the inn and Mrs. Pender 'calling over stairs'. 'If 'e be menfolks, stay down, but if 'e be woman-

233

folk, come oop, I be in me stays.' Naomi and I went up. Of course Mrs. Pender could give us tea, but as for rooms, they reckoned to let come May, but never no earlier. 'But we will have to be at school before that, and we do want to come here,' pleaded Naomi. 'Well do'e now, my hangel?' said the landlady and by the time we had finished tea she had promised to have the rooms ready 'the day following tomorrow'. Sennen was a curious place; a few men went to the mines, but most were fishermen. There were few children—if the family name was not Nicholas, it was Pender. One had to remember which man answered to the name of Bill Pender, William Pender or Pen's Billy.

In the little row of whitewashed coastguards' houses, the men held themselves rather aloof from the village, they 'belonged with' the lighthouse keeper and his mate. I eagerly accepted an invitation to visit the Longships lighthouse with the people who supplied the rations. In big pools on the rocks under water at high tide, there were enormous sea-anemones which Naomi wanted to feed. The men told her they were flowers, but she showed them the anemones grabbing pieces of sandwich offered to them. The next time we went out to the Longships we found the men had over-fed the 'flowers' and several of the pools were full of undigested fragments.

Mrs. Pender made the most delicious home-made bread, large and small loaves called 'mansions' and 'little mansions', and we got milk, butter and eggs from the farm on the cliff, but the butcher would not risk his pony down the Lost Road, and shouted his offers to Mrs. Pender. She shouted her orders back, and all the village knew what we were having to eat and waylaid us to ask how we had enjoyed it! Then during the week before Easter, numbers of French boats came into the bay and hung about in the hopes of there being a catch of grey mullet, which they bought up and on which they made huge profits on the Paris fish market if they got the fish in before the end of Lent. They also bought as much home-made bread as Mrs. Pender could make for them, and unfortunately stood drinks of very fierce brandy to anyone who would accept them. Mrs. Pender rationed her customers most strictly. 'No Michael, you know it's no use asking me. My usual good cup tea and welcome, but no drink of no kind; you've been with the Frenchies already and had more than is good for you.' Michael would settle down to his tea, grumbling even when he was given a 'little mansion' to take home to his wife.

A school friend of Jack's came as a companion a couple of times, but was desperately sick when we took him to the lighthouse, poor little chap. I remember two boys scrambling up from the beach on a stormy morning with loads of seaweed on their backs. The old woman, for whose garden it was intended, called after them, 'Come oop me children', and the captain of the lifeboat joggled my elbow saying, 'Us used to think you was foreign when you first come to Cove, but look to that there! Now us knows that you belong Cornish same as we.'

John didn't enjoy trips to the lighthouse as much as his family did. When there was a fairly heavy swell the rowers once smashed the blades of a couple of oars on a rock which, as Jack said, had 'come up unexpectedly'. John said, 'Now, now, now', exactly as he did when he wanted Jack to 'go easy' with some laboratory apparatus, and the men didn't much like it—with the result that the next time they were taking out a relief they woke me by throwing gravel in at my open bedroom window, and explained that they wouldn't call the doctor as 'twas fairly rough, 'but you and Missy us'll fetch along and welcome.' So a very excited little girl tripped downstairs with me. We had some milk and each carried a 'little mansion' down to Cove with us, and embarked. It *was* rather rough, and I was glad to find that Naomi really enjoyed it and showed no symptom either of sea-sickness or of fear.

Sennen held one disadvantage for me. John and the children adored caves. If there was any sign of a crack in the cliff they were bound to investigate it; and there was one horrible place, a mine, on the point of Cape Cornwall, where every now and then a wave breaking against the cliff would submerge at the entrance, and pour down by a channel in the floor. Of course the noise was deafening and one was drenched as in a thunderstorm. We never got quite to the end of the channel, for the way was partially blocked with falls of the roof, and I have thought since that it was probably built as a way of escape in case of a mine explosion or fire, when normal exits would be blocked. The water which flowed inwards may have made a big pool or found some other outlet, but it was all mysterious, and far better than any Swiss Family Robinson cave, as the children said, and I felt bound to say, 'Isn't it lovely', whatever my feelings might be.

John laughed at me when he discovered how much I hated holes, but I got my own back on the tops of the cliffs, when I had to beg him not to spoil the children's nerve by constant cautions to them, and commands to me not to let them look over the edge. They were neither of them inclined to be giddy, but Naomi had rather a better head than Jack, who, like his father, would walk along a knife edge of rock or timber in a mine, quite unaffected by the yawning gulf beside him, provided it was dark and he could not see the danger. One of the managers told me about this with considerable astonishment.

A catch of grey mullet during Lent was, of course, an enormous stroke of luck for the village. When there was any kind of shoal everyone knew his job and became suddenly intent on it. Watchers on the cliff were doubled, and were constantly semaphoring messages to boat crews waiting below. If the shoal should move into a favourable position, then the crews of the two boats extended the huge net behind the shoal and made for the shore, while the surface of the sea shimmered like silver. We had the good luck to be at Sennen on two occasions when there was a good catch, and I was told all about it. There were men's shares for anyone who worked in the fishing, and widow's shares, and smaller shares for orphans, but if any man was convicted of not having helped in the catch, he lost his share. There was only one excuse accepted—if a

man were on his way to St. Just, seven miles off, to fetch the
doctor.

Piles of fish were made along a bank, behind where the
Atlantic cable had its landing place. One or two elders super-
vized this, and every now and then they picked up a big fish
from a pile and replaced it by a smaller one amidst a good deal
of rather sarcastic language, but no really violent comment.
When the heaps of fish were ready, a large basket was strapped
on to a man's back and everyone threw something into it, a
gaudy hankerchief if he had one, a clasp knife, or if his pockets
were empty, a curiously shaped root or a clump of seaweed.
Then a man was blindfolded and stationed behind the man
with the basket and as they walked along the row of heaps he
picked some article out of the basket and dropped it on a heap
of fish. This caused a good deal of amusement, particularly
when some of the men picked up their fish and went off very
quickly. 'He thinks he'll get a better price from the Frenchies
if he gets his in first, but they know just what the haul has
been and they'll bargain with all of we,' someone explained.
Then I saw Jack picking up a small heap from the end of the
row, and said something about wanting to pay like the
Frenchmen. But the captain of the lifeboat only laughed at
me. 'He've earned his share,' he said. 'Why he been along o'
we out working since six o'clock. He's all in a muck, you see
that he has a good breakfast now, he've earned it.'

And how good the grey mullet was to eat! The French boats
went off with their fish for Paris, and I don't believe all the
French cooking could have been as successful as Mrs. Pender's
slow stewing in milk. Whenever I hear of grey mullet in the
shops I try to get it dressed in the Cornish way. Perhaps it's
no longer fresh enough after twenty-four hours in the train,
but it never seems half so good as it did at Sennen.

On the last year that we went there I kept Naomi for a
fortnight after school expected them both back in Oxford, as
she had been ill and wanted all the sea air we could give her.
At the beginning of our visit that year, the four biggest men of
the village were waiting for us when our fly stopped at the

usual point in the lost road, picked up the carrying chair which I had warned them I should bring, and were off 'over cliff' with her before the fly was dismissed. Six weeks later, when poor Jack was already back at school, Billy Pender came into the sitting-room to say casually, 'Reckoning tomorrow's fine as today, us will take you to the Brissons.'

'The Brissons!' I said, 'why I thought no-one could land there.' I was thinking of the coastguard's tales of how unfortunate shipwrecked people were sometimes washed on to the Brissons by a big wave and couldn't get off again and died of cold and starvation. Billy reassured me, quite unnecessarily, 'Us'll not take you supposing it's not safe,' he said.

The next morning was sunny and quiet. We rowed out and round the Brissons, waiting for the moment when the tide should be right for landing. Until we got fairly close I did not realize why the great rock was always spoken of in the plural. From the shore it seemed one solid mass, but now one saw why the Brissons were spoken of as 'they'. 'They look kindly today' or 'Keep clear of the Brissons, they'll draw you in with this tide.' Between its two parts there was a narrow chasm in which even on a calm day like this the level of the water rose several feet as each wave came in, and fell away with a queer sucking sound before it rose to the level of the sea outside the chasm. It seemed to rest there till the next wave sweeping in started the cycle again. When Billy judged the distance and the angle were right for the attempt, he jumped, turned round and lay flat on his face, digging his toes firmly into some crack, then leaned over and grabbed the gunwale of the boat, the next time she came within reach; 'and now me hangel' and Naomi stood up and was dropped over Billy's back, somewhere between his outstretched legs. For one horrible moment I was separated from my girl, then I jumped, missing Billy's head by inches, and fell forward on to a mass of live shells growing on dead ones, and giving the black rock its curious grey colour. The cleft between the two rocks was so covered by a projection from one of them that you never saw it from the land. We were taking long breaths and looking around us when Billy

238

called to come on, so very carefully we made our way to where he was stroking the head of a puffin as she sat on her nest. 'I'll not take her off, she mightn't go back and the eggs would get cold,' Billy said, 'but come along a bit further and we'll find more.' We found many more gentle puffins, Welsh parrots the fishermen call them, and not so gentle shags or cormorants, which looked as if they would like to peck the intruders, but thought prudence the better part of valour, and turned their heads away so as to lose sight of the temptation.

When we landed I found we had caused some sensation. The captain of the lifeboat congratulated me: 'You two be the only women folk to come alive off the Brissons,' he said. 'That captain's wife they tell you of, what landed, she never came off, not even for her funeral, poor soul, she were washed away. You be alive.'

What nice friendly people they all were! Before we left, one of the coastguards spoke to me about the red coat which Naomi always wore if she was alone on the shore. 'You put that on she for reason, I guess. We always kept the glass on she, and the day the fog came on we was just thinking of going for she, but you got in first before we,' he said.

Index

❅

Index

Index

Index

244

Index

245

Index

Jane Makgill (1) = *Robert Haldane* = (2) MARY ELIZABETH BURDON SANDERSON
(of Cloan d. 1877)

PROF. JOHN BURDON SANDERSON, F.R.S.
m. *Ghetal Herschell*

Margaret Isabella
m. Sir John Makgill, Bt.

Richard Burdon Sanderson
Viscount Haldane, O.M. F.R.S.
(d. 1928)

PROF. JOHN SCOTT HALDANE, C.H., F.R.S. = LOUISA KATHLEEN TROTTER O.B.E.

ROBERT HALDANE MAKGILL, C.B.E.   & others

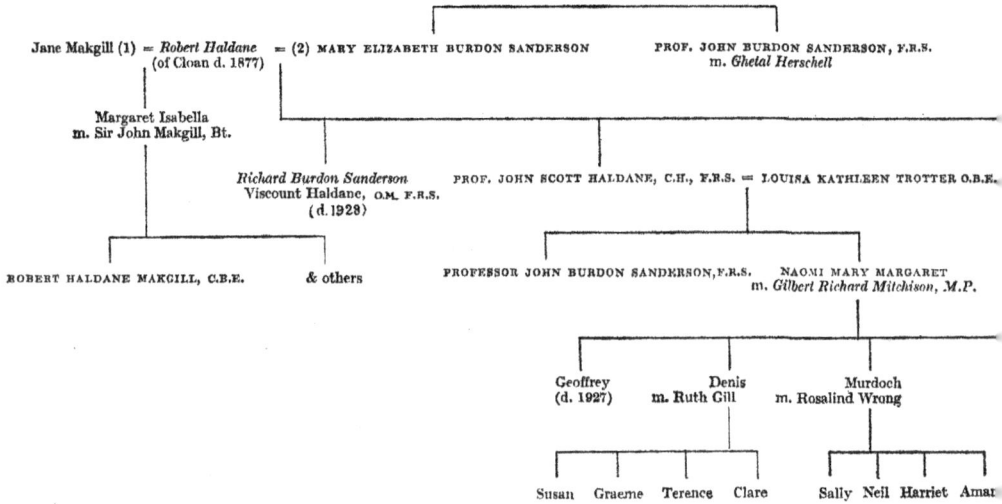

PROFESSOR JOHN BURDON SANDERSON, F.R.S.   NAOMI MARY MARGARET
m. *Gilbert Richard Mitchison, M.P.*

Geoffrey
(d. 1927)

Denis
m. Ruth Gill

Murdoch
m. Rosalind Wrong

Susan   Graeme   Terence   Clare

Sally   Neil   Harriet   Amar

Haldane and Makgill Family Tree.

An extended family tree can be found at
http://www.kennedyandboyd.co.uk/images/NML/tree.pdf

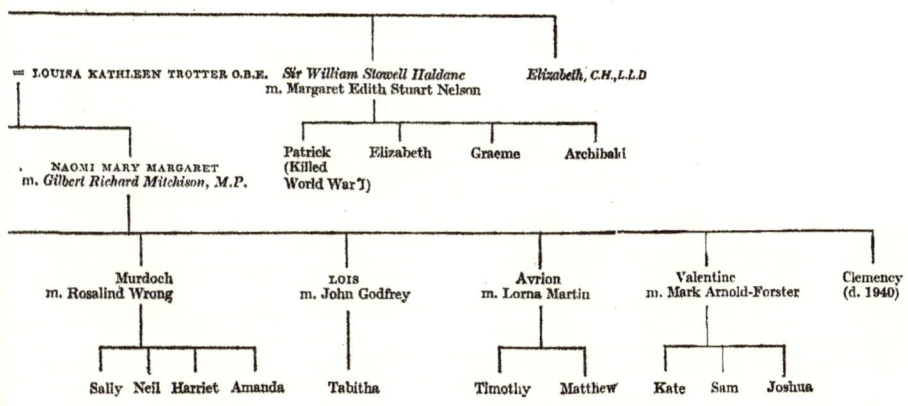

LOUISA KATHLEEN TROTTER O.B.E. ══ *Sir William Stowell Haldane*
m. Margaret Edith Stuart Nelson

Elizabeth, C.H.,L.L.D

NAOMI MARY MARGARET
m. *Gilbert Richard Mitchison, M.P.*

Patrick (Killed World War I)   Elizabeth   Graeme   Archibald

Murdoch
m. Rosalind Wrong

LOIS
m. John Godfrey

Avrion
m. Lorna Martin

Valentine
m. Mark Arnold-Forster

Clemency
(d. 1940)

Sally   Neil   Harriet   Amanda

Tabitha

Timothy   Matthew

Kate   Sam   Joshua